"Anyone who thought they knew everything about the Ripper story will benefit from a reading."
Carl Ryker, Lawton, Oklahoma, USA

"This is not only a deep dive into the historical context of Jack the Ripper's world, but holds cautionary wisdom for modern-day crime-solving… I highly, highly recommend it!"
Esther Perrot, Paris, France

"It's essential reading for readers who crave context over hype."
Kim Olsen-Clark, Chicago, Illinois, USA

"A well-researched book and a wonderful read!"
Toni Gooderham, West Wickham, UK

"Everything you have been told about the killings is questioned… This is a must-read."
Leigh Ann Solomons, Monmouth Junction, New Jersey, USA

"Well researched and informative, and I thoroughly recommend it to everyone."
Alastair Gatt, New Zealand

"What an amazing book—the research is unbelievable."
Meredith Light, Washington, DC, USA

"It is a rare thing to find a book that presents an incredibly detailed, evidence-based analysis of a subject while being wildly entertaining."
John J. Stevens, USA

"The book was fantastic. It gives even more question marks on who and how many may have been Jack the Ripper."
Julia Halliday, Epsom, UK

"I highly recommend it to anyone with an interest in the case."
Kevin Hulsman Groesbeek, Gelderland, Netherlands

"After reading this book, I have no doubt that I now know what really happened."
Ken Hallgring, Neptune, New Jersey, USA

"Shines a light on the precarious status of women (as well as the entire working class) in Victorian England."
Robert Campbell, Burlington, Ontario, Canada

"If you know nothing about Jack the Ripper, read this book. If you think you know a lot about Jack the Ripper – read this book."
Kevin Phelan, Chicago, Illinois, USA

"We found it riveting and were unable to put it down."
Helen & Patrick Mather, Toronto, NSW, Australia

"A meticulously researched exploration of the Whitechapel murders with a fresh perspective on the killer's identity that sets it apart from conventional theories."
Danny Kao, San Francisco & New York, USA

"A captivating book for all fans of the case, which I would highly recommend!"
Sue Horner, Towcester, UK

"The book paints an excellent picture of why these crimes were significant and why they could have happened."
Andrew Gee, Houston, Texas, USA

"If you're looking for a comprehensive, yet utterly readable, look at the Whitechapel murders, *Yours Truly Jack the Ripper* is a great place to start."
Mary Williams, Milwaukee, Wisconsin, USA

"Having read a good few of the very many books about 'Jack the Ripper', this book, in my opinion, is the best. Well researched, it includes details I was previously unaware of."
Bob Grice, Doncaster, UK

"Well researched, it does a fantastic job describing Victorian London and its harsh realities for those unfortunate to have lived in Whitechapel."

Matthew Metcalfe, Acworth, Georgia, USA

"I very much enjoyed reading and especially listening to your book."

Christine Masters, Austen, Texas, USA

"A *tour de force* on an endlessly fascinating subject, reflecting immense knowledge and research in language beautifully composed from front to back... Highly recommended."

Pat Lewis, Vancouver, British Columbia, Canada

"*Yours Truly Jack the Ripper* brings the Whitechapel murders vividly to life while questioning many of the assumptions that have shaped how the story is usually told."

Julie Landis, San Diego, California, USA

"The writing is skilled, absorbing, and hard to put down—I paused only for snack breaks."

Ann Meyer, Minneapolis, Minnesota, USA

"This is an excellent book and I recommend to anyone interested in learning more about the circumstances of these dreadful murders of women in London during 1888."

Andrew Maclean, Hampton, Victoria, Australia

"Considering your book from my perspective as a retired scientist and attorney, I found it very professional and perceptive... Your discussion of the past is certainly pertinent to today."

Sandra L. Story, Chicago, Illinois, USA

"*Yours Truly Jack the Ripper* is a must read for anyone with an interest in Jack the Ripper and Victorian London... The conclusion is stunning and satisfying."

Alicia Kennedy, Long Beach, New York, USA

"Extremely well written and researched; it takes you right into the heart of the 1880s East End, a place nearly as lawless as the Wild West. Compelling read with a new theory that isn't over the top."

Leslie Amos, Romford, UK

"Meticulously researched with a rigorous academic review of available evidence and literature... a narrative format that maintains sensitivity for the victims and their families."

Andrew D.C. Meddick, Miami, Florida, USA

"This meticulously researched yet highly accessible book belongs in every true-crime lover's collection."

Stephen Jackson, Chicago, Illinois, USA

"The book was a fascinating read. It provided phenomenal insight and an excellent account of life and times in 19th-century London's East End... The book was certainly an eye-opener and a must-read for any JTR fan!"

Lynn Southgate, Stuart, Florida, USA

"This is by far the most comprehensive material I have ever encountered on Jack the Ripper. Not only does it shed light on the victims, but on the entire era."

Kefren Mertens, Belgium

"A wonderful addition to any Jack the Ripper library. Walker wields Occam's razor with the precision of a surgeon as he dissects the many myths that surround the infamous murders of 1888. Highly recommended!"

Jon Gossard, Anaheim, California, USA

"The book is fantastic."

Gary Marks, Oldwick, New Jersey, USA

Yours truly Jack the Ripper

How the Victorians created the world's greatest murder mystery

Richard Walker

Yours Truly Jack the Ripper
ISBN 978-1-905315-95-6 (paperback)
ISBN 978-1-905315-96-3 (ebook)
ISBN 978-1-905315-97-0 (hardback)
Also available as an audiobook.
Published in 2026 by Heritage Hunter
www.heritagehunter.co.uk

jacktherippertour.net

A CIP record of this book is available from the British Library.

Contents

Part 1: Dismantling the Mythology

1 The Story Everyone Knows 3
2 Rich and Poor 8
3 'Applauding the Open Class Bias of Magistrates and Judges' 12
4 It Was the Victim's Fault 16
5 The Foundation of Fiction 19
6 Manufacturing a Monster 26
7 The Copycat Theory 30

Part 2: The Victims Revisited

8 Mary Ann (Polly) Nichols 39
9 Homeless 43
10 The Man Beside the Body 46
11 Sunday's Bombshell 50
12 The Day after the Bombshell 54
13 Detective Inspector Abberline on the Case 58
14 How Was Polly Nichols Killed? 62
15 Annie Chapman 67
16 She'd Been Dead for at Least Two Hours 74
17 John Richardson: Eyewitness or Killer? 86
18 Elisabeth Gustafsdotter (Liz Stride) 94
19 The Murder of Elizabeth Stride 98
20 Kate Eddowes 108
21 The Evidence and the Police Failure 114
22 How Might Kate Eddowes Have Been Murdered? 123
23 Mary Jane Kelly 129
24 The Three Who Went Before 141

Part 3: The Dark Side

25 The Women and the Street Gangs 149
26 The Women and Their Jekyll and Hyde World 151
27 A Jekyll and Hyde City 154

Part 4: Suspects

28 The Royal Conspiracy 159
29 Walter Sickert: Artist, Eccentric ... and Killer? 163
30 'Oh, Without a Doubt, a Hundred Per Cent, It's Him' 168
31 Russell's Shawl Story 172
32 The Ease of Creating Suspects 184

Part 5: The World of Jack the Ripper

33 Letters from Hell 189
34 The Writing on the Wall 192
35 The Macnaghten Memoranda 193

Part 6: The Players

36 Queen Victoria 201
37 Prince Albert Victor 205
38 Lord Salisbury 208
39 Henry Matthews 209
40 Sir Charles Warren 210
41 Dr Robert Anderson 213
42 Chief Inspector Donald Sutherland Swanson 217
43 Detective Inspector Frederick Abberline 220
44 Major Henry Smith 223

Conclusion 227
Map 233
Bibliography 235
Index 237

Part 1

Dismantling the Mythology

1

The Story Everyone Knows

In the gaslit streets of Victorian London, a monster stalked the night. Jack the Ripper – the name still sends shivers down spines nearly 140 years later. We know the story: a shadowy figure preying on prostitutes in the dark alleys of Whitechapel, vanishing into the fog after each brutal murder. It's a tale that has spawned countless books, films and theories. Crime writer Patricia Cornwell spent millions trying to prove the killer was the Victorian artist Walter Sickert. Businessman Russell Edwards bought a bloodstained shawl, convinced DNA would finally unmask the Ripper.

There's one problem: the story they and everyone else have heard is wrong.

Tour guides, DNA and Kate Eddowes' shawl

I'm Richard Walker, a London tour guide. The first walk I learned and delivered was the Jack the Ripper tour. It appeared to be an exciting acting challenge, a piece of street theatre in which I would perform a one-man show with a gift of a story to tell.

The most popular guided walk in London is about this unknown serial killer. Viator lists 87 companies offering Jack the Ripper tours. It's a fantastic story combining whodunnit, horror and illicit sex, set in gaslit Victorian London.

And I was fortunate with my timing, as interest in the case surged in the new millennium. Johnny Depp and Heather Graham added a little glamour to the tale in the film *From Hell*, which put the murders back in the headlines in 2001.

In the same year, Patricia Cornwell began her research, and in 2002 she published her book *Portrait of a Killer: Jack the Ripper Case Closed*, which became a bestseller.

Russell Edwards left a Cambridge cinema fired with a new interest kindled by *From Hell*. That new interest led Russell to 'a shawl belonging to Kate Eddowes', and in 2014 he published *Naming Jack the Ripper*.

Both books claimed DNA evidence solved the mystery. Russell Edwards says confidently, 'We have definitely solved the mystery of who Jack the Ripper was. Only non-believers that want to perpetuate the myth will doubt.'

Both writers believe they've solved the case. They can't both be right, though both could be wrong. What is certain is that they've been swept up in a story shaped by Victorian assumptions that continue to influence how we interpret the evidence today.

Exploring my doubts

During the COVID lockdown, I couldn't stop exploring my doubts about these 19th-century crimes against women. Revisiting the books I had read led me to new research, revealing a glaring problem with the standard story. I discovered that much of what we 'know' about these murders rests on assumptions that have never been appropriately challenged.

These were assumptions made by police officers and journalists. They were all men. Men who were working in or reporting on a highly charged situation. The best of us would be challenged.

Even in our more enlightened times, challenges persist and things are far from perfect. The London Metropolitan Police commissioned Louise Casey to investigate after one of its officers abducted Sarah Everard from a London street in March 2021, before raping and murdering her.

The 363-page report details disturbing stories of sexual assaults usually covered up or downplayed, with 12% of women working for the Met saying they had been harassed or attacked at work, and one-third experiencing sexism. The report concluded that the Metropolitan Police is broken and rotten, suffering collapsing public trust and is guilty of institutional racism, misogyny and homophobia.

If in our 21st-century Metropolitan Police Force, we have 'sexual assaults usually covered up or downplayed', what would we expect from the Metropolitan Police shaped by, and dealing with, the culture prevalent in 19th-century Britain?

This matters because the conviction that a murderer was killing prostitutes meant the police ignored another, more likely scenario. This blinkered view of the case almost certainly caused a catastrophic failure to secure justice for the victims.

The conviction arose simply from the question: 'What woman would end up alone at night with a potential killer?' Answer: a prostitute.

There were no cameras to record the moments leading up to and including each murder, so that conviction is a possible explanation, but it is not a fact.

Fact: the first four of the five victims were homeless and frequently had no other choice but to sleep rough, and the fifth victim slept in a room that was not secure.

Fact: the five victims were killed when they were lying down.

Fact: in each case, there was no sign of a struggle.

Fact: in each case, they were killed in a densely populated area within yards of where people slept, and nobody heard a sound.

Fact: the murders took place in an area that was less than one square mile, an area that was heavily patrolled by police, vigilantes and a population that was on full alert, yet the killer(s) escaped every time.

Fact: the simplest explanation is that the women were killed by an opportunist who found an easy target as they slept.

Occam's razor

William of Occam was a Franciscan friar born in Ockham, Surrey, England. He became a significant figure of medieval thought in 14th-century Europe.

Occam's razor, also known as the principle of parsimony, suggests that you should choose the simplest explanation if there is more than one explanation for a phenomenon.

That is Occam's razor. I refer to it in this book, so it's essential to verify whether we can use it on Jack the Ripper.

If you check for where the simplest explanation appears to be wrong, you will find examples.

Darwin's theory of evolution provides a unifying explanation for the tremendous variety of life on earth, all of which evolved over billions of years from a single origin. Darwin's assumption was that individuals within a population of any species vary; the variations are passed down through the generations; and the individuals with the variations best adapted to suit their environment are more likely to survive and reproduce. Once upon a time, there was a single cell adapting with all its might, and four billion years later, we have David Attenborough, all thanks to the power of natural selection. All of which, for me, is a simple explanation for the wonderful variety of life on earth.

However, some have pointed out that while Darwin's assumptions are pretty straightforward, there are mind-bogglingly complex fields of evolutionary biology and genetics, so there is a more straightforward explanation for the variety of life on earth: God.

It is claimed that this shows that Occam's razor may not always give you the correct explanation.

You will have your own opinion, but for me, God requires far more assumptions, complexity and a giant leap of faith than does Darwin.

Writing in *Open Mind*, theoretical physicist Jim Al-Khalili gave another example of where Occam's razor might not work. He asked the physicist Peter Higgs to explain the Higgs boson in 30 seconds.

> He looked at me solemnly and, I have to admit, not particularly apologetically, and shook his head. He explained that it had taken him many decades to understand the physics underlying the Higgs mechanism in quantum field theory, so how could people expect such a complex subject to be condensed into a short sound bite?

I am not familiar with alternative theories to the Higgs mechanism in quantum field theory, so I can't make a decision about which explanation is the simplest.

Occam's razor doesn't say that everything is simple; it says you should choose the simplest explanation when there is more than one, as it is likely to be correct.

Explanations for how something happens in the field of quantum physics are no doubt complex, but other things being equal, the simplest of those complex explanations is likely to be the best choice.

What interested me in Jim Al-Khalili's article was when he warned that 'it is hard to fight the human impulse to look for the simplest account of something we don't understand'.

What I found fascinating about that statement is how many Victorian police officers, journalists and modern-day experts on the Jack the Ripper case have effortlessly overcome 'the human impulse to look for the simplest account of something we don't understand'.

There are numerous examples of where the simplest explanation –

indeed what many would regard as common sense – was ignored.

The book I have written does not wrestle with the Higgs boson, complex fields of evolutionary biology and genetics or whether God exists. It is simply about the murders of several women in 1888, and how those murders were, and are, investigated.

This book examines why the most straightforward explanation was, and is, ignored and what happens when we apply Occam's razor to the Whitechapel murders. When we strip away prejudices and examine the evidence without predetermined conclusions, a different story emerges.

2

Rich and Poor

The 19th century witnessed a significant shift in the way human life was perceived. Religious faith was experiencing a crisis; yet, at the same time, churches were being built in ever greater numbers, and charitable institutions were being founded. There were great scientific leaps, technological advances, huge increases in industrial output, a massive increase in wealth for a select few, and an ever-expanding empire; yet, despite all this activity, poverty flourished.

It is a remarkable coincidence that two books written to highlight the horrific conditions of the working classes in England were published in the same year.

In 1845, Friedrich Engels published *The Condition of the Working Class in England in 1844*. In the same year, Benjamin Disraeli published *Sybil or The Two Nations*. Both books were intended to provoke a serious reaction to the appalling conditions in which three-quarters of England's population lived.

Here is the moment in Disraeli's novel when he sums up the situation in the country.

> 'Yes,' resumed the younger stranger after a moment's interval. 'Two nations, between whom there is no intercourse and no sympathy; who are as ignorant of each other's habits, thoughts, and feelings, as if they were dwellers in different zones or inhabitants of different planets; who are formed by a different breeding, are fed by a different food, are ordered by different manners, and are not governed by the same laws.'
>
> 'You speak of – ' said Egremont, hesitatingly.
>
> 'THE RICH AND THE POOR.'

Disraeli could also have pointed out that the country was divided into two nations, the male and the female. For the poor, life was tough. For the poor who were women, it was very tough.

The Condition of the Working Class in England in 1844 was published in Friedrich Engels' native language, German. The English translation arrived in 1887, one year before the Whitechapel murders of 1888. He wrote:

> Competition is the completest expression of the battle of all against all which rules in modern civil society... In this country, social war is under full headway; everyone stands for himself and fights for himself against all comers, and whether or not he shall injure all the others who are his declared foes depends upon a cynical calculation of what is most advantageous for himself.

In this social war, the weakest suffered most. Engels described the life of some of those at the mercy of everybody as they tried to survive in this world.

> Women often return to the mill three or four days after confinement, leaving the baby, of course; in the dinner-hour they must hurry home to feed the child and eat something, and what sort of suckling that can be is also evident.

Engels included the testimony of several workwomen:

> M. H., twenty years old, has two children, the youngest a baby that is tended by the other, a little older. The mother goes to the mill shortly after five o'clock in the morning, and comes home at eight at night; all day the milk pours from her breasts, so that her clothing drips with it.
>
> H. W. has three children, goes away Monday morning at five o'clock, and comes back Saturday evening; has so much to do for the children then that she cannot get to bed before three o'clock in the morning; often wet through to the skin, and obliged to work in that state.

She said:

> My breasts have given me the most frightful pain, and I have been dripping wet with milk.

And the conditions that Engels described in 1844 did not disappear.

Two Quakers, William Bryant and Francis May, started the Bryant and May company in 1843. In 1888, working conditions in their factory in Bow were appalling.

Social campaigner Annie Besant questioned some of the girls who worked at the factory. On 23 June 1888, she published what she had learned in her weekly paper, *The Link*. She described the factory as a 'prison house' and the match girls as 'white wage slaves' – 'undersized', 'helpless' and 'oppressed'.

These 'white wage slaves' worked from 6:30 a.m. until 6 p.m., with just two breaks, standing all the time.

Annie Besant wrote:

> A typical case is that of a girl of 16, a piece worker; she earns 4s a week, and lives with a sister, employed by the same firm, who 'earns good money, as much as 8s or 9s per week'. Out of the earnings, 2s is paid for the rent of one room; the child lives on only bread-and-butter and tea, alike for breakfast and dinner.

The working conditions included fines and occasional blows.

> The splendid salary of 4s. is subject to deductions in the shape of fines; if the feet are dirty, or the ground under the bench is left untidy, a fine of 3d. is inflicted.
>
> If a girl leaves four or five matches on her bench when she goes for a fresh 'frame,' she is fined 3d., and in some departments, a fine of 3d. is inflicted for talking.
>
> One girl was fined 1s. for letting the web twist round a machine in the endeavour to save her fingers from being cut, and was sharply told to take care of the machine, never mind your fingers.
>
> Another, who carried out the instructions and lost a finger thereby, was left unsupported while she was helpless.
>
> The wage covers the duty of submitting to an occasional blow from a foreman; one, who appears to be a gentleman of variable temper, 'clouts' them 'when he is mad'.

That foreman would not have been the only official dressed in a little brief authority who would have seen casual abuse as a perk of the job. All of this, and the girls frequently suffered from the effects of the white phosphorus used in match manufacturing.

On the website of the Royal College of Surgeons, Susan Isaac wrote:

> Phosphorus necrosis of the jaw, commonly called 'phossy jaw', was a really horrible disease and overwhelmingly a disease of the poor. Workers in match factories developed unbearable abscesses in their mouths, leading to facial disfigurement and sometimes fatal brain damage. In addition, the gums developed an eerie greenish white 'glow' in the dark.

The Quaker employers, Bryant and May, were aware of phossy jaw, but workers who complained of toothaches were told to have their teeth extracted or face dismissal. When these women went on strike in July 1888, they risked everything to escape industrial poisoning and poverty wages.

For many women, life didn't get any better at home. Jack London, in his 1903 book *The People of the Abyss,* wrote:

> The men are economically dependent on their masters, and the women are economically dependent on the men. The result is, the woman gets the beating the man should give his master.
>
> Wife-beating is the masculine prerogative of matrimony. They wear remarkable boots of brass and iron, and when they have polished off the mother of their children with a black eye or so, they knock her down and proceed to trample her very much as a Western stallion tramples a rattlesnake.

If wives may be trampled like a rattlesnake, what then for the degraded women littering the paths of such men as they seek some night-time entertainment? And how did society's officials treat the victims?

3

'Applauding the Open Class Bias of Magistrates and Judges'

George Bernard Shaw wrote in *The Star* newspaper (24 September 1888) about the intense class bias in the law enforcement of the day and the support they received from the 'West-end press, headed by the *St. James's Gazette*, the *Times*, and the *Saturday Review*'.

In a male-dominated world, women at the bottom of society faced a double bias. Both their class and their gender were against them when they faced the magistrate. Frances Jones was only one of many women who suffered repeated violence, only to find the law and the press considered them guilty of the crimes against them.

Jurriaan Maessen and Jonathan Tye, writing in their 2023 online article 'Introducing Edward Buckley: Life & Crimes of a Whitechapel Fiend', which they dedicated to the memory of Frances Jones, show how women, especially those at the bottom of society, were regarded by those in authority, in this case, both a magistrate and a journalist:

> On the 5th September 1885 the East London Observer ran a report on yet another assault on Frances Jones, titled: 'It almost served her right'. The report details an assault which occurred on the previous Wednesday (2nd September) and it turns one's stomach for two reasons in particular: the cowardly violence exerted by Buckley, and the rather nonchalant way it was handled by the court's magistrate:
>
> 'Edward Buckley, of 14, Hanbury-street, Whitechapel, was charged with violently assaulting Frances Jones, 15, Devonshire-street,

> Commercial-road, St. George's-in-the-East. Prosecutrix said about 9.30 on Wednesday night she was in the East London Tavern, in the Whitechapel-road, drinking.'
>
> The prisoner came up to her, without any provocation, and struck her a violent blow in the mouth. She did not say anything to the prisoner. By Buckley: Last Sunday Buckley gave her £3 8s. to go and take a room, so that they might live together. The clothes she was wearing she bought with the money. Mr. John Woolf, the proprietor of the East London Tavern, said he saw Buckley strike and kick the prosecutrix in a most cruel manner. Mr. Biron said practically the prosecutrix had robbed the prisoner of his money, but should not just take the law into his own hands. He would have to find one surety in £10 to keep the peace for six months.

The newspaper heading 'It almost served her right' probably reflected the attitude of many to such incidents; as Jurriaan and Jonathan say, 'it turns one's stomach'.

Another crime against a woman was reported in *The Sunday People* on Sunday, 23 December 1888. The report appears on page 9 and is headed 'Extraordinary Outrage at Dalston'.

> At the Dalston Police Court on Wednesday, before Mr Horace Smith, a woman of shabby genteel appearance, who gave the name of Sarah Delhar, 40, and said she had no home, and no occupation, was charged with being drunk and incapable under the following extraordinary circumstances. Police Constable 434 N deposed that at one o'clock on Wednesday morning, he was on duty in Shacklewell Lane, when he heard screams proceeding from the mews in Dunn Street, Dalston. On hastening to the spot, he found the prisoner lying on a costermonger's barrow in a state of complete nudity.
>
> Mr. Smith: Did she complain of being ill-used?
>
> The constable said she was drunk.

This was an odd way to reply to Mr Smith's question. This homeless woman was discovered stripped of her clothes, and the article says, 'She bore signs of severe ill treatment about the face, and her left eye was almost closed.'

Was the woman drunk or just confused? How reliable a witness was the constable? What follows in the article casts serious doubt over the evidence he gave.

> A person who said her house abutted on the mews now came forward. She was not asked her name.

Given what this witness goes on to say, it is extraordinary that she was not identified.

> She said that soon after midnight, whilst she was in bed, she heard fearful screams, proceeding from the mews. It was some time before she had the courage to move. At length, she went into the room of a lodger whose window overlooked the mews. There she saw a woman lying on a barrow and two men standing over her. She could not see well what they were doing, but she had an idea that Jack the Ripper was at work as the screams continued and the woman was evidently struggling, the witness induced her lodger to open the window. She then called out, and the men ran away. She went with her friend into Shacklewell lane, and there they saw the constable, whose attention they called to the screams.

There are two possibilities: the witness and her friend are not telling the truth, or the policeman is not telling the truth. It's difficult to come up with a reason why the witness and lodger would make this story up.

> They went round with the officer and helped to dress the woman. The prisoner said she was a lone but respectable woman, her late husband having been in a good position in life, she did not know how she got down the mews, but she had been very badly treated, and two rings she was wearing had been stolen. Mr. Horace Smith said he must hear more of this, and he put the woman back for inquiries.

So there it is. The woman was to be put back for inquiries. She was the prisoner. She was to be charged with being drunk and incapable. This homeless woman had been brutally assaulted. The only evidence presented that she was drunk comes from the police officer.

The police officer who was summoned by the witness and her lodger, but who claimed he ran there when he heard her screams, was not to be investigated.

I was alerted to this 'Extraordinary Outrage at Dalston' by my friend and colleague at London Walks, David Tucker. There may be other such instances of women assaulted while sleeping on the streets of the nation's capital that I am unaware of. There were eight others that I do know of, and this book is about what happened to them.

All of these women were assaulted in 1888 and within three miles of where the assault on Sarah Delhar took place. In two of the cases, there were police officers who, like Police Constable 434 N, gave evidence that was contradicted by the statements of other witnesses. As with this case, the contradictions were not questioned. All of these victims were, like Sarah Delhar, between the ages of 38 and 46, homeless and blamed for facilitating the crimes against them.

There is no surprise here; this was a society where middle-aged women who lost their male protector for whatever reason were rendered homeless. And so the 40-year-old Sarah Delhar, homeless and alone, could be dragged from sleep, stripped naked and flung onto a costermonger's barrow, which one of the merry japesters trundled into Dunn Street while his comrade-in-arms won her compliance by well-aimed blows at her face.

Here is another example of Victorian attitudes to impoverished and vulnerable women as seen in Jack London's *The People of the Abyss*.

> Yesterday, Dr. Wynn Westcott held an inquest at Shoreditch, respecting the death of Elizabeth Crews, aged 77 years, of 32 East Street, Holborn, who died on Wednesday last. Alice Mathieson stated that she was the landlady of the house where the deceased lived. Witness last saw her alive on the previous Monday. She lived quite alone. Mr. Francis Birch, relieving officer for the Holborn district, stated that the deceased had occupied the room in question for thirty-five years. When the witness was called on the 1st, he found the old woman in a terrible state, and the ambulance and coachman had to be disinfected after the removal. Dr. Chase Fennell said death was due to blood poisoning from bed sores, due to self-neglect and filthy surroundings, and the jury returned a verdict to that effect.

Jack London says:

> The most startling thing about this little incident of a woman's death is the smug complacency with which the officials looked upon it and rendered judgment. That an old woman of seventy-seven years of age should die of SELF-NEGLECT is the most optimistic way possible of looking at it. It was the old dead woman's fault that she died, and having located the responsibility, society goes contentedly on about its own affairs.

4

It Was the Victim's Fault

After criticism of the police following the murder of the third victim, Elizabeth Stride, Sir Charles Warren, commissioner of the Metropolitan Police, wrote to the Whitechapel Board of Works:

> The public, and especially the residents of Whitechapel, are naturally alarmed at what has taken place, and are impatient as they read from day to day that the murderer has not been apprehended; but the police cannot accomplish impossibilities. The murderer has selected for his victims women who, in their desire to avoid the public gaze, practically assisted him in his diabolical work.

This verdict by Sir Charles has been cited and repeated even in respected works. Philip Sugden sums it up succinctly in his 1994 book *The Complete History of Jack the Ripper*:

> Indeed, his victims, prostitutes all, accustomed to accosting men and taking them to dark or unfrequented byways and yards for sex, greatly facilitated his crimes.

There is no solid evidence to support this. Yet it's repeated as fact across the literature. Here is what Peter Ackroyd writes about the first victim in his 2008 book *Jack the Ripper and the East End*. 'Her name was Mary Ann Nichols, and her throat had been cut. A prostitute living in a doss-house, she was desperately looking for custom.' He then quotes the murdered woman, 'I'll soon get my money, see what a jolly bonnet I have.'

Those quoted words, reported in the sensation-seeking *Star* newspaper, appear in almost every book about this case. How reliable is this evidence? It's never questioned because these comments support the assumption that

Mary Ann, known as Polly, was killed after accosting a client and taking him somewhere dark for sex.

The problem runs deeper than individual details. From the beginning, investigators decided on one explanation – a serial killer murdering prostitutes – which stopped them from considering other possibilities. As Philip Sugden himself warned, 'evidence in conflict with the theory is liable to be suppressed or perverted' and 'fiction is frequently dressed up as fact.'

Yet Sugden and other modern investigators commit the same error.

What the evidence shows

A closer examination of the facts reveals something different. For the coroners who heard all the evidence, only Mary Jane Kelly – who self-described as a prostitute – was recorded as a prostitute on her death certificate. There is no solid evidence that strangers picked up and killed Polly, Annie, Elizabeth or Catherine.

The way these murders were initially presented reflected male Victorian attitudes towards women – attitudes that persist in how the case is still discussed today. To understand why, we need to understand what life was like for vulnerable women in 1888 in London.

Sarah Delhar was a typical example. At the age of 40, she told the magistrate that she had 'no home and no occupation... She was a lone but respectable woman; her late husband having been in a good position in life.' Sarah Delhar was homeless, and she was attacked at night on the streets. She became the plaything of two men who beat her about the face and stripped her naked. On the word of a police officer (you may decide how reliable he was), she was charged with being drunk and incapable.

Like Sarah Delhar, all but one of the women murdered in Whitechapel in 1888 had 'no home and no occupation', and each 'was a lone but respectable woman' whose life changed when, like Sarah Delhar, they lost the protection of their male partner. There were many homeless middle-aged women in 1888.

William Booth, the founder of the Salvation Army, wrote in his 1890 book *In Darkest England and the Way Out*:

> To very many, even of those who live in London, it may be news that there are so many hundreds who sleep out of doors every night... we are apt to forget the multitude outside in the rain and the storm who are shivering the long hours through on the hard stone seats in

> the open or under the arches of a railway. These homeless, hungry people are, however, there, but being broken-spirited folk for the most part, they seldom make their voices audible in the ears of their neighbours.

Polly Nichols, Annie Chapman, Liz Stride and Kate Eddowes, murdered in 1888, were all like Sarah Delhar: homeless and in their forties. But young women were no less vulnerable.

The Maiden Tribute of Modern Babylon

Three years before the Whitechapel murders, campaigning journalist William Thomas Stead wrote *The Maiden Tribute of Modern Babylon*, exposing systematic sexual violence against women and girls. In one chilling interview with an experienced police officer, Stead asked whether actual rapes were 'constantly being perpetrated in London on unwilling virgins, purveyed and procured to rich men at so much a head by keepers of brothels'. The officer's response? 'Certainly, there is no doubt of it.'

When Stead pressed about why nothing was done, the officer explained that once a girl lost her chastity, she became 'a discredited witness'.

This was the context in which the Ripper murders were investigated. In a world where wife-beating was considered a husband's prerogative, where homeless women were routinely brutalised, where the police would regard a rape victim as 'a discredited witness' and murder victims as facilitating the crime against them. Is it surprising that these middle-aged, vulnerable women were immediately labelled as the lowest kind of sex worker?

5

The Foundation of Fiction

The first four murder victims shared a striking vulnerability that made them easy targets. They were particularly susceptible to alcohol's effects at a time when brewers like Young and Truman had built around 20,000 pubs across London. More importantly, their backgrounds had left them uniquely unprepared for life on Whitechapel's brutal streets.

Remarkably, none of these four women grew up in abject poverty. All had fathers who were skilled workers – men who could afford to send their daughters to school until the age of 15. Each of the victims had maintained marriages or partnerships until those relationships collapsed as they approached middle age. Having never learned to navigate the mean streets of Whitechapel, they struggled to survive in ways that children of true poverty would have mastered early on.

Children raised in genuine destitution – sharing eight-by-eight-foot rooms with adult siblings who slept together on floors where morality would be impossible – learned harsh lessons if they survived their first five years. They understood basic survival rules: sleep where others are gathered and avoid places where any drunken thug can use you as their plaything.

However, the early life of the first four victims did provide them with skills that those growing up in abject poverty would have been unable to acquire. They grew up learning how to take care of a home. At school, they would have learned needlework. These skills enabled them to secure char work, particularly for Jewish families in Whitechapel. Beginning a career selling sex in middle age would have been extraordinarily difficult, competing against women who had learned early, some even from childhood, how to survive the brutal 19th-century sex trade.

In Victorian London, being labelled a prostitute by the police carried devastating consequences. It meant arrest, imprisonment, social ostracism and destruction of one's reputation, often based on nothing more than an officer's word. By 1887, this system of arbitrary labelling had reached crisis proportions, with up to 6,000 women arrested annually on prostitution charges.

The Elizabeth Cass case

28 June 1887 was a day of celebration in London. Queen Victoria's Golden Jubilee had brought unprecedented crowds to the West End, and record-breaking sunshine filled the streets with revellers. Among them was Elizabeth Cass, a young dress designer who had recently moved from Stockton-on-Tees to work for Mary Ann Bowman at her Southampton Row premises in Bloomsbury.

Cass had ventured to Regent Street to shop at Jay's department store. As she pushed her way through the jubilee crowds, Police Constable Bowden Endacott, a plain-clothes officer whose speciality was arresting suspected prostitutes, spotted her. Endacott arrested Cass, took her to Tottenham Court Road Police Station, and charged her with solicitation and prostitution.

The next morning at Great Marlborough Street Police Court, magistrate Robert Milnes Newton heard Endacott's testimony that he had observed Cass soliciting on three separate occasions late at night in Regent Street. However, Mary Ann Bowman appeared as a character witness, testifying that her employee had never been out late at night and was 'a young woman of spotless character'.

Faced with conflicting testimony and no corroborating evidence, Newton had little choice but to find Cass not guilty. Yet his warning revealed the impossible position women found themselves in: 'Just take my advice: if you are a respectable girl, as you say you are, don't walk in Regent Street at night, for if you do you will either be fined or sent to prison after the caution I have given you.'

In essence, the magistrate was telling respectable women that public spaces belonged to men and prostitutes – and that the police had the right to determine which category any woman fell into.

Mary Ann Bowman refused to accept this injustice quietly. On 30 June, she wrote a formal complaint to the Metropolitan Police. Her actions caught the attention of Liberal MP Llewellyn Atherley-Jones, who raised the case in Parliament, demanding that Home Secretary Henry Matthews order an inquiry.

Initially, Matthews refused, citing the lack of a conviction. However, Atherley-Jones forced a parliamentary vote on the matter, and the political pressure became too great to ignore. An official inquiry was ordered, and Endacott was suspended from duty.

The inquiry revealed the deep institutional problems within the Metropolitan Police. Commissioner Charles Warren concluded, 'I am not prepared to say that I can see any grounds for accusing PC Endacott of wilful perjury. However, that is a matter on which I think the Public Prosecutors should decide.' This lukewarm response prompted Bowman and Cass to pursue a private prosecution for perjury.

By the time the legal proceedings concluded, Elizabeth Cass had married and become Mrs Elizabeth Langley. Neither she nor Bowman was satisfied with the outcome, but they had achieved something more significant than personal vindication.

The Cass case had exposed the arbitrary nature of prostitution arrests to unprecedented public scrutiny. The press coverage was extensive, and the parliamentary debate had embarrassed the government. Most importantly, it forced Metropolitan Police Commissioner Sir Charles Warren to issue a crucial memorandum: officers were forbidden from labelling women as prostitutes unless the women self-identified as such or irrefutable evidence existed.

The results were immediate and dramatic – prostitution arrests plummeted overnight. However, as we shall see, the memorandum was not adhered to during the investigation into the Whitechapel murders.

Endacott after the scandal: from constable to Ripper suspect

Bowden Endacott continued his police career until 1900. Upon his retirement, the *Police Review and Parade Gossip* offered this assessment:

> In his capacity of a Constable Mr Endacott endeavoured to exercise what influence he could in regard to the purity and morality of the streets, and it was his zeal in this direction that bought him in 1887 into unusual prominence. This was in connection with what was known as the 'Cass' case.

The euphemistic language reveals how the police establishment continued to view Endacott's actions as overzealous rather than fundamentally wrong.

A modern theory

In 2022, researcher Rod Beattie published *Jack the Ripper – The Policeman: A New Suspect*, identifying Bowden Endacott as his prime candidate for the infamous killer. Beattie's theory addresses one of the most perplexing aspects of the Ripper case: how the killer consistently evaded capture despite the massive police presence in Whitechapel.

> With the amount of police officers that had been drafted in to patrol the East End of London as the murders progressed, no one could have continually got away with the attacks unless that person was involved with the police.

Beattie suggests that if Endacott were indeed the killer, the authorities might have discovered his identity but kept it secret to prevent national chaos. The revelation that Jack the Ripper was the same policeman who had nearly brought down the government through the Cass scandal would have been devastating to public confidence in law enforcement.

Rod Beattie joins Arthur Conan Doyle among those who have suggested that a police officer may have committed the murders.

That is one explanation for how the killer got away with these murders in challenging circumstances, but there is another, simpler explanation.

Whether or not Endacott was Jack the Ripper, the Cass case reveals something far more significant about the Whitechapel murders: the unreliability of police labelling practices. Consider how the victims are typically described in Ripper literature:

> The body of Mary Ann, or 'Polly' Nichols, a prostitute, had been found on 31 August 1888 in Buck's Row in Whitechapel. She had been murdered, and her body had been mutilated. A similar murder had taken place two weeks earlier, that of Martha Tabram, also a prostitute.

This matter-of-fact presentation in Rod Beattie's book obscures two crucial questions: what evidence exists that these women were actually prostitutes, and, if they were, how was Endacott able to carry out the murders in the remarkable way that they were committed?

The evidence problem

The truth is that the evidence rests almost entirely on police assertions and contemporary assumptions. Unlike Elizabeth Cass, who had Mary Ann Bowman to defend her character, the Ripper victims were dead when the labels were applied. They had no employers to hire lawyers, no advocates to challenge police characterisations, and no voice to defend themselves.

The police had both motive and opportunity to label the victims as prostitutes. Such classifications served multiple purposes: they suggested the women had engaged in risky behaviour, provided a convenient explanation for why they were out late at night, and implied they had willingly gone with their killer. In essence, labelling victims as prostitutes explained why, despite the many police patrols, the murderer got away with it every time.

For journalists, labelling the victims as prostitutes obviously made a better story.

There is no solid evidence because there was no way of collecting it. As Hallie Rubenhold explains in her 2019 book *The Five: The Untold Lives of the Women Killed by Jack the Ripper*, Commissioner Charles Warren wrote in a letter to the home secretary during the Whitechapel investigation itself: 'We have no means of ascertaining what women are prostitutes and who are not.'

If the police had 'no means' of determining whether women were prostitutes, on what basis were the victims labelled as such?

Evidence, bias and the Jack the Ripper investigation

The popular perception of the Jack the Ripper murders – five prostitutes killed by a serial killer – faces increasing scholarly challenge. This debate crystallised in responses to Hallie Rubenhold's book *The Five*, particularly in discussions on the specialist website Casebook: Jack the Ripper (casebook.org).

While many welcomed Rubenhold's research, some Ripperologists expressed frustration with her challenge to the widely accepted theory of the Ripper. One contributor highlighted what they saw as a crucial omission:

> Here we have Inspector Helson saying that William Nichols had stated that he had stopped paying his wife's support because he had found that she was a prostitute. I don't know whether Hallie

> Rubenhold would classify a statement like that in a MEPO report as being 'hard evidence', but the book makes no mention of Helson's report; it ignores it completely. And that is extraordinary to me because surely her readers deserve to be told what Helson had written so that they can decide for themselves whether or not this theme that runs throughout her book has legs or not.

Steven Blomer in *Inside Bucks Row* quotes Inspector Helson's report of 7 September 1888 and says, 'This report appears to confirm that the authorities officially accepted that she had been living as a prostitute.'

It is extraordinary to me that what a policeman reports an estranged husband has said about a wife could be described as hard evidence.

This is what William Nichols said at the inquest into Polly's death on 3 September, four days before Inspector Helson wrote his report:

> **William Nichols,** printer's machinist, Coburg Road, Old Kent Road, said the deceased was his wife, but they had lived apart for eight years. He last saw her alive about three years ago and had not heard from her since. He did not know what she had been doing in the meantime.
>
> **A Juryman**: It is said that you were summoned by the Lambeth Union for her maintenance, and you pleaded that she was living with another man. Was he the blacksmith whom she had lived with?
>
> **Witness**: No; it was not the same; it was another man. I had her watched.

William Nichols employed a detective to gather evidence that would allow him to stop paying his wife's support. The detective did not find that she had been facilitating her own murder by accosting men for sex. He found that she was living with a man. This is not my definition of prostitution.

This is a contentious issue for serious researchers, and the controversy reflects broader tensions in Ripper research.

Tom Wescott, another dedicated researcher, argues in *Ripper Confidential* (2017):

> The murdered women of Whitechapel have become romanticised to the point that they're often portrayed as anything but what they were. That is not to say they deserved their fate. Nobody does. But if

> we're to hunt Jack the Ripper, we must observe his victims in the same context in which he observed them, and for all intents and purposes, they were addicts and criminals.

Wescott's expertise is undeniable. But since these murders remain unsolved, shouldn't we maintain an open mind throughout our investigation? If we categorically state that our goal is 'to hunt Jack the Ripper', aren't we narrowing our focus dangerously?

Declaring that 'we must observe his victims in the same context in which he observed them' might be sensible if we knew who 'he' was.

The methodology question

This debate highlights a crucial issue in historical research: the distinction between following evidence to draw conclusions and selecting evidence that supports predetermined theories. When we begin with the assumption that Jack the Ripper existed and killed prostitutes, we create a framework that inevitably shapes how we interpret ambiguous evidence.

6

Manufacturing a Monster

Contrary to popular belief about the violent nature of Whitechapel's slums, murder appears to have been remarkably rare. Bruce Paley, in *Jack the Ripper: The Simple Truth* (1995), writes:

> Although there could be no denying that the East End, and Whitechapel especially, had a well-deserved reputation for being a violent, dangerous and unsavoury place, murder itself was actually a surprisingly rare occurrence. In fact, in 1887, the year before the Ripper murders, out of eighty recorded homicides in London, not a single one took place in Whitechapel...
>
> Nor were that year's statistics a fluke. There hadn't been any murders in Whitechapel in 1886 either, out of sixty-eight committed in London, while the reports for 1889 and 1890 each show one murder per year in the district, out of totals of seventy-nine and seventy-four respectively for all of London."

No doubt some murders could have been missed. But what is clear is that while the papers certainly covered the events surrounding the 1887 murder of Miriam Angel by Israel Lobulsk (Lipski), south of Whitechapel in St George's in the East, in some detail, the press coverage of the murders of 1888 was on an altogether different scale.

A dull year desperate for news

When *The Star* launched into London's crowded newspaper market on Tuesday, 17 January 1888, its owners faced a significant challenge; they entered a competitive market. The competition from established newspapers wasn't the only threat to *The Star*'s continued survival. They were entering the marketplace at the very beginning of what was to be a very dull year.

As Paul Begg notes in *Jack the Ripper: The Facts* (2004):

> Eighteen eighty-eight was a very dull year. Most history books don't mention it at all or mention it in passing. There was no cause for anxiety abroad.

This news drought created the perfect conditions for sensational journalism. By autumn 1888, *The Pall Mall Gazette* and *The Star* had become pioneers of what would soon be called 'new journalism'. The belief that 'if it bleeds it leads' certainly applied to their editorial ethos.

In *Jack the Ripper: The Forgotten Victims* (2013), Begg explains:

> They helped to inflate the Whitechapel murders into an often extravagant narrative of shock and horror ... For the "new journalism", the Whitechapel horrors were as much to do with politics and increasing sales as with crime.

Contemporary observer George R. Sims captured this dynamic perfectly. On Sunday, 9 September 1888, he noted that the Whitechapel murders had 'come to the relief of newspaper editors in search of a sensation'. A week later, he observed: 'There isn't much to talk about – We live in dullish times; The only things the newsboys shout are these Whitechapel crimes.'

Just five weeks after *The Star*'s debut, the violence began. Annie Millwood, 38 and homeless, was stabbed multiple times in Spitalfields on Saturday, 25 February 1888. She died five weeks later from her injuries. Three days after Annie's death, Emma Elizabeth Smith, 45, also homeless, was attacked minutes from where Millwood had been assaulted. A blunt instrument had been thrust inside her, causing fatal peritonitis. On Tuesday, 7 August, Martha Tabram, 39 and homeless, was discovered on a building's first-floor landing – again, just minutes from the previous attacks. She had been stabbed 39 times.

These brutal attacks, all committed on Whitechapel's streets in the early hours, perfectly suited *The Star*'s sensational editorial approach. The fact that Whitechapel had experienced no murders for two years made these killings even more dramatic. With each new death, *The Star* grew more skilful at exploiting the horror, and by the year's end – largely thanks to coverage of these victims – it boasted the largest evening newspaper circulation in the country.

The Star and its competitors didn't hesitate to attack police incompetence, maintaining relentless pressure on investigators. But this raises uncomfortable questions: How much more intense would that pressure have been if these victims were daughters of dukes or wealthy merchants? Does pressure diminish when victims are labelled prostitutes? Could that label have been adopted early by police for convenience rather than evidence?

The murders were real, the suffering genuine. But the legend that grew around them may tell us more about Victorian media and society than about any single perpetrator stalking the streets of Whitechapel.

The imperial mindset: how Victorian class prejudice shaped the Ripper investigation

Assistant Commissioner Sir Robert Anderson dismissed the victims as belonging to 'a very small class of degraded women who frequent the East End streets after midnight, in hope of inveigling belated drunkards, or men as degraded as themselves'.

If this was the attitude of a civilised, well-educated senior police officer, what could we expect from the average working man of that era?

Anderson's prejudices weren't personal failings – they were products of imperial ideology. Anderson and his class shared a world view shaped by the conviction that they possessed a divine right to rule both the wider empire and its centre.

This mindset was perfectly captured by Cecil Rhodes, who declared:

> I contend that we are the first race in the world, and that the more of the world we inhabit the better it is for the human race… Remember that you are an Englishman and have consequently won the first prize in the lottery of life ... It is our duty to seize every opportunity of acquiring more territory ... more territory simply means more of the Anglo-Saxon race more of the best the most human, most honourable race the world possesses.

This imperial world view didn't only justify overseas conquest – it shaped domestic attitudes towards society's most vulnerable members. The same ideology that allowed 'civilised' men to use extreme violence to take what they wanted from colonised peoples also determined how they viewed the slumdwellers who lived a five-minute walk away.

These women lived at the heart of the British Empire, yet in the minds of men like Anderson, they could never be seen as members of what they considered 'the first race in the world, winners of the first prize in life's lottery'.

The empire's violence was enabled by technology and greed. As Hilaire Belloc observed: 'Whatever happens, we have got / The Maxim gun, and they have not.'

Meanwhile, as George Bernard Shaw noted, the imperial system maintained enough of its population in poverty to ensure 'a ready supply of recruits' – men who were 'ostensibly heroic and patriotic defenders' but really 'unfortunate men driven by destitution to offer themselves as food for powder for the sake of regular rations, shelter, and clothing'.

This world view created a crucial blind spot in the investigation. Anderson and his colleagues operated from the conviction that they belonged to a fundamentally different species from the victims. This prejudice inevitably shaped how they interpreted evidence and pursued leads.

Importantly, Anderson had never actually met these women. There was no solid evidence they spent their nights 'inveigling belated drunkards'.

Even modern writers struggle to escape these prejudices. Philip Sugden describes the second victim in *The Complete History of Jack the Ripper* as 'Annie Chapman, alias Annie Siffey. A sad, broken-down little prostitute, she lived a precarious and semi-nomadic existence on the streets and in the common lodging houses of Spitalfields.' The language betrays assumptions that would have been familiar to Victorian readers.

The truth was straightforward and tragic. These were women whose lives had collapsed when they found themselves alone and vulnerable in a society that offered them little protection. They experienced first-hand how brutal life could be for women at the bottom of Victorian society, and their lives ended when they were brutally murdered on the streets of the world's wealthiest city in 1888.

Perhaps they wouldn't have disagreed with Percy Bysshe Shelley's observation: 'Hell is a city much like London.'

Understanding this context suggests a different possibility entirely. Rather than seeking a mastermind driven by surgical skill and a mission to eradicate sin, we might consider whether these crimes were committed by men who had internalised the same imperial attitudes that shaped police investigations. Men who, influenced by sensational newspaper coverage and existing prejudices, saw these women as Anderson did – as a 'degraded' class unworthy of protection or even basic humanity.

The question isn't whether the killer was extraordinary, but whether the attitudes that enabled these murders were disturbingly ordinary for their time.

7

The Copycat Theory

The gaslit streets of Whitechapel in 1888 harboured more than just fog and shadows – they concealed a population pressed to the very margins of survival. Spending nights alone on these unforgiving thoroughfares, the unfortunate women who would become victims were easy prey for the thoughtless, careless cruelty of strangers. Men that Oscar Wilde would later describe in *The Soul of Man Under Socialism*:

> Upon the other hand, there are a great many people who, having no private property of their own, and being always on the brink of sheer starvation, are compelled to do the work of beasts of burden,... the man who is poor is in himself absolutely of no importance. He is merely the infinitesimal atom of a force that, so far from regarding him, crushes him: indeed, prefers him crushed, as in that case he is far more obedient.

Yet occasionally, among this teeming mass of the dispossessed, some would become ready for disobedience – to lash out violently at someone they perceived as even more wretched than themselves. Jack London and, indeed, the newspapers of the day make clear that male violence against women was very common.

The impossible logistics

The practical challenges of explaining how all eight attacks on these women occurred, from Annie Millwood on 25 February to Mary Jane Kelly on 9 November, strain credulity when attributed to a single perpetrator. The victims were killed in densely populated streets, under the watchful eye of an increasingly vigilant police force that had flooded the area with constables and plain-clothes detectives.

The Metropolitan Police had deployed hundreds of officers throughout Whitechapel, conducting door-to-door searches, questioning thousands of residents and maintaining round-the-clock patrols. Amateur vigilante groups prowled the streets alongside the professionals, creating an atmosphere of unprecedented surveillance.

Yet somehow, according to the conventional narrative, on each occasion one man was accosted by these hapless victims, and together they evaded the dragnet. Then, within yards of where people lived, he struck with surgical precision and vanished without a trace.

Those convinced it was Aaron Kosminski, the 23-year-old Polish Jew with severe mental health problems, or Walter Sickert, the 28-year-old Victorian painter, or Prince Albert Victor, the 24-year-old royal duke, or James Maybrick, the 50-year-old Liverpool cotton merchant, or any of the other 200-plus suspects who have been proposed over the decades, sensibly focus their investigations on DNA analysis, handwriting comparisons, biographical histories and psychological profiles. They meticulously examine personal correspondence, medical records and alibis. What they consistently avoid is a deep, systematic investigation of the practical mechanics of how these murders were actually committed under such remarkable circumstances.

The investigators of 1888 should not be judged too harshly for their tunnel vision. At the time, the Metropolitan Police were under enormous pressure from the press, the public and political authorities to solve the case quickly. The force's reputation had been badly damaged by their inability to prevent the murders, and Commissioner Charles Warren faced calls for his resignation. Under such circumstances, the single-killer theory offered a conceptually more straightforward investigation model – one perpetrator to catch, one pattern to decode, one mystery to solve.

Journalists found that the mysterious, elusive 'Jack the Ripper' sold more copies than mundane accounts of multiple criminals exploiting vulnerable women. The single-killer theory provided a perfect villain for the penny press: invisible yet omnipresent, brilliant yet mad, sophisticated yet savage. It was a story that sold itself.

A lone voice of reason

In this atmosphere of mounting hysteria and investigative tunnel vision, one writer questioned the received wisdom. Responding to the murder of Mary Jane Kelly – the fifth and most ghastly – *The Daily News* of Saturday, 10 November 1888, offered this remarkably insightful analysis:

> Whitechapel has on horror's head horrors accumulated ... Of course we do not suggest that this is any conclusive evidence that this murder was done by the hand which may have committed some or all of the other crimes. There is a ghastly imitativeness in the crime, a horrible 'fashion' which may be set going in murder, and which reveals itself with the mechanical servility of any other imitativeness and any other fashion… Therefore it is not to be hastily assumed that all the murders were done by the one hand.

This anonymous writer's use of the phrases 'ghastly imitativeness' and 'horrible fashion' demonstrates a sophisticated understanding of how violence can spread through communities like a contagion. The writer reveals an appreciation for how spectacular crimes can establish templates that inspire copycat behaviour.

The writer's analysis was far ahead of its time, anticipating by decades what criminologists would later name the copycat effect. More importantly, it challenged the fundamental assumption that was already hardening into conventional wisdom – that these crimes must be the work of a single perpetrator.

This prescient journalist wasn't alone in recognising the possibility of 'ghastly imitativeness' in the Whitechapel attacks. Significantly, this view was shared by Dr George Bagster Phillips, the highly respected district police surgeon who had personally examined several of the victims and crime scenes. Phillips possessed the medical expertise and first-hand experience to make informed judgements about the murders.

While Dr Thomas Bond, the consulting surgeon, brought in to provide a comprehensive analysis, concluded that 'the five murders were no doubt committed by the same hand,' Phillips maintained his dissenting opinion. As Donald Rumbelow notes in *The Complete Jack the Ripper* (1975), 'He did not believe that all the Whitechapel killings had been the work of one man.'

This professional divide within the medical establishment reveals that even contemporary experts with direct access to the evidence were far from unanimous in their conclusions.

On one tour, when I suggested the Jack the Ripper murders might be copycat murders, a man burst out laughing at the absurdity that five different murderers could be prowling Whitechapel simultaneously. The writer for *The Daily News* anticipated such reactions:

> The natural inclination of everybody would be to hope that the murders and mutilations are the work of some solitary wretch with a positive mania for women's blood. It would be better that such were the explanation than to believe that one murderer hacked a woman to pieces, and that several other murderers followed and improved upon his example.

The miraculous mystery

Unappealing as it may be, the copycat killer idea offers the most straightforward explanation to this mystery:

> The whole neighbourhood has been thrown into alarm and consternation. Every man and woman in the entire region must have been aroused to watchfulness and to activity. Yet the murders have been going on just the same – and we do not hear of any clue to the perpetrator of the latest any more than to the perpetrator of the earliest. If we are to accept what is certainly the general opinion, that the last five murders at least are the work of one hand, then the wonder becomes all the greater that one man can keep on doing such things, deed after deed, without being discovered. That such a man should again and again succeed in entrapping a woman into some lonely place and there slaughter her and yet never be seen, never be noticed, never be suspected by anyone because of blood marks on his hands or his clothes, would certainly seem to border on the miraculous.

Miraculous indeed! This leads the writer back to his theme:

> Of course, there is the other possibility to which we have already drawn attention, that some at least of the later crimes may have been the mere outcome of man's perverted imitativeness.

Evidence of imitativeness

There can be little doubt about 'man's perverted imitativeness'. The term 'copycat killer' first appeared following the crimes attributed to Jack the Ripper. There was a significant increase in replicated crimes following the

1888 murders, and *The Daily News* of Saturday, 10 November shows the copycat criminal was alive and well, even before the murder of Mary Jane Kelly on Friday, 9 November:

> The newspapers have been full of cases of men who threatened their wives, or their sweethearts, or women who were neither their wives nor sweethearts that they would treat them in the Whitechapel way… Practical jokers in the East-end have frightened women almost out of their senses by brandishing knives and proclaiming themselves to be 'Jack the Ripper.' One such frolic actually caused a poor nervous woman to lose her life. While a mania of this kind is in the air we may expect to find mimicry take the form of earnest as well as of jest.

Mimicry in earnest and in jest. Perhaps crime is always in earnest for loved ones left behind, while it may be jest for the criminal – a merry jape settling in the jester's brain, 'while a mania of this kind is in the air'.

The multiple perpetrator theory

The possibility that different individuals committed the murders gains credibility when we consider how the press described each killing in graphic detail. These vivid accounts could have served as blueprints, allowing subsequent killers to build upon their predecessors' methods. The apparent similarity in modus operandi might not indicate a single perpetrator, but rather the power of imitation in an age of sensational journalism.

And so, 'while a mania of this kind is in the air', a man who knows a tiny territory and the military precision of the police patrols stumbles on an easy target.

The copycat effect: modern understanding of an ancient phenomenon

Today, behavioural scientists and criminologists recognise the pattern observed by the writer for *The Daily News* as the 'imitation', 'contagion', or 'copycat' effect. This phenomenon has been extensively studied and documented, revealing the powerful role that media coverage plays in inspiring similar crimes. Loren Coleman writes in his 2004 book *The Copycat Effect*:

> And what it deals with is the power of mass communication and culture to create an epidemic of similar behaviours.

The mechanism is straightforward yet profound: spectacular crimes receive extensive media coverage, which inadvertently provides detailed instruction manuals for potential imitators. The coverage often includes specific details about methods, locations and victim selection that can inspire copycat attempts. In the case of the Whitechapel murders, the press provided extensive coverage of the locations, the nature of the wounds, and the circumstances of discovery – all information that could enable imitation.

The phenomenon has deep historical roots. Sociologist David P. Phillips coined the term 'Werther Effect' after Johann Wolfgang von Goethe's 1774 novel, *The Sorrows of Young Werther*. Coleman explains the connection:

> In the story, the youthful character Werther falls in love with a woman who is promised to another... He then dresses in boots, a blue coat, and a yellow vest, sits at his desk with an open book, and, literally at the eleventh hour, shoots himself. In the years that followed, throughout Europe, so many young men shot themselves while dressed as Werther and seated at their writing desks with an open copy of The Sorrows of Young Werther in front of them that the book was banned in Italy, Germany, and Denmark.

This literary precedent demonstrates that the copycat effect was already known about more than a century before the crimes attributed to 'Jack the Ripper'. The Werther suicides reveal how detailed media descriptions of self-destructive behaviour can inspire waves of imitation, even when the original inspiration is fictional rather than factual.

The overlooked possibility: why the copycat theory was ignored

If the concept of 'man's perverted imitativeness' was already recognised in 1888, why didn't the contemporary investigators, or modern ones, consider it as an explanation for the Whitechapel murders? The answer lies in the seductive power of the single-killer narrative and the investigative momentum it generated.

The single-killer theory had become so deeply embedded in both official and public consciousness that many writers and researchers forgot how surprised some contemporaries were by this assumption. The idea that one brilliant, elusive madman was stalking the streets of Whitechapel captured imaginations in a way that multiple unconnected killers could not.

George R. Sims, a prominent journalist and social commentator, writing on Sunday, 9 September 1888, suggested that the idea the murders were committed by the same killer was the creation of a talented journalist:

> The Whitechapel murders, which have come to the relief of newspaper editors in search of a sensation, are not the kind of murders which pay best. The element of romance is altogether lacking... The best element in the cases for newspaper purposes is that they are similar to a murder which was committed near the same spot some time previously, and this enables the talented journalist to start the idea that the four crimes are by the same hand. Given this idea, and 'the maniac who lures women into lonely spots and cuts them up' speedily assumes a definite shape.

The reference to 'the talented journalist' who started 'the idea that the four crimes are by the same hand' suggests that the single-killer theory may have been more a product of journalistic imagination than investigative analysis. Once 'the talented journalist' had planted the seed of a single killer, that killer inevitably assumed a definite shape.

The form became three-dimensional less than three weeks after Sims wrote his article. A letter arrived at the Central News Agency on Thursday, 27 September 1888, signed with the name that would become synonymous with the case: 'Jack the Ripper'. It gave the theoretical killer a name and made the single-killer theory almost impossible to challenge.

Most experts believe that the letter was written by a journalist to keep the story going. It worked. The writer of the letter called 'Jack the Ripper' his trade name; we would call it a brand name. I doubt that any advertising company could come up with a better one.

One 'talented journalist' starts 'the idea that the four crimes are by the same hand' and then he or another names him. It is clever. It is the ultimate murder mystery because we don't know who the killer is, yet we do know. He's *Jack the Ripper*.

Part 2

The Victims Revisited

8

Mary Ann (Polly) Nichols

Mary Ann Nichols is remembered today because many experts believe her to be the first victim of a serial killer known as Jack the Ripper. In the pre-dawn darkness of Friday, 31 August 1888, her body was discovered in Buck's Row – a shadowy lane tucked behind Whitechapel train station.

Inspector John Spratling's official report, filed that same morning, documented the grim discovery: at 3:45 a.m. Police Constable John Neil found a woman lying motionless on her back, her throat slashed from ear to ear in a savage display of violence. When Dr Rhys Llewellyn arrived to examine the scene, he discovered the horrific extent of the attack – her throat had been severed from left to right with two distinct cuts on the left side, completely severing the windpipe, gullet and spinal cord. Bruising marked her face: what appeared to be a man's thumbprint on her right lower jaw and a longer bruise across her left cheek. Most shocking of all, her stomach had been torn open with deliberate brutality.

A week later, when investigators had pieced together her identity, a police report began: 'Deceased identified as Mary Ann Nichols, a prostitute, who separated from her husband nine years ago.'

For many historians and investigators, the reason that this 43-year-old woman was out on the mean streets of Whitechapel in the middle of the night appears straightforward: she was a prostitute, as both police records and contemporary newspapers matter-of-factly reported.

Ripper expert Martin Fido characterises her as 'a drab little woman' who 'drank her husband's wages', asserting that 'it was established that she was practising prostitution'.

The authoritative *Jack the Ripper CSI: Whitechapel* provides the broader context that seems to support this conclusion:

> In the mid-nineteenth century, London's East End was a hotbed of tension and desperation. These harsh economic circumstances had driven many women to prostitution as their only means of survival. It was into this savage landscape that Jack the Ripper emerged to hunt his prey.

She facilitated her own murder. What were the police or indeed the wider society supposed to do? But did Mary Ann Nichols actually become a prostitute?

A different beginning

Born on Tuesday, 26 August 1845 and christened Mary Ann Walker, she was affectionately known as Polly from her earliest childhood years. Her father, Edward, was a skilled blacksmith who had found steady, respectable work in London's thriving print industry around Fleet Street – a detail that immediately sets the record straight. Polly was no victim of the crushing, generational poverty that trapped so many East End families. Hers was a typical working-class household where personal virtue and family reputation were not just valued but fiercely protected.

Edward Walker and his family occupied a social position measurably above the appalling, dehumanising conditions that slum children endured daily in London's most notorious districts. But even in those desperate neighbourhoods, it would be a grave mistake to assume that virtue and reputation meant nothing to the residents.

During the 1800s, Bethnal Green had earned its reputation as one of the most dangerous and degraded areas of the entire East End, so notorious that Charles Dickens chose it as the perfect setting for the criminal lair of Bill Sykes in *Oliver Twist*. Yet even there, as Michelle Higgs demonstrates in

A Visitor's Guide to Victorian England (2014), working-class women were far from the morally loose stereotypes often portrayed in sensationalist accounts:

> For many working-class women, retaining their virtue and reputation was very important to increase the chances of a good marriage. Mrs Layton, born in Bethnal Green in 1855, worked in domestic service and her story is told in Margaret Llewelyn Davies' *Life As We Have Known It.* After a two-year engagement, Mrs Layton recalled: 'The man that I had promised to entrust my future life to made improper suggestions to me, and when I refused tried to overcome me by force. I am thankful I succeeded in defeating him. From that moment I lost all respect for him and, in spite of all his protestations of regret and promises that it should not occur again, I told him I would never forgive him, and broke off the engagement there and then.'

Rather than compromise her principles for marriage, she broke off the engagement immediately – a decision requiring tremendous courage in an era when spinsterhood often meant destitution.

This was the world into which Mary Ann 'Polly' Nichols was born, though her early years offered more promise than most.

A childhood above the abyss

Social reformer Charles Booth defined abject poverty as families surviving on less than a pound a week. In London's East End, tens of thousands existed on fractions of that amount. Thousands of children were born into genuine destitution, sharing tiny, vermin-infested rooms where older siblings slept on floors while parents conceived new children in the same cramped space. As campaigner Andrew Mearns observed, morality became nearly impossible under such conditions. Desperate parents sometimes pushed children into petty theft or prostitution.

The statistics were horrifying. William Thomas Stead, editor of *The Pall Mall Gazette*, documented 'one district with 43 brothels containing 428 women and children, many not 12 years of age, working as prostitutes'. To expose how easily children could be purchased for sexual exploitation, he bought 13-year-old Eliza Armstrong from her mother for £5.

Polly Nichols definitely didn't become a child prostitute. Her father, Edward Walker, earned more than double Booth's poverty threshold – enough to provide his daughter with opportunities that remained rare for working-class girls. Edward could afford to send Polly to school.

This was no small privilege. Although education wouldn't become compulsory until 1876, Polly received schooling until the age of 15 – extraordinary for Britain's working class, especially for girls. Most girls fortunate enough to receive any education learned only to read; Polly mastered both reading and writing.

At 15, Polly avoided the typical path into domestic service – a route fraught with danger for young women. Female servants were often vulnerable targets for males in the household seeking to seduce or rape them. Those who became pregnant struggled to find respectable work afterwards; for many, prostitution became the only option for survival.

Instead, Polly remained at home, managing the household for her father and older brother while they earned the family's income. This arrangement continued until she was 18, when she married William Nichols, a Fleet Street printer. As Mary Ann Nichols – or simply Polly – she settled into domestic life, managing the home for her husband, father, brother and eventually their three children. The family remained crowded in Edward Walker's house until Polly reached the age of 30.

In 1876, the Nichols family achieved something remarkable – they convinced the Peabody Trust, a charitable housing association, of their exemplary moral character and stable income, securing tenancy in newly built flats in Southwark. That July, they moved to Stamford Street, marking the first time in 30 years that Polly had lived anywhere but her father's house.

Here, in their own space, Polly bore her fourth and fifth children. But prosperity couldn't prevent the arguments that began tearing her marriage apart. William claimed Polly had developed a drinking problem – the apparent source of Martin Fido's dismissive characterisation of her as a 'drab little woman who drank her husband's wages'.

Historian Hallie Rubenhold offers a more nuanced perspective:

> Whatever Polly's habits, they couldn't have been as uncontainable as her husband implied. If they were, the superintendent would have noticed and taken steps to remove the Nicholses, as happened with other problem-drinking tenants.

Polly's father, Edward Walker, provided an alternative explanation at his daughter's inquest: William had begun an affair with Rosetta Walls, a younger woman whose husband had gone to sea. Whatever the truth, on 29 March 1880, 34-year-old Polly walked out of the Peabody flats forever.

9

Homeless

Polly's desperation became clear when she sought refuge in the Lambeth Union Workhouse. These institutions, designed to sweep the poor from public view, were deliberately appalling, as Charles Dickens had exposed in his novels. Jack London's account of spending a night in one captures their horror: he was forced to strip naked and enter a communal bath that had already washed all the day's previous entrants.

The workhouse represented everything Polly would have feared: being treated with contempt, prisoner-like clothing, hard physical labour, inadequate food and prohibition of alcohol. Yet she had nowhere else to turn.

Thomas Taverner, the relieving officer at Lambeth Union Workhouse, interviewed William Nichols and ordered him to pay five shillings' weekly maintenance. The five shillings allowed Polly to leave the workhouse. This arrangement lasted a year until William hired a detective who presented evidence that Polly was sharing a room with George Crawshaw at Holloway. As Rubenhold notes:

> William was absolved of financial responsibilities and on 28 July 1882, he and his paramour packed their belongings, took his children by their hands, and bid goodbye to Stamford Street. The superintendent noted William Nichols had been a 'good tenant' but 'left in debt' – the words 'good tenant' were later struck through.

When maintenance payments ceased, Polly endured nearly a year in the Lambeth Union Workhouse before she could no longer bear it. She found temporary refuge with her father and her brother's family, though the arrangement proved difficult for everyone involved.

In 1884, she moved in with Thomas Stewart Drew, a widowed

blacksmith with three daughters who offered her what seemed like a settled home. For two years, this arrangement provided stability.

Then tragedy struck. In June 1886, Polly's older brother – her only sibling – suffered third-degree burns when a paraffin lamp burst into flames as he tried to extinguish it. His terrible death devastated Polly, possibly damaging her relationship with Drew. By November 1886, they were no longer together.

Once again, Polly faced the streets alone, with nowhere to go but the Lambeth Union Workhouse.

The year 1887 began with eager anticipation of a celebration. Queen Victoria's Golden Jubilee on 20–21 June brought grandees from around the world, streets bloomed with decorations, and crowds cheered the grand procession through London.

Yet this pageantry masked a harsher reality – in 1887 it was now 14 years into 'The Long Depression', which had begun with 'The Panic of 1873'. That massive financial crash, which began in Vienna, spread throughout Europe and across the Atlantic, triggering 20 years of British economic stagnation that hit those at the bottom of society with devastating force.

The contrast became stark five months after the jubilee's pomp. Thousands gathered in Trafalgar Square on Sunday, 13 November 1887, to protest the appalling conditions that existed. Two thousand Metropolitan Police officers armed with truncheons, supported by 400 Household Cavalry troops, broke up the demonstration. The violent clashes between police and demonstrators on that day earned it the name of 'Bloody Sunday'.

For Polly, the cold, wet months at the end of 1887 meant tramping for work and sleeping rough in doorways and stairways. By 16 April 1888, desperation drove her to the Renfrew Road Workhouse. The enforced absence of alcohol may have helped stabilise her – by 12 May, she was deemed suitable to serve in the respectable middle-class home of Mr and Mrs Cowdry.

During her first week in service, she contacted her father for the first time in two years:

> I just write to say you will be glad to know that I am settled in my new place and going alright up to now… It is a grand place with trees and gardens back and front. All has been newly done up. They are teetotallers and very religious, so I ought to get on. They are very nice people, and I have not much to do.

A secure place to sleep, three meals a day, and the comfort of a proper home must have felt miraculous after her desperate existence on the streets.

But perhaps the devout couple's rigid moral expectations proved too much for Polly. On 12 July 1888 – just two months after her hopeful letter – Sarah Cowdry wrote to Renfrew Road Workhouse reporting that Polly had absconded with £3 10s worth of clothing.

By early August, Polly had found refuge at Wilmott's Lodging House at 18 Thrawl Street – a women-only establishment that offered the illusion of safety in Whitechapel's labyrinth of desperation. For three weeks, she clung to this last vestige of respectability, but then the inevitable happened: Polly's money ran out.

On Thursday, 30 August 1888, as if the city itself sensed the approaching horror, a thunderstorm swept across London's East End, followed by a relentless drizzle that turned the cobblestones treacherous and the air bitter. The temperature plummeted to an unseasonable 8°C, 46°F – cruel weather for a woman forced to sleep rough.

Polly took refuge in the kitchen of Wilmott's. This was not uncommon; the next victim, Annie Chapman, like Polly, tried to get a few hours out of a cold and wet night. Both women were eventually turned out onto the streets.

Within minutes of where Polly was turned out, three women had been brutally attacked: Annie Millwood in February, Emma Elizabeth Smith in April, and Martha Tabram just three weeks earlier, on 7 August. But that was Polly's problem, not the deputy keepers.

An hour later, at 2:30 a.m., Ellen Holland met Polly. Ellen was out that hour because there was a huge fire blazing at the docks; entertainment was thin on the ground in Whitechapel at that time, so thousands were out enjoying the spectacle. By 2:30, Ellen was making her way back to her bed when she met Polly at the corner of Whitechapel High Street and Osborn Street. St Mary's Church clock struck the half hour as she watched her friend disappear eastward into the darkness.

At 3:15 a.m., Police Constable John Neil walked eastward down Buck's Row. The street lay empty and silent.

When he returned 30 minutes later, Mary Ann 'Polly' Nichols lay dead on the cobblestones.

On Thursday, 6 September 1888, Polly was buried in an unmarked grave in the City of London Cemetery. For 108 years, she lay forgotten, her story dissolved into the larger mythology of the Ripper murders.

In 1996, cemetery authorities added a commemorative plaque bearing her name.

10

The Man Beside the Body

Polly Nichols was murdered in front of a pair of wooden gates on Buck's Row's south side. The eight-foot high gates were attached to a house that formed the end of an eastward-running row, with a bedroom window less than four yards from where she died. Behind that window lived a very light sleeper who heard nothing. Directly opposite lived a woman who was awake at the time of the murder. She, too, heard nothing. The *Evening News* of Saturday, 1 September 1888, captured the eerie quiet:

> Mrs. Green, Mr. and Mrs. Perkins, the watchman in Schneider's tar factory, and the watchman in a wool depot, which are both situated in Buck's-row, agree that the night was an unusually quiet one for the neighbourhood.

Two men worked through the night in a Winthrop Street yard just behind the murder site. They heard nothing.

The area was heavily patrolled. PC John Neil walked Buck's Row every half hour. About 120 yards east, PC John Thain patrolled Brady Street and checked the east end of Buck's Row every half hour. Both officers served in the J Division, which was responsible for Bethnal Green, located east of Whitechapel. About 200 yards west of the murder site, PC Jonas Mizen of H Division patrolled Baker's Row, and every half hour, he checked the west end of Buck's Row.

None of these people – residents, workers or police – saw the victim or killer arriving or leaving.

The timeline

Divisional Inspector Spratling recorded that day:

> PC 97J Neil reports at 3:45 a.m. 31st of August. He found the dead body of a woman lying on her back with her clothes a little above her knees with her throat cut from ear to ear… PC obtained the assistance of PCs 55H Mizen and 96J Thain.

The phrasing is significant: PC Mizen is listed first, suggesting he arrived to assist before PC Thain. The report also notes: 'a bruise, apparently of a thumb being on the right lower jaw, also one on the left cheek.'

The inquest opened on Saturday, 1 September 1888, and *The Daily Telegraph* reported PC Neil's testimony on Monday, 3 September:

> Yesterday morning I was proceeding down Buck's-row, Whitechapel, going towards Brady-street. There was not a soul about. I had been round there half an hour previously, and I saw no one then.

He doesn't mention a time at any point. Inspector Spratling wrote in his report: 'PC 97J Neil reports at 3:45: He found the dead body of a woman.' Not many people had watches, so timings would have been based on public clocks that everyone could see. Some clocks might have been running a couple of minutes slow, while others were running a couple of minutes fast.

Dr Llewellyn would have had a watch, and in his statement, he said he was 'called about four o'clock', but he doesn't say if that was when he received a knock at the door, or when he had dressed and left his house, or did he mean that was when he arrived at the crime scene?

One comment about time that gives us a reference point is when, in his evidence, the doctor said, 'I believe she had not been dead more than half an hour.' PC Neil didn't miss the killer by much, and this is confirmed by him because he said there was 'blood oozing from a wound in the throat', and in answer to a question from the coroner, he said: 'There was a pool of blood just where her neck was lying. It was running from the wound in her neck.'

From the doctor's information, the earliest time that death could have occurred was 30 minutes before he examined the body.

What happened in those 30 minutes?

PC Neil could have walked up Court Street from Whitechapel Road; at that point, he was only a minute and a half west of the body.

> I examined the body by the aid of my lamp, and noticed blood oozing from a wound in the throat. She was lying on her back, with her clothes disarranged. I felt her arm, which was quite warm from the joints upwards. Her eyes were wide open. Her bonnet was off and lying at her side, close to the left hand.

Even for a police officer, this would have been a shocking situation to face in a dark and silent lane, and the minute and a half he had been in Buck's Row would now be three minutes. PC Neil then saw PC Thain's light at the east end of Buck's Row. He said he called, but he didn't use his whistle.

PC John Thain was a 34-year-old married man answering a call from a fellow police officer who hadn't used his whistle, but let's assume he didn't dawdle. At a fast walk, maybe 4 miles an hour (2 yards per second), another minute had passed. A minimum of four minutes since PC Neil entered Buck's Row.

Then PC Neil said, 'I said to him, "Run at once for Dr Llewellyn".' This was not a life-saving situation; the victim was dead. But again, let's assume PC Thain didn't dawdle. Going west for 100 yards, then south down Court Street for 60 yards, crossing Whitechapel Road diagonally to 152 Whitechapel Road is another 60 yards. At a brisk pace, PC Thain would have been knocking on the door to wake the doctor two minutes after leaving the crime scene. So, a total of six minutes at a minimum would have passed since PC John Neil arrived in Buck's Row.

38-year-old Rhys Llewellyn had to get out of bed, answer the door, receive the information, return to his room and get dressed. He was a Victorian gentleman, so dressing was not as straightforward as it is today. His underwear would have consisted of a combination suit or separate drawers and a vest. He would need to attach a stiff collar to his shirt with collar studs. Then he put on his trousers, waistcoat, morning coat, socks, and boots that would need lacing, and then he tied his cravat.

Also, he knew he was not being called to save someone's life.

By the time he had picked up his bag and closed his front door, it was 10 minutes since PC Thain knocked. A total of 16 minutes.

Dr Llewellyn had just got out of bed, so we might allow him four more minutes to get to the crime scene, another minute to examine the body and decide that 'she had not been dead more than half an hour'.

For 21 of those minutes, PC John Neil had been in Buck's Row. The killer had a maximum of nine minutes.

Nine minutes in which he worked in silence, getting her onto the ground without a struggle. There was no blood on the front of Polly's clothes; it was all gathered beneath her. The killer made sure the left carotid artery was pointing down to the cobbles so that the last beat of her heart pumped the blood straight down, not over him. There was also no blood spread around, so she had to have been positioned on her left side.

This killer was not working in a frenzy.

Then he rolled her onto her back, and just below the cut he had made on the left of her throat, he took his knife across, cutting almost back to the spine. Then he repositioned himself to lift her skirts above her waist. She was wearing stays, so he'd have to move them somehow, either by pushing them up her body or cutting them to loosen them.

Then Dr Llewellyn said, the abdomen was mutilated:

> Two or three inches from the left side was a wound running in a jagged manner. It was a very deep wound, and the tissues were cut through. There were several incisions running across the abdomen. On the right side, there were also three or four similar cuts running downwards.

All accomplished in complete silence without a struggle, and leaving only two small bruises on the face.

By the time he stood up to admire his work, a minimum of two minutes must have passed. Now he had to leave Buck's Row. If he went east, it was 120 yards to Brady Street. He was unlikely to run, but walking briskly at four miles per hour, he would cover two yards per second and reach Brady Street in one minute. Going west to Baker's Row would take two minutes. From the moment he killed Polly to the time he had cleared Buck's Row, the minimum time taken would have been three minutes.

He could have been exiting Buck's Row less than six minutes before PC Neil arrived.

Dr Llewellyn said, 'I believe she had not been dead more than half an hour.' Not more than half an hour, so it could have been a couple of minutes less, which could mean the killer was leaving just four minutes before PC Neil arrived. Certainly not much more because the blood was still flowing when he arrived at the crime scene.

The killer had a tiny window of opportunity in which to commit the murder.

Do we know what happened in those few minutes? Yes.

11

Sunday's Bombshell

Friday's newspapers reported the discovery by PC John Neil, and on Saturday, he gave his evidence at the inquest, which was reported in Saturday's newspapers.

Everything changed on Sunday, 2 September 1888 – yet remarkably, I have never read a book that mentions this. As Paul Begg notes, 'Accounts of the crimes themselves decreased. For example, only one-fifth of Don Rumbelow's book actually discussed the crimes!'

What changed that Sunday?

Lloyd's Weekly published a massive 6,500-word investigation into Polly Nichols' murder. Buried halfway through:

> REMARKABLE STATEMENT
> On Friday night Mr. Robert Paul, a carman, on his return from work, made the following statement to our representative. He said: It was exactly a quarter to four when I passed up Buck's-row to my work as a carman for Covent-garden market. It was dark, and I was hurrying along, when I saw a man standing where the woman was.

This is more than two days after Polly Nichols was murdered, but not until Sunday does the world learn that a man was standing where Polly Nichols lay dead.

Robert Paul gave his 'Remarkable Statement' to a journalist at *Lloyd's Weekly* on the day of the murder. The journalist would have been delighted to have a scoop. But he had a problem: the paper he worked for was a weekly, and his story wouldn't appear for two days. Fortunately, the man who handed him the story kept quiet. Maybe money changed hands.

What is important is that the man standing where Polly lay also kept quiet. Why?

The interview with Robert Paul continued:

> He came a little towards me, but as I knew the dangerous character of the locality I tried to give him a wide berth. Few people like to come up and down here without being on their guard, for there are such terrible gangs about. There have been many knocked down and robbed at that spot. The man, however, came towards me and said, 'Come and look at this woman.'

Robert Paul was describing an event that took place in those crucial minutes before PC John Neil stepped out of Court Street and into Buck's Row.

For how many of those minutes was Robert Paul in Buck's Row?

He walked the full length of Buck's Row, that is over 300 yards, so even at a fast pace, it will take nearly three minutes. Add to that the fact that he was stopped by the man by the body.

> I went and found the woman lying on her back. I laid hold of her wrist and found that she was dead and the hands cold. It was too dark to see the blood about her. I thought that she had been outraged, and had died in the struggle. I was obliged to be punctual at my work, so I went on and told the other man I would send the first policeman I saw.

He would have been in Buck's Row for about four minutes. He didn't see or hear anybody else during that time, apart from the man by the body.

That is four of those crucial minutes when the murder took place. The killer did not strike in the four minutes that Robert Paul was in Buck's Row, or Paul would have seen the murder being committed, so the murder had to have taken place before Robert Paul entered Buck's Row and saw a man standing by the body.

Continuing with Robert Paul's statement.

> I saw one in Church-row, just at the top of Buck's-row, who was going round calling people up, and I told him what I had seen, and I asked him to come, but he did not say whether he should come or not. He continued calling the people up, which I thought was a great shame, after I had told him the woman was dead.

Now here is a bombshell. A police officer knew that two men had been at the crime scene before PC John Neil discovered the body. How lucky was that *Lloyd's Weekly* journalist?

The journalist knew, when he heard Robert Paul's story, that there were two other men in a position to sell this story. He knew journalists from every rival newspaper were swarming through Whitechapel, desperate for information about this murder. He also knew that detectives were calling house to house seeking information. Despite all this, *Lloyd's Weekly* got its scoop.

Why did those two men remain silent for more than two days?

A police officer was informed about a potential crime in the area. Three women had been attacked within half a mile of where he was told there was a woman who appeared to be dead. It was less than four weeks since Martha Tabram was discovered with 39 stab wounds. The police were being heavily criticised for their failure to catch the killer.

In an ideal world, the police officer would insist that these two men accompany him to the scene of the crime and, at the same time, would summon assistance by blowing his whistle. Then, when he discovered the woman had had her throat cut, he would search these two men for a weapon.

It wasn't an ideal world, but at the very least, we would expect PC Jonas Mizen to take the names and addresses of the two men. PC Mizen didn't do that; he was tapping on windows to wake people up for work: a service for which he received a payment and that is what he continued to do.

What did PC Mizen do when he realised that the woman he was told about was not just one of the many homeless women sleeping on the streets that night in Whitechapel, but another victim of a monster who was making the headlines?

He knew the two men were bound to talk, so he had better confess right away.

Recently promoted Divisional Inspector John Spratling of J Division wrote his report on the day of the murder:

> PC 97J Neil reports at 3:45 AM 31st of August. He found the dead body of a woman lying on her back with her clothes a little above her knees with her throat cut from ear to ear ... PC obtained the assistance of PC's 55H Mizen and 96J Thain.

He doesn't mention the two men. He does record that PC Mizen gave assistance and places his name ahead of PC Thain. Anybody unaware of any other facts might reasonably assume PC Mizen responded with urgency.

The day after the murder, Saturday, 1 September, the inquest opened. Only one senior police officer was named. He was Inspector James Henry Helson, who had been in charge of the J Division of the Metropolitan Police since 1887. There were only three witnesses: Polly's father, PC Neil and Dr Llewellyn. The evidence presented omitted Robert Paul and the man beside the body, even though PC Jonas Mizen knew they had been at the crime scene before PC Neil.

By the end of Saturday, the police might be pleased to note that neither of the men had revealed their story. A story that may alert a journalist to another example of police incompetence.

Hopefully, any modern-day detective would see the man who was standing by the body as somebody who had the opportunity to commit the murder.

Is there a plausible reason why the police in 1888 didn't consider this?

Rather than seeing a man who undoubtedly had the opportunity to murder Polly, they see two men who told a police officer about a possible murder. Would the killer do that?

Additionally, they asked the question: what kind of woman would end up in a dark lane with a man she didn't know? The answer must be a prostitute. Polly accosted a client, and he killed her. She was walking from the west while the unknown man was walking from the east; therefore, she could not have accosted him, so they must not waste precious time on him. What was important was to close ranks around PC Jonas Mizen.

But then, after more than 48 hours of silence, *Lloyd's Weekly* revealed all. Sunday, 2 September must have been a busy day for the H and J Divisions.

Monday's inquest opened with Inspectors Helson and Abberline and Detective-Sergeant Enright.

Detective Inspector Abberline, who missed the first day of the inquest, was now on the case. PC Jonas Mizen, who also missed the first day, was present, and so was the mystery man. But not Robert Paul, the crucial witness who dropped the bomb. If I were a police officer, I would have ensured that Robert Paul was at that inquest.

12

The Day after the Bombshell

> **Police-constable Mizen** said that at a quarter to four o'clock on Friday morning he was at the crossing, Hanbury-street, Baker's-row, when a carman who passed in company with another man informed him that he was wanted by a policeman in Buck's-row, where a woman was lying. When he arrived there Constable Neil sent him for the ambulance. At that time nobody but Neil was with the body.

It's a very short statement, and fortunately for PC Mizen, Robert Paul had not been summoned, so PC Mizen's brief statement that he was wanted by a policeman was not challenged. And Robert Paul's comment that 'He continued calling the people up' was not mentioned.

The next witness then gave evidence.

The Daily Telegraph reported on Tuesday, 4 September 1888:

> **Charles Andrew Cross**, carman, said he had been in the employment of Messrs. Pickford and Co. for over twenty years. About half-past three on Friday he left his home to go to work, and he passed through Buck's-row. He discerned on the opposite side something lying against the gateway, but he could not at once make out what it was. He thought it was a tarpaulin sheet. He walked into the middle of the road, and saw that it was the figure of a woman.

Robert Paul didn't see him 'in the middle of the road'. Robert Paul said, 'I saw a man standing where the woman was.' It was dark. Buck's Row was about 20 feet wide. Would Charles Cross make out any more detail if he were 10 feet away than he did when he was presumably around 15 or 16 feet away?

> He then heard the footsteps of a man going up Buck's-row, about forty yards away, in the direction that he himself had come from. When he came up witness said to him, 'Come and look over here; there is a woman lying on the pavement.' They both crossed over to the body, and witness took hold of the woman's hands, which were cold and limp. Witness said, 'I believe she is dead.'

Was anybody among the Met's finest listening to this while running a finger down an open copy of *Lloyd's Weekly*? Ready to interrupt the witness by waving his copy of *Lloyd's Weekly* in the man's face and showing Robert Paul's words to the man, 'I laid hold of her wrist and found that she was dead and the hands cold.' Well, that didn't happen, so the man who was found standing next to a woman who had been murdered minutes before continued:

> He touched her face, which felt warm. The other man, placing his hand on her heart, said 'I think she is breathing, but very little if she is.'

You decide which of these two men is making things up and why.

> Witness suggested that they should give her a prop, but his companion refused to touch her.

Philip Sugden in *The Complete History of Jack the Ripper* said Robert Paul suggested 'they prop her up, but Cross would not touch her'. Of course, if Cross had just killed her and cut her throat to the spinal column, moving her risked her head falling off. However, let's return to Cross and his statement.

Just then, they heard a policeman coming.

Robert Paul didn't mention hearing a policeman. If Cross heard a policeman, why didn't he tell that policeman about the woman?

> Witness did not notice that her throat was cut, the night being very dark. He and the other man left the deceased, and in Baker's-row they met the last witness, whom they informed that they had seen a woman lying in Buck's-row. Witness said, 'She looks to me to be either dead or drunk; but for my part I think she is dead.' The policeman said, 'All right,' and then walked on.

Which conversation happened? Robert Paul told *Lloyd's Weekly* about 14 hours after Polly was murdered:

> I told the other man I would send the first policeman I saw. I saw one in Church-row, just at the top of Buck's-row, who was going round calling people up, and I told him what I had seen, and I asked him to come, but he did not say whether he should come or not. He continued calling the people up, which I thought was a great shame, after I had told him the woman was dead.

And which conversation would the police prefer? Continuing with the statement of Charles Cross:

> The other man left witness soon after. Witness had never seen him before.
>
> Replying to the coroner, witness denied having seen Police-constable Neil in Buck's-row. There was nobody there when he and the other man left. In his opinion deceased looked as if she had been outraged and gone off in a swoon; but he had no idea that there were any serious injuries.

Coroner: Did the other man tell you who he was?

Charles Cross: No, sir; he merely said that he would have fetched a policeman, only he was behind time. I was behind time myself.

Again, this is not what *Lloyd's Weekly* reported. Robert Paul said. 'I told the other man I would send the first policeman I saw.'

A Juryman: Did you tell Constable Mizen that another constable wanted him in Buck's-row?

Charles Cross: No, because I did not see a policeman in Buck's-row.

Okay, I've no quarrel with that. The witness is telling the truth.

The mystery deepens

Here, two days after the murder, the public learned for the first time that there was 'a man standing where the woman was'. This raises profound questions.

More puzzling still: when Robert Paul told a policeman what he'd seen, why did the man beside the body remain invisible until Sunday's newspaper revelation?

This detail is crucial because Robert Paul places a man at the crime scene during those vital minutes when Polly Nichols had just been murdered. Of the 200+ Jack the Ripper suspects proposed over the decades, not one can be definitively placed in that unique position at that critical moment.

The two-day silence about the man beside the body represents the most significant overlooked clue in the Jack the Ripper case.

Somebody was lying: Cross, Mizen or both?

PC Mizen didn't act urgently – he didn't even take the names and addresses of the men. Of course, claiming he was told that a policeman was already there would explain what otherwise might look like negligence; the other police officer had taken details, and PC Mizen didn't need to rush since someone was handling the situation. Senior officers might also collude to avoid providing the press with more evidence of police incompetence.

The man standing beside the body in Buck's Row when Robert Paul arrived was invisible all Friday and Saturday. He appeared only after Robert Paul's Sunday revelations in *Lloyd's Weekly*.

13

Detective Inspector Abberline on the Case

Why didn't Abberline ensure that Robert Paul testified at the inquest? Why didn't he verify Charles Cross's account against Robert Paul's statement in *Lloyd's Weekly*?

It doesn't take Sherlock Holmes to realise that there were numerous contradictions in the evidence given by Robert Paul, Charles Cross and PC Jonas Mizen, yet no one seemed interested in resolving them. And I repeat, Charles Cross was found standing over the body in the few minutes when a knife sliced through the carotid artery of a 43-year-old homeless woman.

Abberline attended the inquest's second day – we know this because he was mentioned regarding Polly's undergarments. When the coroner requested that her stays be examined more carefully, 'on the suggestion of Inspector Aberline [*sic*], the clothes were sent for.' That was the only time Abberline's name appeared on the day that Charles Cross gave his testimony.

The police requested a two-week pause to gather evidence.

The Witnesses' Addresses:
Edward Walker: 15 Maidwell Street, Albany Road, Camberwell
Henry Tomkins: 12 Coventry Street, Bethnal Green
William Nichols: Coburg Road, Old Kent Road
Emily Holland: 18 Thrawl Street
Robert Paul: 30 Forster Street, Whitechapel
Charles Cross: no address recorded – only that he worked for Pickford's

Abberline could have tracked Cross down. As Christer Holmgren notes in *Cutting Point* (2021), *The Star* gave his address as 22 Doveton Street, Cambridge Road, Bethnal Green.

When the inquest reopened after two weeks, Abberline made his only substantive contribution:

> **The Coroner**: There was a man who passed down Buck's Row when the doctor was examining the body. Have you heard anything of him?
>
> **Inspector Abberline**: We have not been able to find him.

Two weeks after Robert Paul's revelation about finding a man beside the body, the only comment made by Abberline referred to someone who passed by after the police had gathered at the scene of the crime. What about the man standing beside Polly while her blood was still flowing?

The unanswered questions

Critical questions remained unasked:

- Why did Charles Cross and PC Mizen stay silent for two days?
- Why did Mizen lie about a policeman already being present?
- Which man refused to help sit Polly up?
- Who said they thought she was dead?
- Which of them actually informed PC Mizen?
- Why was Cross's address omitted from the official record?

This isn't nitpicking. According to Dr Llewellyn, someone murdered Polly just minutes before PC Neil discovered her, while her blood still flowed. A witness placed a man beside the body during those crucial minutes. The man admitted being there. This scenario is unique among all the attacks of 1888.

Why did Charles Cross stop?

Whitechapel teemed with homeless people seeking rest wherever they could find it. When did you last stop after midnight to examine a rough sleeper? People do stop, but they will be a police officer or volunteers working for a homelessness charity. This man wasn't about to offer aid, advice or resuscitation, and he didn't; instead, he told a policeman. He didn't need to wait to inform the next passerby in order to do that.

Cross's behaviour defies logic. Why would someone late for work stop to examine a woman in a gateway? He claimed he initially thought it was 'a tarpaulin sheet' but then 'saw that it was the figure of a woman'. In that case, most people who were late for work would be on their way.

When did you last see someone standing over a rough sleeper, waiting to inform the next passerby? In 1888 London, with many more homeless people than today, such behaviour would have dramatically extended your journey time.

Cross claimed urgency – he was 'behind time' for work. *The Daily Telegraph* reported he left home 'about half-past three', while *The Star* said 3:20 a.m. At the inquest, he testified: 'I heard the footsteps of a man going up Buck's Row, about forty yards away.' *Lloyd's Weekly* quoted Robert Paul: 'It was exactly a quarter to four when I passed up Buck's Row.'

The walking times don't add up.

I went to 22 Doveton Street, set my stopwatch and walked as though I were late for work. It took me six minutes to get to the spot where Polly was murdered. If Cross left at 3:20 a.m., he took 25 minutes. If he left at 3:30, he took 15 minutes.

The police had two weeks to investigate a man who took 15 or 25 minutes to complete a six-minute walk, yet apparently never questioned this discrepancy.

The name that wasn't

Recent research revealed a startling fact: in 1888, no one named Charles Cross was listed at 22 Doveton Street. However, Charles Lechmere was listed there. Obviously, the police didn't even do this basic check.

When Charles Lechmere was an infant, his father abandoned the family. At the age of 7, his mother married Police Constable Thomas Cross. In the 1861 census, young Charles appeared as 'Charles Cross' – but this was the *only* official document in over 100 that recorded him with that surname until he testified about finding Polly's body.

As Christer Holmgren writes:

> Going by the more than one hundred signatures we have, he always called himself Lechmere. His children went by that name, his wife did, his post would reasonably have had that name on it, and so on.

The police accepted the name 'Charles Cross' without verification. They had six days between Monday, 3 September and Annie Chapman's murder on Friday, 8 September to investigate the contradictions, but they never checked this man's address or story.

This is how Philip Sugden reports the discovery of Polly Nichols' body in *The Complete History of Jack the Ripper*:

> At about 3:40 on the morning of Friday, 31st August, a carman was walking to work along Bucks Row, Whitechapel. He was Charles Cross of 22 Doveton St, Cambridge Heath Rd, Bethnal Green, and he had worked at Pickford's for more than twenty years. Buck's Row seemed deserted. Cross was on the north side of the street and was walking towards Bakers Row. The morning was chilly and still very dark.

He goes on to explain how Cross saw what he thought was a tarpaulin before realising it was a woman, at which point Robert Paul arrived.

This description appears in every book covering the Buck's Row events. Yet the only evidence for this version comes from the man discovered beside a woman who had just been brutally murdered – a woman whose blood was still flowing. A man who didn't reveal himself for two days, used a name abandoned since childhood, and took 15 or 25 minutes for a six-minute walk.

Ex-Superintendent Dr Andy Griffiths stated in the Channel 5 documentary *Jack the Ripper: The Missing Evidence* (2014) that the police wouldn't be looking for anyone else if this murder happened today.

14

How Was Polly Nichols Killed?

Setting aside whether Polly earned her living selling sex, there's no evidence she picked up a client after leaving Ellen Holland at 2:30 a.m. Police and modern researchers have reasoned that someone killed her in a dark lane, then asked what kind of woman would end up in a dark lane with a man she didn't know. Their answer: a prostitute. But this isn't evidence – it's merely a possible explanation built on an assumption. The actual evidence suggests she didn't pick up a client at all.

First, her route contradicts the theory. When she left Ellen Holland, Polly didn't head west towards the red-light district. She didn't make for Commercial Street, Aldgate High Street or St Botolph's Church – so popular with men seeking women that locals dubbed it the Prostitutes' Church. Instead, she turned her back on all that and walked east. Buck's Row lay deep inside Whitechapel's residential area, well away from the killing fields where three homeless women had already died after being brutally attacked.

Second, Buck's Row wasn't the unfrequented location researchers claim. Philip Sugden argues in *The Complete History of Jack the Ripper* that the victims 'greatly facilitated his crimes' because they were 'prostitutes all, accustomed to accosting men and taking them to dark or unfrequented byways and yards for sex'.

Buck's Row around 3:30 a.m. was certainly dark, but hardly unfrequented. Consider who was nearby: men working in a yard in Winthrop Street, three watchmen at Buck's Row businesses, three police officers conducting half-hour patrols, two women living within yards (one a light sleeper, one awake) at the time, and two men heading to work who would arrive within minutes of the murder. This doesn't describe an isolated killing ground.

Third, Dr Llewellyn said he believed death occurred not more than 30 minutes before he examined Polly's body. There was a lot that needed to be done between the time the knife went in and Dr Llewellyn's arrival. It's difficult to imagine there was time for Aaron Kosminski, Walter Sickert or any other suspect to carry out this murder and mutilation and then disappear before Charles Cross (Lechmere) entered Buck's Row.

Fourth, the medical evidence defies the client scenario. Dr Llewellyn testified that the victim was killed while lying down, without a struggle and in complete silence. He noted only minor facial injuries:

> On the right side of the face there is a bruise running along the lower part of the jaw. It might have been caused by a blow with the fist or pressure by the thumb. On the left side of the face, there was a circular bruise, which also might have been done by the pressure of the fingers.

How would a client arriving with a prostitute manage this feat? The next four victims were also killed while lying down, dying without struggling or screaming.

Donald Rumbelow observes that outdoor prostitutes provided their services standing against walls – they wouldn't leave themselves at a client's total mercy by lying down, nor would clients want to lie on the grimy East End streets.

Neither Rumbelow nor Sugden satisfactorily explains how a client convinced Polly to lie down and then killed her without producing a sound or struggle, leaving only two minor facial bruises.

Tom Wescott attempts an explanation in *Ripper Confidential*:

> If we disregard the notion that the Ripper stood Polly up and delivered a 'one-two' punch on the right jaw and left cheek then what we're left with as the most plausible explanation is that he kneeled to her right, next to her head and grabbed her face with his left hand, applying great pressure to hold it steady as he inflicted the second and deepest of his throat wounds.

But Wescott doesn't explain how the killer got Polly onto the ground to begin with – silently and without a struggle. Remember, a light sleeper lived nearby, and another woman was awake. Both, along with other witnesses, reported it was an exceptionally quiet night. Did Polly and her supposed client communicate in sign language? However you attempt to explain it, attacking someone who remains silent and doesn't struggle presents a significant challenge.

'Who do you think the killer was?'

At the end of my Jack the Ripper tour, one question usually comes up. 'Who do you think the killer was?' My reply is that it is impossible with the information we have to be certain who carried out these murders. Then what usually follows is, 'But you are our tour guide, and you've studied this, so who do you *think* it was?' That person has paid me to share what I have discovered about this case, and so I provide an answer.

There will be readers who will not be interested in writers who theorise about who the killer was; however, I also know there will be readers who will feel that, having paid money for a book on this case, they will expect me to tell them who I *think* it was.

For the brutal murder of Polly Nichols, I can think of two alternatives. You may be able to come up with a third.

Scenario one

A serial killer (Walter Sickert, Aaron Kosminski, James or Michael Maybrick, or another of the many suspects that you prefer) systematically targets prostitutes – possibly Annie Millwood, Emma Elizabeth Smith and probably Martha Tabram. Three weeks after the stabbing of Martha Tabram 39 times, Polly Nichols walks east in the early morning hours. Throwing caution to the wind despite the recent violence, she accosts a stranger and persuades him to accompany her silently to Buck's Row.

They arrive at the gates. Still without speaking, he stuns her with a face punch or grabs at her throat, or pulls out a bottle of chloroform and wrestles her to the ground, all without producing a single scream, choking sound or sign of struggle, while causing only two minor bruises.

He cuts her throat, mutilates her abdomen and departs seconds before Charles Cross (Lechmere) mistakes her body for a piece of discarded canvas. As Sugden writes: 'Polly seems to have died, then, only minutes before Cross came upon her, and it is entirely on the cards that he unwittingly scared her attacker away.'

Scenario two

A 43-year-old homeless woman turns her back on the activity around Spitalfields and walks away from the area where three homeless women had been brutally attacked.

Attacks Polly is all too well aware of, thanks to the sensational accounts in the newly launched *Star* newspaper, and in other newspapers desperate to maintain market share. Sensational accounts that reached a crescendo following the 39 stab wounds on Martha Tabram. The newspapers have successfully whipped up a frenzy of mass hysteria, which creates, in the words of Loren Coleman, 'an epidemic of similar behaviours'.

Polly makes her way to a pair of wooden gates near residential housing, but finds them locked and eight feet tall. Desperately tired, she lowers herself against them and closes her eyes.

If we accept PC Neil's testimony about his final patrol down Buck's Row, Polly arrived after 3:15 a.m. Around that time, whether you're standing watch on a ship or living among Whitechapel's homeless, the desire to escape into sleep becomes overwhelming.

Charles Lechmere – who gave his name to the inquest as Charles Cross – left his home at 22 Doveton and was in Brady Street in time to see PC Neil moving towards Whitechapel Road. He made his way along Buck's Row, where Polly was lying in a gateway. At a time when we know a 'kind of mania is in the air' exciting 'man's perverted imitativeness' to wakefulness.

She was already lying on the ground. No struggle required to position her there. She was asleep, making it simple to prevent screaming by clamping his left hand over her mouth while pinching her nostrils closed between thumb and forefinger to cut off her breathing. Simultaneously, his right hand gripped her jaw to prevent her head from thrashing side to side, which might allow her to break free and scream. His right hand's grip left a thumb-shaped bruise on her lower right jaw and finger marks on her left cheek. Starved of oxygen, her body went limp.

Once she was unconscious, he rolled her onto her left side, drew his knife and severed the left carotid artery. Her heart's final beats pumped blood straight down onto the cobblestones – exactly as the doctor described. This explains how the doctor knew she was killed while lying down: despite the throat wounds, no blood appeared on the front of her clothing. Instead, it pooled beneath her, meaning the killer would have had minimal blood on himself.

He then rolled her onto her back, slashed her throat wide open, lifted her skirts and began the abdominal mutilation. Then he heard Robert Paul's hobnailed boots approaching on the cobblestones. Two choices: flee in his own hobnailed boots, alerting every police officer in the area, or bluff it out. 'Look, there's a woman lying here.'

In this scenario, she was already prone – no struggle to get her down.

She was asleep – no problem preventing screams or breathing. It represents the simplest, most commonplace explanation.

Polly becomes another rough sleeper attacked on the streets of the country. Not unusual even in our 'enlightened times'. The BBC News on Thursday, 12 June 2025, reported:

> **A number of attacks and threats against rough sleepers in a town has sparked a police investigation and left a charity concerned somebody could die.**
>
> Five homeless people suffered violence or threats in Shrewsbury in the past week with some of them needing hospital treatment, Shrewsbury Ark posted on Facebook.
>
> One person reported being stabbed and a member of the Ark's support team said: 'We're genuinely worried someone will die.'
>
> A West Mercia Police spokesperson said they were aware of several vulnerable people in the town centre being attacked 'in recent weeks' and an investigation was under way.
>
> A spokesperson for the Ark said many rough sleepers felt reluctant to speak out 'due to fear and vulnerability'.
>
> But they said one woman, who wanted to remain anonymous, said she was woken at 03:00 BST on one recent night when she was punched in the head by a man who had been walking with a woman.

Shrewsbury is not unique. The homeless charity, Crisis, reports: 'People sleeping on the street are almost 17 times more likely to have been victims of violence and 15 times more likely to have suffered verbal abuse in the past year compared to the general public.'

Sky News reported on Tuesday, 5 December 2023: 'Jerrid Joseph Powell, 33, is accused of killing three rough sleepers in Los Angeles.'

The simplest explanation

While absolute certainty isn't possible after 137 years, the second scenario explains the evidence more simply than any alternative. The question then is, why didn't the Metropolitan Police consider it?

15

Annie Chapman

Eight days after the murder of Polly Nichols, the day after her funeral, and following intense media coverage of the earlier attacks, another woman's body was discovered in Whitechapel.

For investigators in 1888 and for many experts in recent times, this was another reason to dismiss Charles Lechmere. The man standing by Polly's bleeding body. The man who called himself Charles Cross. Six days after explaining himself at an inquest, would he be bold enough to get himself accosted by another prostitute and cold-bloodedly murder her?

That logic ceases to be logic, of course, if investigators removed the blinkers that focused their search on a single assassin on a mission to rid the world of prostitutes.

The victim was Annie Chapman. She was found in the yard behind 29 Hanbury Street on Saturday, 8 September 1888.

The *Daily News* of Monday, 10 September 1888, captured the hysteria that followed the discovery:

> The excitement has been intense. The house and the mortuary were besieged by people, and it is said that during a part of Saturday people flocked in great numbers to see the blood-stained spot in the yard, paying a penny each. In the White-chapel-road 'Lines on the Terrible Tragedy' were being sold, and men with the verses round their hats were singing them to the tune of 'My Village Home.' A wretched waxwork show had some horrible picture out in front, and people were paying their pence to see representations of the murdered woman within.

The ghoulish spectacle had real consequences. Dr Phillips reported that he and his assistant were 'out of their beds nearly all Saturday night in attendance of cases of assault, some of them of the most serious character, arising directly or indirectly out of the intense excitement'.

Such was the brutal legacy of Annie Chapman's murder – not just another victim, but the catalyst for a public frenzy that would define the Jack the Ripper phenomenon.

Annie Chapman: a different beginning

Annie Eliza Smith was born in September 1841 to parents Ruth Chapman and George Smith. Both had grown up in rural Britain before moving to London. George Smith was strong and healthy, untainted by the capital's choking air. Although underage, he enlisted in the prestigious Lifeguards regiment.

One advantage of military life was access to regimental schools. Like many army children, Annie received a proper education until the age of 15, learning to read and write, and excelling at needlework that would serve her throughout her life.

Annie's childhood unfolded in an area far removed from the grimy streets of Whitechapel. Between the genteel squares of Kensington and the royal grandeur of Windsor, she inhabited a world of relative privilege and possibility. Yet even elegant Kensington could not shield families from Victorian England's greatest enemy: disease.

In 1854, tragedy struck with devastating swiftness. Within three terrible weeks, four of Annie's five siblings perished – three claimed by scarlet fever, one by typhus. The Smith household, once filled with children's laughter, fell silent except for the sounds of grief.

Ruth bore two more daughters and, in 1861, welcomed a son. By then, 20-year-old Annie had found employment as a housemaid, while her father had risen to become valet to his commanding officer.

In 1862, when his commanding officer left the army, 43-year-old George also left to continue as his valet. But the following year, while visiting Wrexham on business, George was discovered in his hotel bed, his throat cut by his own razor.

Whether driven by despair, drink or demons that only he could see, George Smith's suicide shattered his family's carefully constructed world. Ruth, left to navigate widowhood, moved to 29 Montpelier Place in Knightsbridge, where she could supplement her income by taking paying guests.

It was here that Annie met her future husband, John Chapman, a coachman employed by a wealthy family. They married on 1 May 1869 at All Saints Church, Knightsbridge.

The alcohol epidemic

Ten years after their wedding, the Chapmans moved with their two daughters to Windsor, where John had secured a prestigious position as head coachman to Francis Tress Barry. Barry's estate commanded magnificent views of Windsor Castle, and the position promised security and respectability.

But Annie carried within her a burden that would prove heavier than any external hardship: an addiction to alcohol.

She was far from alone in this struggle. All five of the Ripper victims would seek alcohol's temporary refuge. But Annie's dependence ran deeper than most.

Victorian England had created an alcohol-saturated culture. Technological advances in brewing and distilling, combined with aggressive modern advertising, transformed alcohol into a mass-produced commodity targeting an ever-expanding consumer market. Victorian society organised itself around alcohol consumption – beer houses, gin palaces, oyster bars, private clubs and public houses competed for custom from dawn until the small hours.

Political battles raged around the 'drink question'. The Liberal Party aligned itself with temperance campaigns seeking radical licensing reforms, while the Conservative Party championed the drink trade, defending citizens' rights to purchase and consume alcohol. The enormous fortunes of the profitable brewing and distilling families made it an unequal contest, one that was further exacerbated by government revenue from alcohol sales, regardless of which party held power.

The result was staggering; in London, Annie Chapman would never be more than a five-minute walk from a drink. Today, with a population of 9 million, London maintains 3,500 pubs. In 1888, with fewer than 5 million residents, it supported 20,000 drinking establishments.

Annie Chapman: a life beyond the headlines

After Annie's murder, a letter appeared in *The Pall Mall Gazette*, 1 May 1889. It was written by Annie's sister Miriam:

> Just before I was six years old, my father cut his throat, leaving my mother with five children, three girls older, and one child younger than myself.

Their father's suicide, which the family attributed to alcoholism, left a profound mark on the Chapman sisters. Determined to break the cycle, they all signed temperance pledges, vowing never to touch alcohol. Yet despite their best efforts, Annie would struggle with the very demon that had destroyed their father.

> We tried to persuade the one given to drink to give it up. She was married and in a good position. Over and over again, she signed the pledge and tried to keep it. Over and over again, she was tempted and fell.

Annie's alcoholism exacted a devastating toll. Of the eight children she bore, six died – their deaths linked to her drinking. When her 12-year-old daughter succumbed to meningitis, Annie's grief increased her dependency. Her sisters, desperate to save her, arranged for her admission to the Spelthorne Sanatorium in Feltham, West London. Her husband, John Chapman, agreed to pay a shilling a week for the year-long treatment.

The sanatorium worked – initially. Annie returned home transformed, a sober wife and mother. But sobriety proved fragile. A few months later, John had to take his master out in harsh winter weather. Suffering from a bad cold with snow falling, he fortified himself with hot whisky. That single kiss goodbye became Annie's undoing.

'It was of no use,' she confessed to Miriam. 'No one knew the fearful struggle unless I can keep out of sight and smell, I can never be free.'

The relapse sealed Annie's fate. Francis Barry insisted that she leave. John arranged for her to receive 10 shillings a week in London.

Annie briefly lived with her family, but as Miriam observed, 'She would always keep out of our way, but she must and would have the drink.' Unable to drink without facing her family's disapproval, Annie made the painful decision to leave.

Descent into the abyss

Jack London captured the reality of London's underclass in *The People of the Abyss*: 'Nowhere in the streets of London may one escape the sight of abject poverty; five minutes' walk from almost any point will bring one to a slum.'

Annie's descent began in Notting Hill, just north of Hyde Park. On Charles Booth's poverty map, the area was coloured black and described as 'hopelessly degraded'. For Annie, this move represented her first step down – not into Alice's rabbit hole, but into what Jack London called the 'Abyss'.

As historian Hallie Rubenhold observes, Victorian society showed no mercy to women who fell from grace:

> A woman who was 'drunk and disorderly', who embarrassed herself in public, who demonstrated no regard for her appearance, who did not have a respectable home or a husband or family to regulate her conduct, was judged to be as much of a degenerate as a prostitute. They became one and the same: outcast women.

Annie's precarious position as a lone woman in Victorian London demanded that she find male protection, despite still being legally married. She paired up with Jack Sievey, who made wire sieves – perhaps drawn by her steady ten-shilling weekly allowance. In 1884, they moved to Whitechapel and took lodgings in a doss house on Dorset Street.

Jack London described these establishments with unflinching clarity:

> While 300,000 people of London live in one-room tenements, and 900,000 are illegally and viciously housed, 38,000 more are registered as living in common lodging houses known in the vernacular as doss houses ... life in them is degrading and unwholesome.

Their new address was at Crossingham's on Dorset Street, a street that was filled with doss houses, earning it the nickname 'Dossit' Street. Despite fierce competition, Dorset Street won the grim title of 'worst street in London'. Social reformer Charles Booth called it the worst street he'd ever seen, while the local police inspector declared it London's worst for poverty, misery and vice.

At Crossingham's, Annie found a friend in Amelia Palmer, who described Annie as 'a very respectable woman whom she had never heard use bad language ... straightforward and a very clever and industrious little body when she was sober.'

This testimony reveals a woman far more complex than the stereotypes of her time, suggesting someone who retained dignity and industriousness despite her circumstances.

In December 1886, catastrophe struck: the 10 shillings suddenly stopped and Annie learned that her husband John was gravely ill. In the depths of winter, she walked 25 miles to Windsor, arriving shortly before his death but not staying to witness it. Miriam described John Chapman as 'a white-haired, broken-hearted man' when he died of cirrhosis on Christmas Day 1886, aged just 45.

The loss devastated Annie completely. As Amelia Palmer observed, 'she seemed to give up altogether.' With no more money arriving, Jack Sievey moved on, leaving Annie to navigate an increasingly hostile world alone.

The final months

Annie briefly took up with 'Harry the Hawker', then began a steadier relationship with Edward Stanley, a brewery worker known as 'Ted' or 'the Pensioner'. Though Stanley claimed to have known Annie for two years, they only began part-time cohabitation during the summer of 1888. Perhaps it was these relationships that led Timothy Donovan, keeper of the doss house, to describe Annie as a prostitute.

When she couldn't pay her bed money, Donovan turned a middle-aged woman in very poor health onto Whitechapel's cold, wet streets – streets where three women had already been attacked that year and Polly Nichols had been murdered and mutilated just eight days earlier.

Amelia Palmer had noted a transformation in Annie. She became 'a pitiful case marked by drink and despondency, hunger and sickness,' and yet Annie continued to work. She did crochet work and made antimacassars to sell at Stratford Market – a commitment that required an eight-mile round trip and standing all day in all weather, despite her poor health.

Even in her final days, Annie spoke of going hop-picking in Kent, clinging to a hope for seasonal work. But the evening before her murder, when Amelia Palmer asked if she'd walk to Stratford Market the next day, Annie replied that she was too ill to do anything.

Hours later, a knife sliced through her carotid artery, but her story – one of childhood trauma, addiction, loss and survival – reminds us that behind the headlines was a woman who had once been a respectable wife and mother, who had fought her demons and lost, who had tried to maintain her dignity even in the depths of poverty, and who had died not as a symbol but as a human being whose life had mattered.

Annie Chapman's story illustrates the precarious nature of Victorian women's lives and the thin line between respectability and destitution. Her tragic end should not overshadow the resilience she showed in the face of overwhelming odds.

16

She'd Been Dead for at Least Two Hours

The geography of the terror was remarkably compact. The first two victims on the nights they had their doss money slept in a Spitalfields doss house – Annie's in Dorset Street and Polly's in Thrawl Street. The third and fourth women murdered – Liz Stride and Kate Eddowes – also found shelter in a doss house, but in Flower and Dean Street. The fifth victim, Mary Jane Kelly, slept in a rented room in Miller's Court, just off Dorset Street. All five were sleeping within a five-minute walk of each other.

In 2008, the Metropolitan Police at Scotland Yard created a geographical profile of Jack the Ripper, concluding he lived within a five-minute walk of all his victims and a 20-minute walk of each murder site. In 1888, the police had no idea about geographical or any other kind of profiling.

They faced another disadvantage: an overreliance on eyewitness evidence. Even today, eyewitness testimony seems compelling – someone was there, they saw what happened, surely they must be reliable. However, forensic science, particularly since the advent of DNA testing, has revealed that eyewitness evidence may be psychologically compelling but scientifically unreliable.

The eyewitness reliability problem

On my second Jack the Ripper Whitechapel Walk, only two people had booked. As we set off from our starting point, the husband turned to me and said, 'I'm really excited about this tour.'

When I asked if he had any particular reason, he replied, 'Well, for 25 years I worked homicide in the Bay Area.'

At Brick Lane, as I was about to describe the events surrounding the murder of Annie Chapman, I began discussing the problems with eyewitness evidence. He interrupted me. 'Richard, let me tell you something – you could get four eyewitnesses describing the same scene, and you would get four completely different stories. Eyewitness evidence is totally unreliable.'

The fragility of eyewitness evidence

In the USA, the Innocence Project has shown that 73% of the 239 convictions overturned through DNA testing since the 1990s were based on eyewitness evidence. Kirk Bloodsworth's case exemplifies this problem: convicted of rape and murder in 1984, largely on the testimony of five eyewitnesses, he served nine years before DNA testing proved his innocence.

More recently, in the UK, the conviction of Peter Sullivan – dubbed the 'Beast of Birkenhead' – was overturned in 2025 after Peter had spent 38 years in prison. His 1986 conviction for murdering Diane Sindall had relied primarily on eyewitness evidence, which was later contradicted by new DNA findings.

These cases illustrate why eyewitness testimony, while potentially valuable, requires careful scrutiny rather than automatic acceptance. Research consistently shows that we are poor at recognising the faces of people who are unknown to us and that we've seen only briefly, and that interviewing and questioning can contaminate memories. The more times witnesses recount events, the more likely their memories become distorted as they unconsciously 'fill in blanks' to create coherent narratives.

This modern understanding of eyewitness unreliability becomes crucial when examining the investigation into Annie Chapman's murder, where witness testimony would create more confusion than clarity.

In *Jack the Ripper: Scotland Yard Investigates* (2006), Donald Rumbelow and Stewart Evans write:

> On the night of her murder, Annie was again on the streets, desperately trying to raise a few pennies to pay for a bed ... That night, she had no money. The nightwatchman, John Evans, saw her leave about 1.45 a.m. after he asked if she could pay for a bed ... There are no known further sightings of her until around the time of her murder. Her movements remain a mystery, but she may merely have been sleeping rough somewhere.

Two starkly different possibilities emerge from this account: either Annie spent her final hours desperately trying to earn money for lodging, or she simply found somewhere to sleep rough. The gap in her timeline – from 1:45 a.m. until her discovery – would become central to the investigation.

Annie's body was discovered at 6:00 a.m. in the yard behind 29 Hanbury Street, lying with her head near the steps that led to the yard. Dr George Bagster Phillips, the divisional police surgeon, examined the scene 20 minutes later. His assessment was precise; as *Jack the Ripper: Scotland Yard Investigates* explains, Dr George Bagster Phillips 'saw the body at 6.20 a.m. and he then gives it as his opinion that death occurred about two hours earlier, viz: 4.20 a.m.'

The crime scene told a chilling story. Annie had entered the yard alive, made no cry for help, showed no signs of a struggle and was killed while lying down. Death came when her left carotid artery was severed. But this time, the killer's work was more extensive and horrific – her clothes were pulled up, her stomach ripped open, her intestines pulled out and thrown over her shoulder. A complete post-mortem examination revealed that her uterus had been cut out and taken away.

A question that often gets asked about these murders is whether the killer was a doctor. Would it require a great deal of medical skill to remove a uterus?

At the inquest into the murder of Annie Chapman, Dr George Bagster Phillips said:

> I am of the opinion that the length of the weapon with which the incisions were inflicted was at least five to six inches in length – probably more – and must have been very sharp. The manner in which they had been done indicated a certain amount of anatomical knowledge.

So, not necessarily a highly skilled surgeon. In the case of Mary Ann (Polly) Nichols, Dr Llewellyn believed the killer possessed only 'some rough anatomical knowledge'. Elizabeth Stride had only her throat cut, so no medical skill was required. In the case of Kate Eddowes, there was extensive mutilation, and like Annie Chapman, her uterus was removed, but also her left kidney.

At the inquest, the coroner asked Dr Brown if the removal of the kidney would require special knowledge.

Dr Brown: It would require a good deal of knowledge as to its position, because it is apt to be overlooked, being covered by a membrane.

Coroner: Would such knowledge be likely to be possessed by someone accustomed to cutting up animals?

Dr Brown: Yes.

In our modern world, few get to see anybody 'cutting up animals'. It was different in Whitechapel in 1888. Samuel Barnett, the rector of St Jude's church in Whitechapel, wrote in *The Times* on 19 September 1888:

> At present, animals are daily slaughtered in the midst of Whitechapel, the butchers with their blood stains are familiar among the street passengers, and sights are common which tend to brutalise ignorant natures. For the sake of both health and morals, the slaughtering should be done outside the town.

In the 1960s, I worked in a slaughterhouse in Winnipeg. It was very instructive. I doubt that I would be able to match the skill I observed, but then again, Kate Eddowes' killer didn't display great precision. Dr Brown said, 'The uterus was cut away with the exception of a small portion.'

The first doctor to arrive at the scene of Kate Eddowes' murder was Dr George Sequeira. His opinion was 'that the murderer had no design on any particular organ of the body. He was not possessed of any great anatomical skill.'

Dr Thomas Bond, who, with Dr George Bagster Phillips, performed the post-mortem examination of the fifth and final victim, Mary Jane Kelly, and wrote a report on all five murders, concluded:

> In each case, the mutilation was inflicted by a person who had no scientific or anatomical knowledge. In my opinion, he does not even possess the technical knowledge of a butcher, horse slaughterer, or any person accustomed to cutting up dead animals.

From the evidence of the doctors involved in these cases, it is clear that it did not require a doctor to perform any of these murders.

The popularity of the doctor theory – with its angel of mercy-turned-evil demon theme – may well have drawn inspiration from Robert Louis Stevenson's *The Strange Case of Dr Jekyll and Mr Hyde* (1886). The stage adaptation starring Richard Mansfield opened at the Lyceum Theatre in London's West End on 4 August 1888. Three days later, the body of

Martha Tabram was discovered in London's East End. She had been stabbed 39 times.

The production was originally scheduled to close on 29 September, after which Mansfield planned to stage other plays. He initially followed this plan, introducing other productions in early October, but then, by popular demand, reintroduced Dr Jekyll and Mr Hyde to his schedule between 10 October and 20 October. The play was running when Polly Nicholls was murdered on 31 August and when Annie Chapman was murdered on 8 September.

Dr Phillips determined that Annie was sober at the time of death but in desperately poor health, malnourished and in the advanced stages of tuberculosis. Drawing on more than 20 years of medical experience, he estimated she had been dead 'for at least two hours' and added 'probably more'.

Then, evidence emerged that would challenge this estimate.

An hour after Annie's body was discovered, a market porter arrived at the crime scene. He was John Richardson, the 35-year-old son of the landlady at number 29, and he told the police that he had visited the yard that morning on his way to work as a porter at Spitalfields Market. He said he didn't enter the yard but stood in the doorway checking the cellar door padlock, and Annie wasn't lying there then. He said that was at 4:45. If Richardson was telling the truth, then obviously Annie couldn't have been murdered before 4:20.

Then, on day four of the inquest, 11 days after the murder on 19 September, Albert Cadosch testified:

> I live at 27, Hanbury-street, and am a carpenter. 27 is next door to 29, Hanbury-street. On Saturday, Sept. 8, I got up about a quarter past five in the morning, and went into the yard. It was then about twenty minutes past five, I should think. As I returned towards the back door I heard a voice say "No" just as I was going through the door. It was not in our yard, but I should think it came from the yard of No. 29. I, however, cannot say on which side it came from. I went indoors, but returned to the yard about three or four minutes afterwards. While coming back I heard a sort of a fall against the fence which divides my yard from that of 29. It seemed as if something touched the fence suddenly.

The coroner asked, 'And you had not the curiosity to look over?' Cadosch replied, 'No, I had not.'

Philip Sugden in *The Complete History of Jack the Ripper* (1994) says this testimony was 'very important indeed'. For me, this testimony is far too vague to be regarded as 'very important'.

Donald Rumbelow appears to agree with me because Albert Cadosch doesn't appear in *The Complete Jack the Ripper* (1975), nor does Paul Begg include him in *Jack the Ripper: The Facts* (2004). He does mention him in *The Complete and Essential Jack the Ripper* (2013), which he wrote with John Bennett. They ask:

> Had Cadosch heard the murder taking place? Despite this, the residents of no. 29 heard nothing out of the ordinary until the commotion surrounding the discovery of the body erupted around 6.00 a.m.

This suggests that Begg and Bennett also considered the evidence too vague to make a decision.

On the same day that Cadosch gave evidence, another eyewitness arrived and gave evidence. Evidence that can't be described as vague. As Rumbelow and Evans write in *Jack the Ripper: Scotland Yard Investigates*:

> At 5.30 a.m. Mrs Elizabeth Long saw a man and a woman talking near to 29 Hanbury Street. She heard the man say, 'Will you?' and the woman replied, 'Yes' ... If the evidence of Mrs. Long is correct that she saw the deceased at 5.30 a.m., then the evidence of Dr. Phillips as to probable time of death is incorrect ... hence the evidence of Mrs. Long which appeared to be so important to the Coroner, must be looked upon with some amount of doubt, which is to be regretted.

Perhaps this need not be regretted if they could show that the doctor was wrong. After all, Mrs Long's evidence supports the idea that Annie Chapman was 'desperately trying to raise a few pennies to pay for a bed'.

Rumbelow and Evans explain that body temperature should be taken rectally with environmental temperature recorded simultaneously, 'if the body temperature is to have any meaning. Dr Phillips did neither'.

They also note that doctors often disagreed when calculating times of death, citing the case of Mary Jane Kelly, where 'estimates made by Dr Thomas Bond and Dr George Bagster Phillips ... were 3 to 4 hours apart'.

A flawed comparison

Choosing Mary Jane Kelly's time of death as a comparison is odd. Estimating Kelly's time of death was far more difficult than Annie Chapman's case. Kelly's mutilation was far greater – flesh was removed from her legs and abdomen, her breasts had been sliced off, every internal organ had been cut out and placed outside her body, and she wore only a thin slip.

Then there is the added difficulty of estimating the time of death. The police surgeons couldn't have access to Mary Jane Kelly's body until 1:30 p.m., so the autopsy only began at 2:00 p.m. (around 10 hours after her presumed death). Both doctors agreed that an accurate time estimation was impossible.

A better comparison

Kate Eddowes offers a better comparison. If Mrs Long's evidence is correct and she saw Annie Chapman alive at 5:30 a.m., then allowing time for the killer and his victim to reach the front door of 29, move quietly through the passageway to the back door, position themselves in the backyard, and then for the killer to execute the murder in complete silence without a struggle, Annie would have been dead about 40 minutes when Dr Phillips examined her.

Dr Phillips said: 'The body was cold, except that there was a certain remaining heat, under the intestines, in the body. Stiffness of the limbs was not marked, but it was commencing.'

Dr Brown first examined Kate Eddowes's body in Mitre Square at 2:20, around 45 minutes after Kate was murdered. *The Daily Telegraph* reported: 'The body had been mutilated, and was quite warm – no rigor mortis.'

On the night of Annie's murder, the temperature dropped to 8°C (46°F). On the night of Kate Eddowes's murder, the temperature was colder at 6°C (43°F).

Kate's body was more mutilated than Annie Chapman's, and lying in a more exposed position, and, to repeat, on a colder night, yet 45 minutes after her murder, she was described as 'quite warm – no rigor mortis'.

This comparison shows Dr Phillips was right to be confident that Annie Chapman 'had been dead for at least two hours, probably more'.

It would take more than a rectal thermometer to convince me that Dr Phillips was wrong.

The problem for many is that Dr George Bagster Phillips' evidence doesn't support the prostitute theory, whereas Mrs Long's evidence does.

Mrs Long's eyewitness evidence

Mrs Long's evidence continues to influence modern interpretations of the Annie Chapman murder. As recently as 2019, the BBC's *Jack the Ripper: Case Reopened*, which was presented by Emilia Fox and supported by a team of experts, accepted that Annie was last seen alive talking to a man near 29 Hanbury Street at 5:30 a.m. This timing forms the foundation of their analysis, demonstrating how deeply embedded Mrs Long's testimony has become in Ripper scholarship.

Given the scarcity of solid evidence in the Jack the Ripper mystery, any potential glimpse of the killer deserves serious consideration. However, we must maintain scientific rigour and not allow a good story to override a careful analysis of the facts.

Mrs Long: the celebrated witness

Elizabeth Long occupies a unique position in Ripper literature as she provides what *The Ultimate Jack the Ripper Source Book* calls 'the first probable sighting of the killer'. Philip Sugden emphasises her importance, writing that her evidence is 'crucial' because she positively identified Annie Chapman at the mortuary and that 'her companion was almost certainly the murderer'.

This interpretation supports the prevailing theory that Annie Chapman, like the other victims, was a prostitute who 'greatly facilitated' her own murder by 'accosting men and taking them to dark and unfrequented byways and yards for sex'.

However, this narrative depends entirely on accepting Mrs Long's testimony at face value.

The location problem

The first issue with Mrs Long's account involves the location itself. If Annie Chapman was indeed at 29 Hanbury Street at 5:30 a.m., she was neither in a 'dark' nor 'unfrequented' location. Sugden's own research confirms this:

> The sun rose at 5:23, there were already plenty of people about. Spitalfields Market had opened at five, at which time the western end of Hanbury Street had been clogged with vehicles.

This creates a paradox. Sugden acknowledges that 'when the killer and his victim entered the yard of No. 29, moreover, the house itself was rapidly coming to life' and 'in slaughtering Annie when and where he did the murderer had thus taken an extraordinary risk'.

The scenario requires us to believe that Jack the Ripper – typically described as cautious and calculating – would commit his most brutal murder so far in broad daylight, behind a house that was rapidly coming to life and located on a busy street crowded with market traffic.

The reliability questions

Philip Sugden in *The Complete History of Jack the Ripper* says, 'At about five that same morning, she [Mrs Long] left her home at 32 Church Street to go to Spitalfields Market'.

Here is part of the transcript from the inquest:

> **Mrs. Elizabeth Long**: I was passing down Hanbury-street, from home, on my way to Spitalfields Market. I knew the time, because I heard the brewer's clock strike half-past five just before I got to the street. I passed 29, Hanbury-street. On the right-hand side, the same side as the house, I saw a man and a woman standing on the pavement talking. The man's back was turned towards Brick-lane, and the woman's was towards the market. They were standing only a few yards nearer Brick-lane from 29, Hanbury-street. I saw the woman's face. Have seen the deceased in the mortuary, and I am sure the woman that I saw in Hanbury-street was the deceased.

Mrs Long's testimony was not given until 11 days after the murder because she didn't make it to the first week of the inquest. She only made it to the second week because she didn't think her crucial evidence was crucial enough to take to the police until three days after the murder. This story was good enough to grant her a view of the dead body of Annie Chapman the next day, four days after passing a woman in a crowded street as she was on her way to work.

If I were in Mrs Long's place, I might remember this woman's face if she were famous or somebody I knew, or I knew she was about to be murdered. Otherwise, why would I remember every stranger's face I passed on a busy street as I made my way to work?

Mrs Long then described the man whom Annie was accosting.

> I did not see the man's face, but I noticed that he was dark. He was wearing a brown low-crowned felt hat. I think he had on a dark coat, though I am not certain. By the look of him he seemed to me a man over forty years of age. He appeared to me to be a little taller than the deceased.

Coroner: Did he look like a working man, or what?
Mrs Long: He looked like a foreigner.
Coroner: Did he look like a dock labourer, or a workman, or what?
Mrs Long: I should say he looked like what I should call shabby-genteel.

Reporting that to the police three days after passing this man in a crowded street is very impressive. Now, what makes Mrs Long's feat truly awe-inspiring is how she dealt with the coroner's next question.

Coroner: Was it not an unusual thing to see a man and a woman standing there talking?
Mrs Long: Oh no. I see lots of them standing there in the morning.
Coroner: At that hour of the day?
Mrs Long: Yes, that is why I did not take much notice of them.

Think of what you were doing three days ago. Picture the busiest street you walked down. Now, visualise any of the people you passed. Think hard.

If you passed Donald Trump or a close friend, you might remember passing them, but Mrs Long didn't know Annie Chapman or the man. Can you match Mrs Long's detailed description of the 'foreigner' with any of the people you passed three days ago on a busy street, whom you did not take much notice of?

On my daily excursions, I couldn't describe anyone I'd passed 10 minutes earlier because, like Mrs Long, I don't 'take much notice of them'.

Was she a strong enough witness to overturn Dr Phillips's expert opinion? Given modern studies on false memory and eyewitness unreliability, Mrs Long's recall seems remarkable.

The police were sufficiently interested to grant her mortuary access, where she identified the murder victim as one of the faces she 'did not take much notice of' four days earlier during her half-hour walk to work. Impressive.

The medical evidence conflict

Dr Phillips, the police surgeon who examined Annie Chapman's body, concluded she had been dead 'at least two hours, probably more' when he examined her at 6:20 a.m. This would place her death around 4:20 a.m. or earlier, well before Mrs Long's claimed 5:30 a.m. sighting.

Dr Phillips' professional assessment, based on a night-time temperature of 8°C (46°F) and Annie's body being cold, meant she had been dead for at least two hours, which is backed up by the fact that Kate Eddowes' body, which had lain out on a colder night for 45 minutes, was warm.

The implausible timeline

Accepting Mrs Long's testimony requires believing an implausible sequence of events. Annie Chapman was described by Dr Phillips as being in very poor health: 'far advanced in disease of the lungs and membranes of the brain ... There was no appearance of the deceased having taken alcohol, but there were signs of great deprivation.'

The evening before her death, Annie told Amelia Palmer: 'I feel too ill to do anything.'

Yet if Mrs Long was correct, after being ejected from Crossingham's lodging house before 2:00 a.m., this desperately ill woman supposedly spent three and a half hours searching the streets before finally encountering a potential client at 5:30 a.m. – in broad daylight, on a busy street clogged with market traffic.

A simpler alternative

Could Mrs Long have fabricated her story to get 15 minutes of fame and free mortuary access?

Possibly, because the evidence suggests a different scenario. Annie Chapman was well acquainted with 29 Hanbury Street. Landlady Amelia Richardson was interviewed by *Lloyd's Weekly* (Sunday, 16 September 1888):

> Our representative on Friday again visited 29, Hanbury-street, and saw Mrs. Richardson, who is naturally greatly shocked that such a terrible crime should have been committed there.
>
> As her rooms are used for prayer meetings once a week, both she and the landlord are very angry at anything like a slur on the respectability of the house. 'When I saw the murdered body I was so shocked

> I did not like to look particularly at her face, but I have no doubt it is the dark woman that used to come round with cotton and crochet work, and I have bought off her many times when she has said that she has been hard up. She used to come round to these houses, and other neighbours used to buy off her too, and lend her money when she said she had not enough for her lodgings.'
>
> She then expressed her great indignation that her son, John, should have told the coroner that people came into the house, for improper purposes.

Annie knew the house was divided into several rented rooms, meaning the front and yard doors remained unlocked. Was she soliciting on the streets for over three hours? Or did she spend about 20 minutes walking to 29 and then huddle down between the steps and the fence to sleep?

Did John Richardson arrive to check the cellar door padlock, holding open the door that was hiding sleeping Annie? Did he leave only for another man to arrive and see her? Was it irresistible fun, and who'd miss one more drab little woman?

17

John Richardson: Eyewitness or Killer?

John Richardson, who claimed the yard was empty at a quarter to five, lived a two-minute walk from 29 Hanbury Street in John Street, now Dray Walk, within five minutes of where the five victims lived.

For 11 days post-murder, the police were interested in Richardson because he changed his story. At about a quarter to seven on the morning of the murder, he left Spitalfields Market to return to 29 Hanbury Street, saying he'd just heard about the murder. Inspector Chandler reported that, 'He said he came to the back door and looked down to the cellar, to see if all was right, and then went away to his work.' That was at a quarter to five.

His mother was recalled and questioned about this, and she said 'she had never missed anything, and had such confidence in her neighbours that she had left the doors of some rooms unlocked. A saw and a hammer had been taken from the cellar a long time ago.'

Strange that the mother was unconcerned about theft, but John was. Had he been calling in every day since the saw and hammer went missing 'a long time ago'?

The yard door hinged on the left and opened into the yard, so he couldn't have known what was on the side of the yard where Annie was found if he stood in the doorway without entering the yard.

So when he appeared on the inquest's second day, he changed his story:

> The yard door was shut. I opened it and sat on the doorstep, and cut a piece of leather off my boot with an old table-knife, about five inches long.

The next day, Inspector Joseph Chandler was giving his evidence, and the coroner questioned him about John Richardson.

> **Coroner**: Did you see John Richardson?
>
> **Inspector Chandler**: I saw him about a quarter to seven o'clock. He told me he had been to the house that morning about a quarter to five. He said he came to the back door and looked down to the cellar, to see if all was right, and then went away to his work.
>
> **Coroner**: Did he say anything about cutting his boot?
>
> **Inspector Chandler**: No.
>
> **Coroner**: Did he say that he was sure the woman was not there at that time?
>
> **Inspector Chandler**: Yes.
>
> **By the Jury**: The back door opens outwards into the yard, and swung on the left hand to the palings where the body was. If Richardson were on the top of the steps, he might not have seen the body.
>
> **Inspector Chandler**: He told me he did not go down the steps.

This was the day after Richardson gave his evidence. Why did the coroner ask Inspector Chandler about Richardson cutting his boot? Was he wondering if Richardson made up that story to explain how he was able to see that part of the yard that the door would have concealed?

Richardson was very clear about what happened:

> After cutting the leather off my boot I tied my boot up, and went out of the house into the market.

No two ways about what he did in the yard. And to do the cutting, he used 'an old table-knife, about five inches long'. A good choice because an old table knife couldn't possibly have performed the surgery carried out on Annie Chapman, and he tells quite a story about rabbits and carrots to explain why he was carrying such an uninspiring knife.

But then there is a problem for John: 'At this stage, the witness was dispatched by the coroner to fetch his knife.'

Sometime later, the same day:

> **John Richardson (recalled)** produced the knife – a much-worn dessert knife – with which he had cut his boot. He added that as it was not sharp enough he had borrowed another one at the market.

A short time earlier, he had told a convincing tale.

> The yard door was shut. I opened it and sat on the doorstep, and cut a piece of leather off my boot with an old table-knife, about five inches long. After cutting the leather off my boot I tied my boot up, and went out of the house into the market.

How did he get that wrong? Had he just imagined that he cut the leather, tied up his boot and then went to work? Instead, he borrowed a knife at Spitalfields Market.

Well, that would be no problem because an essential tool for any market porter was a sharp knife. Did the police ask John why he was carrying this blunt knife to work rather than his porter's knife? This was an essential for anyone in this occupation, as evidenced by this quote from a porter who worked for four decades at Spitalfields Market until it stopped selling fruit and vegetables in 2012.

> A Spitalfields Market porter of forty years standing, Jimmy Huddart is proud to display the clothing of his trade… In the pocket of his apron *Jimmy always kept his porter's knife.* [My emphasis]
> **spitalfieldslife.com 16 March 2025**

The Richardson question

The reason John Richardson's evidence has been accepted is that it supports the evidence of Mrs Long. Evidence in line with the story that Annie was accosting a man who was a prostitute killer.

Accepting Mrs Long's evidence means accepting that Annie Chapman, even though the night was over, was so desperate to get her doss money, she forgot that within five minutes of 29 Hanbury Street three women had been brutally attacked and that for eight days the newspapers had been filled with the gory details of a fourth woman, Polly Nichols, who had been murdered and mutilated just half a mile away.

Accepting Mrs Long's evidence also means accepting that in broad daylight, Annie Chapman accosted a man at 5:30 a.m., led him from the busy street to the front door of a house that was coming to life with people getting ready for work, tiptoed through the passageway and entered the yard. Then the killer got her on the ground in complete silence without a struggle, severed the left carotid artery, cut her throat, lifted her skirts, performed surgery on her abdomen, removed and secreted her uterus, pocketed his knife and left the yard, passing through the passageway and out the front door before John Davis discovered Annie Chapman's body just half an hour after Mrs Long heard Annie say, 'Yes'.

Accepting Mrs Long's evidence also means believing eyewitness evidence from a witness about a couple she had passed in the early morning on her way to work. That is a couple she did not take much notice of, indeed, so little notice she didn't think to report it to the police until three days after the event.

Accepting Mrs Long's evidence also means that 40 minutes after Annie was murdered, her body had lost all of its heat, while Kate Eddowes, in the same amount of time on a colder night, was still warm.

The only reason for anyone to believe Mrs Long's evidence is to confirm their theory that Annie was a prostitute.

Mrs Long's evidence must be rejected, and it raises a serious question around John Richardson.

Comparing the facts around the death of Annie Chapman with the facts around the death of Kate Eddowes proves Annie was dead when John Richardson claims he went to the yard. Why did John Richardson go to such lengths to prove the body was not there?

You may be able to think of several reasons, but I can think of only one. Sometime before 4:20 a.m., he murdered Annie Chapman. Then, when he was at work, he realised that any of the neighbours at or near 29 might tell the police that they had seen the landlady's son entering and leaving in the early morning, so he presented the police with his alibi.

The alibi didn't satisfy the police, especially after the changes to his story; however, the police lost interest in John Richardson when, 11 days post-murder, Mrs Long told the inquest she'd seen Annie Chapman alive at 5:30 a.m. By that time, Richardson had been working at Spitalfields Market for half an hour surrounded by witnesses. Unlike Mrs Long, who was walking down Hanbury Street half an hour late for work.

As Philip Sugden said, 'At about five that same morning, she left her home at 32 Church Street to go to Spitalfields Market.'

Worth noting: Church Street is now Fournier Street, and number 32, where Mrs Long lived, is a convenient two-minute walk from Spitalfields Market and less than three minutes from 29 Hanbury Street.

Why, having left home at 'about 5 in the morning', was she walking down Hanbury Street at 5:30? What was Mrs Long doing for those other 27 minutes? We don't know because nobody asked why. Or why, when she said, 'I left home at about 5 o'clock,' she deliberately made herself late for work by taking a half-hour detour.

The persistence of fantasy

There's no evidence showing what happened to Annie Chapman after leaving Crossingham's at 1:50 a.m. until her body was found at 6:00 a.m. This lack of evidence hasn't stopped lurid descriptions from appearing in our modern age.

William Beadle, in his 2010 *Jack the Ripper – Unmasked*:

> But, as dawn came up on Saturday, 8 September 1888, she had neither money nor lodgings. Instead, she had walked the grimy collection of mean little thoroughfares ... for hour after hour, going round and round the same dark, dispiriting places like the circle of the suicides in Dante's inferno. Five thirty found her in Hanbury Street with at last the prospect of earning some money, by renting out her disease-ravaged little body.

Bruce Robinson in *We All Love Jack: Busting the Ripper* (2015):

> Mrs Chapman was a forty-seven-year-old nothing with progressive lung disease that would probably have killed her if the Ripper hadn't. In the early hours of Saturday, 8 September 1888, in want of four pennies for a bed, she went out hawking the only thing she had.

Both writers show remarkable faith in Mrs Long's eyewitness evidence and total acceptance that Annie's body could move from warm to cold in 40 minutes, though Kate's remained warm, despite Kate being more mutilated and lying in a more exposed position on a colder night.

Occam's razor or conspiracy theory?

Bruce Robinson is very angry with the Victorian elite, who were prepared to go to any lengths to protect their position at the top of the heap, which meant protecting the Masonic Order's reputation. Bruce Robinson said he 'learned to loathe much of what was the Victorian governing class'. He certainly includes enough of his research to persuade me to agree.

If possible, Bruce is even more confident than William Beadle, Patricia Cornwell or Russell Edwards that he has identified the monster. He dismisses the idea that James Maybrick wrote a diary, as Shirley Harrison claims in her 1993 book *The Diary of Jack the Ripper*, and instead claims that these murders were ritualistic murders committed by James Maybrick's brother, Michael Maybrick. Bruce claims the mutilations were inflicted as part of a Masonic ritual that he says Dr George Bagster Phillips tried to hide.

> Phillips 'thought that he had better not go into further details of the mutilations, which could only be painful to the feelings of the jury and the public'. The jury wasn't here for a lullaby, and this was tosh.

Dr Phillips resisted revealing exactly how Annie Chapman's body had been mutilated, but Coroner Wynne Baxter was determined, and eventually, Dr Phillips reluctantly described the results of the post-mortem examination. Bruce believes Dr Phillips' reluctance is explained when it is revealed that Dr Phillips was a Freemason.

> The rules of the 'Funny Little Game' were chosen by the dominant player, and were exclusively Freemasonic. It was a clever strategy by a clever psychopath. Freemasonry was an arena in which the killer was omnipotent, and the System was most exposed. To protect itself, the system was obliged to protect him – and that's about the size of the mystery.

The problem is that Coroner Baxter was also a prominent Freemason, a member of the South Saxon Lodge No. 311. If the argument was about protecting Freemasonry, then at the very least, these men could have had a quiet discussion rather than a public falling-out.

I can suggest another reason for Dr Bagster Phillips's reluctance, as this commentator in *The Daily News* of Saturday, 10 November 1888, offered as food for thought.

> Whitechapel has on horror's head horrors accumulated… The same kind of mutilation which put the trade mark of the assassin on other corpses is shown in the body of the young woman who was murdered yesterday. Of course we do not suggest that this is any conclusive evidence that this murder was done by the hand which may have committed some or all of the other crimes. There is a ghastly imitativeness in the crime, a horrible 'fashion' which may be set going in murder, and which reveals itself with the mechanical servility of any other imitativeness and any other fashion… Therefore it is not to be hastily assumed that all the murders were done by the one hand, or that the last murder was the work of the same criminal as any of the former.

Surely the writer was not the only person who could see, in these brutal attacks on easy targets, a 'ghastly imitativeness'. Dr George Bagster

Phillips also believed it.

> I (Dr Thomas Bond) am of the opinion that the murder was performed by the same person who committed the former series of Whitechapel murders. However, Dr Phillips disagreed with this conclusion. He did not believe that all the Whitechapel killings had been the work of one man.
>
> *The Complete Jack the Ripper* by Donald Rumbelow

You may prefer to agree with Bruce Robinson that Annie Chapman was ritualistically murdered, but I do not believe that Dr Phillips was part of some Freemasonic cover-up. I believe he did not want to reveal any more detail than was necessary for the sensible reason that the inevitable headlines that would follow could provoke another assassin into action.

Early police reports said that Polly Nichols had been disembowelled. That was not correct. Her abdomen had been mutilated, but her internal organs had not been pulled out. Annie Chapman was the first of the Whitechapel murder victims to have been disembowelled. Did the police reports suggest an 'improvement' that was picked up by the next perpetrator to join the game?

Dealing with the result of yet another horror, was Dr Phillips thinking not only of what the papers had printed about the police misreporting, but also of the article that appeared in *The Pall Mall Gazette* the day before the brutal attack on Annie Chapman? It was written by William Westall and titled *A Precedent for the Whitechapel Murders.*

It described events in Bavaria, around 80 years before the murders of 1888, when two women had been lured to a remote cottage where they were brutally murdered. William Westall makes the point that, like Martha Tabram and Polly Nichols, these women had been 'frightfully mutilated'. Westall then adds that both women had been disembowelled. The day after that, Annie Chapman became the first Whitechapel victim to be disembowelled.

The simplest explanation for Dr George Bagster Phillips' reluctance at the inquest was a humane desire not to inflame an already appalling situation.

Bruce Robinson sees it differently. But I have to agree with the reviewer in *The Guardian*: 'If he's wrong – well, it's still a bloody good read.'

And I think Gavin Corbett was about right with his review in *The Irish Times*: 'Withnail & I cult director Bruce Robinson tackles Jack the Ripper in this exhaustively researched, immensely entertaining – and bonkers – investigation.'

Fortunately, *They All Love Jack: Busting the Ripper* is readily available for you to decide. You are, of course, free to believe that three days before reporting to the police, Mrs Elizabeth Long had seen the Freemason Michael Maybrick, or the Liverpool cotton merchant James Maybrick, or the artist Walter Sickert, or the Polish Jew Aaron Kosminski, or any of a score of other possible killers being accosted by Annie Chapman in broad daylight surrounded by busy market day activity.

If only Dr Phillips had been carrying a rectal thermometer, you might even believe that John Richardson murdered Annie as she slept when Hanbury Street was still dark and Spitalfields had yet to come to life.

The simplest explanation remains: Annie Chapman, exhausted and desperate, sought shelter in a yard she knew, fell asleep and was murdered by an opportunist who found her there, not by a client she'd spent hours seeking in increasingly busy streets while desperately ill.

18

Elisabeth Gustafsdotter (Liz Stride)

At one o'clock on the morning of Sunday, 30 September 1888, Louis Diemschutz turned his pony and cart into Berner Street. The little pony clip-clopped down the cobbled street through wind and rain, then turned into an entrance leading to a small yard. The pony shied and wouldn't go further.

It was pitch dark, so Louis climbed down and felt his way forward with his whip. The whip touched something in the entranceway. He bent down and struck a match – almost immediately, the wind and rain blew it out. But in that brief flare, he saw a woman. Unable to make out details, he went indoors to fetch a light. He discovered the woman was dead, her throat cut open.

The victim was Elizabeth Stride, and many believe she was the third woman to be killed by Jack the Ripper. But Elizabeth's story began far from the grim streets of Whitechapel.

A different beginning

Born on 27 November 1843, and christened Elisabeth Gustafsdotter, she was raised in Torslanda on Sweden's west coast. Like Polly Nichols and Annie Chapman before her, her father had skilled work – he was a farmer who ensured his daughter attended school and went to the local Lutheran church on Sundays.

Like many girls with rural backgrounds, Elisabeth moved to the nearest large town as a teenager, finding domestic service work in the port of Gothenburg. In March 1865, Gothenburg police learned that Elisabeth had become guilty of 'lecherous living' – she was six months pregnant. This meant attending the police clinic, stripping naked and joining a line of other naked women waiting for examination. She never revealed the father's identity.

Unfortunately, this young woman wasn't only pregnant. Regular inspections revealed that she showed all the signs of syphilis. She was kept in Gothenburg's venereal disease hospital for treatment. After 17 days, she went into premature labour – her baby daughter was stillborn. Quite a lot for any young person to deal with.

Things didn't improve because respectable work became unavailable once she was added to the 'register of shame'. Elisabeth became a prostitute in Gothenburg.

Escape to London

A German musician from the Gothenburg Orchestra and his wife were among those prepared to help 'fallen women', offering Elisabeth a place in their home as a maid. Through this couple, Elisabeth found employment with a wealthy British family returning to London.

Nine months after her daughter's birth and death, 22-year-old Elisabeth Gustafsdotter left Sweden. On an icy February morning in 1866, she boarded a ship in Gothenburg and sailed to London.

Elisabeth worked as a maid in a respectable Gower Street lodging house. Soon after, she met John Stride, a 47-year-old carpenter. On 7 March 1869, they married at St Giles-in-the-Fields on Denmark Street, and Elisabeth Gustafsdotter became Elizabeth or Liz Stride.

They moved to Poplar in the East End and opened a coffee shop. Unfortunately, it didn't thrive, so in 1871, they relocated in search of a location with less competition. By autumn 1873, they had to sell the lease of their second coffee shop. These business failures depleted their savings and left them in debt, ultimately straining their relationship so that they separated. By late 1881, like Polly Nichols and Annie Chapman, Liz Stride moved to Whitechapel, settling in a doss house at 32 Flower and Dean Street.

Flower and Dean Street's attractive name derives from two bricklayers, John Flower and Gowan Dean, who built its houses in the late 17th century. However, it didn't live up to its attractive-sounding name; it competed with Dorset Street for the title of the 'worst street in London'.

Liz's final six years were spent desperately trying to survive. She'd learned English so well that some Whitechapel acquaintances believed her to be English. She also learned some Yiddish – there was a Jewish population in Gothenburg, so she may have picked up the language there.

Her Yiddish would have improved in Whitechapel, which had a large Jewish population, mainly centred around Brick Lane. They were recent Eastern European refugees, many of whom had little to no English. Communicating in Yiddish helped Liz find work among the Jewish population – char work, or casual domestic service. Work was readily available on the Jewish Sabbath from Friday sunset to Saturday sunset.

A troubled relationship

In 1885, Liz began living with dock worker Michael Kidney. They rented rooms on Devonshire Street, later relocating to Fashion Street, situated between Commercial Street and Brick Lane. Both enjoyed drinking and could become angry and violent when intoxicated. She reported Kidney's brutality to the police in June 1887, but then withdrew charges – a typical pattern among couples trapped in poverty.

As Jack London wrote in *The People of the Abyss*:

> The men are economically dependent on their masters, and the women are economically dependent on the men. The result is that the woman gets the beating that the man should give his master, and she can do nothing. There are the kiddies, and he's the breadwinner, and she dare not send him to jail and leave herself and children to starve.

The final decline

Towards late September, she returned to the Flower and Dean Street doss house. One regular who'd known Liz on and off for five or six years said she and Michael Kidney had 'had words'.

On Saturday, 29 September 1888, she was paid sixpence for cleaning the doss house, and the deputy keeper stated that she had visited the Queen's Head pub on Commercial Street. After that, there is no solid evidence to tell us what she did until she was discovered lying in the dark entrance to a small yard off Berner Street.

Like Polly Nichols and Annie Chapman, Liz Stride was a woman in her forties who'd been married, separated from her husband and lived precariously in Whitechapel and Spitalfields. Like them, she'd had her throat cut. But unlike them, she hadn't had her stomach ripped open.

Some researchers claim this was because Liz Stride wasn't a Jack the Ripper victim – they believe she was killed by someone else, possibly Michael Kidney. Others say she hadn't been disembowelled because Jack the Ripper was interrupted by the man who discovered her body.

'The Double Event'

Less than an hour after Elizabeth Stride's body was discovered, the body of another homeless woman, 46-year-old Catherine or Kate Eddowes, was discovered less than a mile away in Mitre Square in the City of London. Thus 30 September became known as the night of the 'Double Event'.

19

The Murder of Elizabeth Stride

Annie Millwood, Emma Elizabeth Smith, Martha Tabram, Polly Nichols, Annie Chapman, Liz Stride and Kate Eddowes – seven homeless women who were brutally attacked on the streets by a complete unknown.

Commenting on the 'Double Event' in *The Complete Jack the Ripper*, Donald Rumbelow writes, 'Always there was the question of the killer's motive. The victims were too poor to be worth robbing; what they had in common was that all were prostitutes.'

Three assumptions are wrapped in that statement: first, that one individual committed these murders. Second, the killer must have had a motive. Third, the victims were all prostitutes.

As has been said, we cannot say for sure that the same individual committed these murders. As already pointed out, at least one contemporary commentator had doubts, arguing that it might not be one monster's work. The *Daily News* of Saturday, 10 November 1888, reported, 'There is a ghastly imitativeness in the crime, a horrible "fashion" which may be set going in murder, and which reveals itself with the mechanical servility of any other imitativeness and any other fashion.'

'The most difficult crime to track is the one that is purposeless'

As Sherlock Holmes observed in *The Naval Treaty*: 'The most difficult crime to track is the one that is purposeless.' Some crimes defy rational explanation because their motives are incomprehensible to ordinary people.

Consider a contemporary parallel: as I write, two men stand trial at Newcastle Crown Court for felling the Sycamore Gap tree with a chainsaw. The felling of this century-old landmark, cherished by locals and tourists alike, made it into the newspapers. It was even reported in *The Washington Post* and *USA Today*. Beyond the widespread distress, many wondered what could possibly motivate such an act.

The psychology resembles that of a child who ties a can to a cat's tail, or his older brother, who checks for witnesses before launching a kick at a homeless person. To healthy minds, these acts appear motiveless because they are driven neither by money nor by revenge.

Elizabeth Gaskell describes a motive for random acts of wickedness in her 1855 novel *North and South*: 'Many in the crowd were mere boys; cruel and thoughtless, – cruel because they were thoughtless.' Thoughtlessness doesn't necessarily end when boys become men.

Manufacturing comprehensible motives

Perhaps to make the Whitechapel murders more digestible, commentators have proposed various motives. Some have suggested the attacks were gang-related, brutal warnings to prostitutes who refused to pay protection money. Others have proposed a messianic killer driven to punish women of ill repute. Both theories require accepting that the victims were indeed prostitutes.

These explanations created compelling narratives that journalists could exploit, and newspaper sales soared with descriptions rivalling the era's best horror fiction.

Before she was murdered, Elizabeth Stride had spent some nights at a Flower and Dean Street lodging house. Multiple witnesses confirmed she left between 7:00 and 8:00 p.m. on Saturday, 29 September 1888. After that, no one who knew her saw her alive again.

Five or six hours later, at 1:00 a.m. on Sunday, 30 September 1888, her body was discovered half a mile southeast in Dutfield's Yard off Berner Street. The location was next to the International Working Men's Educational Club, where 30 to 40 people remained after an evening meeting. Less than an hour later, the mutilated body of Kate Eddowes was discovered in Mitre Square.

These two brutal attacks naturally spread fear but also fascination. The *Morning Post* included this comment in an article published just three days after the two murders on Wednesday, 3 October 1888.

> Theories, of course, abound, and everybody who can twist the most ordinary occurrence so that it may appear to have the remotest connection with the crimes hastens to communicate it to a police officer.

Philip Sugden says:

> By contrast with the previous murders, the killing of Elizabeth Stride produced a bumper crop of witnesses who claimed to have seen the victim in company with a man shortly before her death.

This bumper crop of eyewitnesses remains part of the Jack the Ripper story to this day.

All the witnesses gave their eyewitness accounts at the inquest on the same day, five days after the murder. Five days of intense media coverage. All of the witnesses provided detailed descriptions despite poor lighting conditions.

And there was an additional problem, as this piece in the *London Evening Standard* of Monday, 12 November 1888, illustrates:

> During yesterday a large number of people called at the mortuary and asked permission to look at the remains. All such requests were, of course, refused.

All of the eyewitnesses who backed up the story that Liz Stride was accosting her killer were granted permission to look at the remains.

The dramatic events surrounding the discovery

Club steward Louis Diemschutz returned home on his pony and cart around 1:00 a.m. When his pony refused to enter Dutfield's Yard, he investigated and found Stride's body near the club wall. After confirming the worst with other club members, Diemschutz ran east along Fairclough Street while Morris Eagle ran north to Commercial Road; both men were shouting for help. The Berner Street beat was patrolled by PC William Smith. At no point on the beat was he more than 200 yards from the crime scene.

Morris Eagle said he found two constables at the corner of Grove Street, about 200 yards from the scene of the crime. One was Constable Henry Lamb, who testified at the inquest on Tuesday, 2 October:

> Last Sunday morning, shortly before one o'clock, I was on duty in Commercial-road ... when two men came running towards me and shouting… Arriving at the gateway of No. 40 I observed something dark lying on the ground ... I turned my light on, when I found that the object was a woman, with her throat cut ... I sent the other constable for the nearest doctor… On my arrival there were about

> thirty people in the yard, and others followed me in ... I then blew my whistle for assistance.

Five days after the murder and three days after PC Lamb gave his testimony, PC Smith testified on Friday, 5 October 1888.

> **PC William Smith**: I was in Berner-street about half-past twelve or twenty-five minutes to one o'clock, and having gone round my beat, was at the Commercial-road corner of Berner-street again at one o'clock. I was not called.
>
> When I came to the spot two constables had already arrived. The gates at the side of the club were not then closed. I do not remember that I passed any person on my way down.
>
> I saw that the woman was dead, and I went to the police-station for the ambulance, leaving the other constables in charge of the body. Dr. Blackwell's assistant arrived just as I was going away.

Consider the timeline: men were running 200 yards and shouting at 1:00 a.m. Then PC Lamb and others ran 200 yards back to the scene, where PC Lamb said he found about 30 people in the yard. 'I sent the other constable for the nearest doctor, and a young man who was standing by, I dispatched to the police station to inform the inspector what had occurred.' He moved the people back so he could examine the body, and only then did he blow his whistle for assistance. The constable ran 150 yards to 100 Commercial Road. Dr Blackwell's assistant answered the door, informed Dr Blackwell. The assistant then threw on his clothes and made his way 150 yards to arrive only moments after the beat policeman turned up. PC Smith, the beat policeman, heard none of this.

I've walked PC Smith's beat. The perimeter takes less than 12 minutes to complete, and no point is more than 200 yards from the murder site.

Where was PC Smith during this extended period of shouting, running and whistle-blowing in the heart of his patrol area?

The coroner, Wynne Baxter asked, 'Had you noticed any man or woman in Berner-street when you were there before?'

> **PC William Smith:** Yes, talking together.
>
> **Coroner**: Was the woman anything like the deceased?

Put yourself in this man's place. He is giving evidence a week after an event where he saw and heard nothing. Now he is standing before a magistrate immediately after William Marshall, a labourer at an indigo warehouse, and James Brown, a dock labourer, have just acquitted themselves well, answering the magistrate's questions. William Smith is a police officer with every reason to avoid giving answers like, 'I'm not sure. It was dark at the time.'

PC William Smith: Yes. I saw her face, and I think the body at the mortuary is that of the same woman.

Coroner: Are you certain?

PC William Smith: I feel certain. She stood on the pavement a few yards from where the body was found, but on the opposite side of the street.

Coroner: Did you look at the man at all?

PC William Smith: Yes.

Coroner: What did you notice about him?

I've just returned from walking to my local shops in broad daylight. I passed several men, but I couldn't describe or pick out any of them from a line-up because I don't pay much attention to people I pass on the street.

PC William Smith: He had a parcel wrapped in a newspaper in his hand. The parcel was about 18in. long and 6in. to 8in. broad.

Coroner: Did you notice his height?

PC William Smith: He was about 5ft. 7in.

Coroner: His hat?

PC William Smith: He wore a dark felt deerstalker's hat.

Coroner: Clothes?

The coroner is doing a great job. He couldn't be more helpful in prompting PC Smith's memory.

PC William Smith: His clothes were dark. The coat was a cutaway coat.

Coroner: Did you overhear any conversation?

PC William Smith: No.

Coroner: Did they seem to be sober?

PC William Smith: Yes, both.

Coroner: Did you see the man's face?

PC William Smith: He had no whiskers, but I did not notice him much. I should say he was twenty-eight years of age. He was of respectable appearance, but I could not state what he was. The woman had a flower in her breast. It rained very little after eleven

> o'clock. There were but few about in the bye streets. When I saw the body at the mortuary, I recognised it at once.

'I did not notice him much.' Well, considering that statement, I would give PC Smith a very high score for observation and recall.

So, given that detailed description of the man who was with the victim just before she was murdered, did PC Smith ensure that he immediately gave that description to his colleagues when he arrived at the scene and 'saw that the woman was dead'? The killer couldn't have gotten far when PC Smith arrived at the scene.

Sadly, he couldn't alert colleagues because he didn't immediately link the dead woman to the woman he claimed he had seen within yards of the crime scene a mere half hour before he arrived and saw 'that the woman was dead'. It was much later: 'When I saw the body at the mortuary, I recognised it at once.'

Let's be fair. A beat policeman's job was tough and poorly paid. Imagine spending hours walking the same circuit of less than one mile in one of London's poorest districts in the early hours of a dreary autumn night in 1888. Would you be on heightened alert, resisting the temptation to find a quiet place to take refreshment, determined to remember every face during the long, weary hours?

The level of detail given by all of these witnesses becomes more remarkable when we consider the conditions. The moon was waning at one-third brightness, and heavy rain had lasted until midnight; thick cloud cover blocked what little moonlight remained. Berner Street's only illumination came from four gas lamps spread over more than 100 yards, primitive flames that provided far less light than modern electric street lighting or even modern gaslights.

Compare the witness statements to Morris Eagle's honest response when asked if he saw anyone in Berner Street: 'I dare say I did, but I do not remember them.' This seems the natural reply of someone not blessed with PC Smith's apparently superhuman powers of observation and recall.

The evidence of Israel Schwartz

Israel Schwartz was a witness who did not attend the inquest, but that hasn't stopped him from becoming a star witness. Some writers, like Russell Edwards, believe that Schwartz identified the man he saw with Liz Stride, 20 months later at a meeting arranged by the police. Russell Edwards believes Israel Schwartz's evidence is important because:

> From a distance of only tens of feet away, he saw Elizabeth Stride being attacked by a man, just fifteen minutes before her body was found only yards from the scene.
>
> Schwartz was on his way to his new home and was walking towards the gateway of Dutfield's Yard at about 12.45 a.m. The report of what he saw was written down in a statement taken by Chief Inspector Donald Swanson.

The statement explains that Israel Schwartz reached the gateway where the murder was committed and saw a man stop and speak to a woman standing in the gateway. The man tried to pull the woman into the street, but he turned her round and threw her down on the footway, and the woman screamed three times, but not loudly.

The problems with Schwartz's account

It's fortunate for Russell's case that she didn't scream loudly, because otherwise somebody would have heard it, and nobody did. If a woman is being attacked, I can believe she would scream. I'm not sure why she would scream 'but not loudly'. I'm not even sure how anybody can scream 'but not loudly'.

On crossing to the opposite side of the street, he saw a second man standing and lighting his pipe.

By the time *The Star* newspaper interviewed Israel Schwartz, the attacker was now 'half-tipsy', and rather than dragging her from the gateway and throwing her onto the footway, 'The Hungarian saw him put his hand on her shoulder and push her back into the passage.'

The Star also reported that rather than the 'second man standing lighting his pipe', the Hungarian stated 'positively that he saw a knife in the second man's hand'.

There's another problem. Schwartz claimed he was walking towards the gateway of Dutfield's Yard at about 12:45 a.m. Morris Eagle was returning at 12:40 a.m., and Joseph Lave said he went down into Dutfield's Yard at about 12:40 a.m. and walked about in the open air for five minutes or more. Neither Eagle nor Lave mention the couple or Israel Schwartz.

And the *Evening News* of 1 October 1888 reported that Fanny Mortimer, who lived two doors along from the murder site, said:

> I was standing at the door of my house nearly the whole time between half-past twelve and one o'clock this Sunday morning and did not notice anything unusual.

Despite this, it is Schwartz's account that is used to explain the timing around this murder in many investigations, including – again – BBC's *Jack the Ripper: Case Reopened.*

There was an incentive for these eyewitnesses who backed up the story that Liz Stride was accosting a client; unlike many others who wanted to view the remains in the mortuary, they were granted permission.

The medical evidence

On Wednesday, 3 October 1888, *The Daily Telegraph* reported the second day of the inquest, Tuesday, 2 October 1888. The first doctor to arrive was Dr Blackwell:

> The deceased was lying on her left side obliquely across the passage, her face looking towards the right wall... The neck and chest were quite warm, as were also the legs, and the face was slightly warm. The hands were cold. The right hand was open and on the chest, and was smeared with blood. The left hand, lying on the ground, was partially closed and contained a small packet of cachous wrapped in tissue paper. The appearance of the face was quite placid.

The fact that her 'face was quite placid', and her hand still held 'a small packet of cachous wrapped in tissue paper' would seem to indicate that, as with the case of Polly Nichols and Annie Chapman, Liz Stride didn't struggle and certainly wasn't thrown to the ground.

> The blood was running down the gutter into the drain in the opposite direction from the feet.... I examined the clothes, but found no blood on any part of them.

Again, like Polly and Annie, she must have been killed when lying on the ground:

> **Coroner**: Did you form any opinion as to how long the deceased had been dead?
>
> **Blackwell**: From twenty minutes to half an hour when I arrived.

Blackwell said, 'I consulted my watch on my arrival, and it was 1.16 a.m.' Meaning Liz Stride was murdered sometime between 12:45 and

12:55. Close to the time that Morris Eagle was returning through the yard and Joseph Lave was spending five minutes taking the air.

Juror: Can you say whether the throat was cut before or after the deceased fell to the ground?

Blackwell: The blood would have spurted about if the act had been committed while she was standing up.

Coroner: A hand might have been put on her nose and mouth?

Blackwell: Yes, and the cut on the throat was probably instantaneous.

A left hand clamped over the mouth, and the nostrils closed between thumb and forefinger, while the right hand gripped the knife that was simultaneously plunged into the left carotid artery of a woman sleeping, is something easily achievable.

The preferred explanation is that the client that Liz Stride had managed to find, or a jealous boyfriend, accompanied her to Dutfield's Yard and got her onto the ground silently and without a struggle. Then they carried out the murder.

The more straightforward explanation for how the victim could have ended up on the ground without a struggle and without crying out is that she was lying down asleep or falling asleep when a stranger took his opportunity.

Juror: Was there any trace of malt liquor in the stomach?

George Bagster Phillips: There was no trace.

From that, it would appear she didn't end up lying where she was found because she was drunk. However, Liz Stride had been treated for syphilis in Gothenburg when she was 21. The treatment at that time was with mercury, which was not a cure. It wasn't until the 20th century that a successful cure was discovered. Penicillin was the real breakthrough in curing the disease.

Liz Stride was 44 when she was murdered. By then, the third stage or tertiary syphilis may well have been causing behavioural changes. The symptoms of tertiary syphilis will depend on which part of the body the infection spreads to. It may affect the brain, nerves or blood vessels. Symptoms can include personality changes, delusions, dementia, paralysis and loss of coordination. Those conditions may have played a part in how she ended up lying in Dutfield's Yard.

It would be the work of seconds for a passerby to bend, cut her throat, move on and lose the knife. Morris Eagle, Joseph Lave or any one of the 30 men at the club could have exited by the side door into Dutfield's Yard and disappeared back into the club without anybody in Berner Street, including Fanny Mortimer, knowing anything about it.

Elizabeth Stride was buried on Saturday, 6 October 1888, at East London Cemetery, Plaistow, London. The funeral was paid for at the expense of the parish.

20

Kate Eddowes

Catherine Eddowes, or Kate Eddowes, is regarded by many as Jack the Ripper's fourth victim. PC Edward Watkins said he discovered her body at 1:44 a.m. in Mitre Square in the City of London. He had walked through the square at 1:30, and he said it was clear. Fourteen minutes later, he walked back into the square and found her body. He said, 'She was ripped up like a pig in a market.'

The timing was extraordinary: Liz Stride's body had been found at 1:00 a.m., and less than an hour later, Catherine Eddowes lay dead in Mitre Square.

Catherine Eddowes was born in Wolverhampton on 14 April 1842 and was christened with her mother's name. Catherine Evans was one of seven children who lacked formal education but found work as a cook at the Peacock Inn in Wolverhampton. Little Catherine became known as Kate. She was part of a big family; her mother gave birth to 12 children though only 10 survived beyond their teenage years.

Kate's father, George Eddowes, was a skilled tinplate worker who had served a seven-year apprenticeship, learning to produce pots, pans and kettles. The year after Kate's birth, George became involved in an industrial dispute and served two months of hard labour for his part in the strike. With little opportunity to work in Wolverhampton, the family moved to London, boarding a canal boat for a two-day journey along the Grand Union Canal.

As a skilled worker, George would earn more than double the £1 a week that Charles Booth considered the dividing line between abject poverty and simply being poor.

An education cut short

Unlike her four older sisters, who were expected to find work and contribute to the family budget, Kate received something precious in Victorian England: an education. George managed to enrol her at the Dowgate School near his workplace, where she studied needlework, arithmetic, reading and writing. Her education even included attending services at St Paul's Cathedral.

In June 1851, 9-year-old Kate joined other pupils for a visit to the Great Exhibition in Hyde Park. For children whose daily existence bore no resemblance to the entertainment value offered in the magnificent Crystal Palace, it must have been an extraordinary day – a glimpse of a world beyond their cramped London lodgings.

But Kate's promising start ended abruptly. When she was 13, her mother died of tuberculosis. Two years later, her father also died, leaving the younger children as orphans in Bermondsey Union Workhouse. 15-year-old Kate took a train back to Wolverhampton to live with relatives.

The descent begins

Her aunt and uncle found Kate work in a tinplate factory – hardly what her education had prepared her for. She endured long hours in deplorable conditions, and on her way home from work, she began visiting the local pubs. Her growing recklessness extended to stealing from her workplace, causing a rift with her relatives. At 19, she walked 14 miles to Birmingham to live with another aunt and uncle, but she couldn't escape the tinplate factories that dominated the industrial landscape.

Then Kate met Thomas Conway, a handsome young Irishman recently invalided out of the Royal Irish Regiment with a sixpence daily pension. Unable to cope with heavy labour due to his poor health, Conway supplemented his meagre income as a travelling peddler, selling scissors, ribbons and toys while entertaining villagers with gossip and tales.

For Kate, this nomadic life might have seemed more romantic than factory work. She soon discovered the harsh reality: missing meals and sleeping rough were regular features of a peddler's existence.

Motherhood and misery

Just days after Kate's 21st birthday on 8 April 1863, her first child, Catherine Annie Conway, was born in a Great Yarmouth workhouse. As historian Hallie Rubenhold notes in *The Five*, these institutions were so infested that 'the gas jets were regularly left on to deter the rats'.

After years wandering the country, Thomas decided to try London, where Kate's second child, Thomas Lawrence Conway, was born. Two years later, in March 1869, Kate gave birth to her daughter Harriet.

Like many families in their situation, they faced starvation. Baby Harriet died of malnutrition.

Thomas left London in search of work, while Kate and her surviving children entered the Greenwich Union Workhouse. The cycle of poverty and institutional dependence had begun in earnest.

The workhouse years

Life showed no signs of improvement over the following years. In August 1873, Kate returned to a workhouse, giving birth to her second son, George Alfred Conway, in the Southwark Workhouse. Three years later, she gave birth to her third son, Frederick, at the Greenwich Union Workhouse.

Entering the workhouse meant passing through what inmates called 'the archway of tears' – being stripped of clothing and personal belongings before entering a communal bath. While Kate and her children moved in and out of these institutions, Thomas drifted in and out of London seeking employment. Kate increasingly turned to alcohol for comfort, which prompted Thomas – a teetotaller – to beat her severely.

As conditions deteriorated, Kate often sought help from her older sister Emma. But Emma and their eldest sister, Harriet, eventually cut ties completely when Kate refused to give up drinking. Finally, at the end of 1881, Kate left her family permanently. When she had fourpence for a bed, she stayed at a doss house at 55 Flower and Dean Street, where she met John Kelly.

A different kind of partnership

John Kelly proved less violent than Thomas Conway and, from Kate's perspective, a better partner because he shared her fondness for alcohol. He worked in the markets, while Kate took on char work among the Jewish families around Brick Lane. Their income remained unreliable, forcing them to alternate between workhouse casual wards and sleeping on the streets.

Like thousands of East Enders, Kate and John looked forward to the hop-picking season as a brief escape from the foul air and squalid slums. In 1888, they walked out of London into Kent's fields to pick hops. Farmers paid only pennies but provided barrels of beer and cider, as well as dry barns for sleeping.

Unfortunately, 1888 proved a poor year for the harvest. Many pickers returned to London hungrier and more destitute than when they'd left. Kate and John arrived back on Thursday evening, 27 September 1888, penniless. They spent the night in the casual ward at Thavies Inn on Shoe Lane.

The last days

The next day, John earned sixpence at Spitalfields Market – probably enough for alcohol. That evening, Kate pawned John's boots for two shillings and sixpence, using the money to buy food, more alcohol and a bed for John.

There's no record of where Kate slept on Friday night. With no money, she only had two choices: a workhouse casual ward or sleeping rough. This exchange at the inquest suggests it was the latter.

> **Coroner:** When did you see her next morning?
> **John Kelly**: About eight o'clock. I was surprised to see her so early...
> **A Juryman**: Is not eight o'clock a very early hour to be discharged from a casual ward? There are some tasks – picking oakum – before you can be discharged.
> **John Kelly**: I know it was very early.

Given that sunrise was at 6:08 a.m., Kate's early appearance suggests she had slept on the streets.

Seeking safety

Knowing that homeless women had been attacked and killed in Whitechapel, Kate may have deliberately crossed into the City of London for protection. The City maintained its own police force, and everyone in London knew that Annie Millwood, Emma Elizabeth Smith, Martha Tabram, Polly Nichols and Annie Chapman had all been attacked and killed in Whitechapel, where the Metropolitan Police held responsibility.

Mitre Square lay just two or three minutes from Houndsditch, where John last parted from Kate, and though only a 10-minute walk from Flower and Dean Street, it fell within the City's supposedly safer jurisdiction.

In 1888, Mitre Square wasn't really a square at all but a small, irregularly shaped space. One corner offered a particularly sheltered, dark spot – exactly where Kate's body would be discovered on Sunday morning.

The final hours

After parting from John Kelly on Saturday afternoon, Kate walked down Houndsditch towards Aldgate. By 8:30 p.m., she was helplessly drunk and collapsed outside 29 Aldgate High Street. PC Louis Robinson said that he 'sat her against the shutters, but she fell down sideways. With the aid of a fellow constable, I took her to Bishopsgate Police Station. There she was asked her name, and she replied "Nothing." She was then put into a cell.'

A little after midnight, she woke and began singing to herself. When she asked about release, she was told she could leave when capable of looking after herself. She claimed that she was, and at 1:00 a.m., the police released her onto the streets.

A community's farewell

On 8 October 1888, her body was carried through the streets lined with mourners to Ilford Cemetery. Her funeral drew not only daughters and sisters, cousins, aunts and uncles, but hundreds of East Enders who gathered at the grave to pay their respects to a woman they recognised as one of their own.

It's worth noting that, despite the appalling conditions that had developed in 1888, decency persisted. As Reverend Samuel Barnett of St Jude's wrote to *The Times* on 19 September 1888:

> The greater part of Whitechapel is as orderly as any part of London, and the life of most of its inhabitants is more moral than that of many whose vices are hidden by greater wealth.

His wife, Henrietta, defended the 'abandoned women' with particular eloquence:

> Only those who know them personally and intimately, as I did by the hundred, can know the readiness to help, the capacity for sacrifice, the generosity of heart, and the disregard of self that survives all the horrors of their lives.

Catherine Eddowes was not simply 'Jack the Ripper's fourth victim'. She was a woman whose life began with promise and education, whose circumstances led her down a path of increasing vulnerability until she found herself alone and defenceless in the early hours of Sunday, 30 September 1888.

21

The Evidence and the Police Failure

The evidence consistently contradicts the accepted narrative that Kate Eddowes was killed while servicing a client. The medical testimony, timeline constraints and witness accounts all point to a simpler explanation.

At the inquest, questions were asked about Kate's character. John Kelly said, 'I have been living with her for seven years… I never knew she went out for any immoral purpose… She never brought me money in the morning after being out at night.'

The deputy at Cooney's doss house was also questioned:

Frederick William Wilkinson: I am the deputy of the lodging-house at Flower and Dean-street. I have known the deceased and Kelly during the last seven years. They passed as man and wife, and lived on very good terms. They had a quarrel now and then, but not violent ... I believe she got her living by hawking about the streets and cleaning amongst the Jews in Whitechapel.

Coroner: Did you know she was in the habit of walking the streets at night?

Comments from witnesses that these women 'walked the streets' are cited as evidence of prostitution. This exchange between the coroner and John Kelly shows that this term didn't automatically imply prostitution:

John Kelly: I never knew she went out for any immoral purpose. She occasionally drank, but not to excess. When I left her she had no money about her. She went to see and find her daughter to get a trifle, so that I shouldn't see her walk about the streets at night.

Coroner: What do you mean by "walking the streets?"

John Kelly: I mean that if we had no money to pay for our lodgings we would have to walk about all night.

It is obvious that 'walking the streets' was not necessarily a euphemism for prostitution. We might also be careful about how we interpret what was meant when a woman was described as an 'unfortunate'. There was no shortage of women in Whitechapel in 1888 who could very definitely be described as unfortunate. How can we know that every time that term was applied, it was meant to indicate the woman was also a prostitute? So far as Kate Eddowes was concerned, Frederick Wilkinson said, 'I never knew her to be intimate with any particular individual except Kelly, and never heard of such a thing.'

Most writers on the subject have been highly sceptical of both John Kelly and Frederick William Wilkinson. In *The Complete History of Jack the Ripper* (1994), Philip Sugden writes:

> Kate's friends and acquaintances insisted that she was not a prostitute. During the winters she worked as a charwoman for the Jews or hawked trifles about the streets… John Kelly told the inquest that although Kate sometimes drank to excess, she did not solicit… Wilkinson had never known or heard of her 'being intimate with anyone but Kelly.' Such protestations carry little conviction. Kelly would have been anxious to scotch any suggestion that he lived off Kate's immoral earnings and Wilkinson that he ran a disreputable house.

Sugden dismisses evidence suggesting Kate was not a prostitute, stating that, 'Such protestations carry little conviction.' Yet, in the same book, he accepts 'Mrs Long's evidence as crucial' evidence indicating Annie Chapman's 'companion was almost certainly the murderer'. This demonstrates a selective bias in his assessment of evidence, favouring what supports his preferred theory while dismissing conflicting accounts.

The timeline

The timeline of Kate's final hours, constructed from inquest testimony, reveals fundamental problems with the accepted narrative:

- 8:30 p.m. Saturday: PC Lewis Robinson found Kate so intoxicated in Aldgate that she required two constables to transport her to Bishopsgate Police Station.

- 12:55 a.m. Sunday: Sergeant Byfield ordered her release check. Kate was discharged at 1:00 a.m.
- 1:45 a.m. Sunday: Kate's mutilated body was discovered in Mitre Square.

At 8:30 p.m., Kate was so drunk she couldn't walk unassisted. Four hours later, at 1:00 a.m., would she realistically be capable of navigating London's dangerous streets?

The police perspective and its flaws

The prevailing police narrative at the time often suggested that protecting these women from attack was challenging because they deliberately put themselves at risk. This perspective was a convenient way to shift blame.

Yet here we have a woman murdered less than 45 minutes after being released onto the streets, not by a doss house deputy, but by a serving police officer from Bishopsgate Police Station.

Does the 'prostitute' narrative perhaps serve to mitigate what looks suspiciously like a catastrophic failure of police duty? Is the evidence that suggested she desperately sought a client more readily accepted than a simpler explanation: that alcohol, a cold night and homelessness led her to a sheltered, quiet corner to find temporary respite?

The celebrated eyewitness

Witnesses came forward claiming to have seen Kate less than 10 minutes before her murder. One of the most 'celebrated' was Joseph Lawende:

Joseph Lawende: I reside at No. 45, Norfolk-road, Dalston, and am a commercial traveller. On the night of Sept. 29, I was at the Imperial Club, Duke-street, together with Mr. Joseph Levy and Mr. Harry Harris. It was raining, and we sat in the club till half-past one o'clock, when we left. I observed a man and woman together at the corner of Church-passage, Duke-street, leading to Mitre-square.

Coroner: Were they talking?

Joseph Lawende: The woman was standing with her face towards the man, and I only saw her back. She had one hand on his breast. He was the taller. She had on a black jacket and bonnet. I have seen the articles at the police-station, and believe them to be those the deceased was wearing.

Let's scrutinise Joseph Lawende's account. He gave his evidence a full 11 days after the event. He had no foreknowledge that a murder would occur as he passed Church Passage. He only recalled the couple when police were conducting house-to-house inquiries in the days after the murder.

Lawende states the woman wore a black jacket and bonnet, with one hand on the man's chest. This scene unfolded a mere five-minute stroll from St Botolph's without Aldgate, infamously known in the 19th century as the 'Prostitutes' Church' due to the hundreds of women who would parade there seeking business. The actual number of women wearing black jackets and bonnets that night is, of course, unknown.

It was a dark, rainy night, lit only by faint gaslight. Could Lawende definitively ascertain the jacket was black? Or might it have been dark brown or navy blue? Was it patterned or plain? In such poor light, how reliable could his identification truly be?

While it's commendable that he remembered anything at all, his claim, 'I have seen the articles at the police station, and believe them to be those the deceased was wearing', relies on being shown some dark clothing draped in the mortuary a day or two later. Is this a positive identification of the woman?

Crucially, they wouldn't let Joseph see her body, only her clothes – what purpose could this serve, since he explicitly stated he hadn't seen her face? Mrs Long didn't make that mistake. She told the police she saw Annie Chapman's face, so she was given permission to see Annie's body.

The description

The Times on Tuesday, 2 October, reported that Lawende described the man as being 'of shabby appearance, about 30 years of age and 5ft. 9in. in height, of fair complexion, having a small fair moustache, and wearing a red neckerchief and a cap with a peak'.

The man was directly beneath the gaslight, meaning the peak would have cast a shadow over the man's face. How could he tell what colour the man's neckerchief was in those conditions? And it is remarkable that he could see not only the man's small moustache but also that it was fair.

The coroner asked him if he would recognise the man again.

Joseph Lawende: I doubt it. The man and woman were about nine or ten feet away from me.

Coroner: You were not curious enough to look back and see where they went.

Joseph Lawende: No.

Like Mrs Long, he wasn't curious enough to look back, so he didn't take much notice. It's impressive. Remember where you were last night. Can you remember anybody you passed? Someone you were not curious about? Could you now describe them in as much detail as Joseph Lawende described this man?

His friend Joseph Hyam Levy says, 'I did not take any notice of them.' The one thing we can take from his statement is the time: 'We got up to leave at half-past one on Sunday morning, and came out three or four minutes later. I saw a man and woman standing at the corner of Church-passage, but I did not take any notice of them.'

This corroborates Lawende's timing: 'It would be twenty-five minutes to two o'clock when we passed the man and woman.'

The next person to see Kate was PC Edward Watkins.

PC Edward Watkins: I was on duty at Mitre-square on Saturday night. I have been in the force seventeen years. I went on duty at 9.45 upon my regular beat. That extends from Duke-street, Aldgate, through Heneage-lane, a portion of Bury-street, through Cree-lane, into Leadenhall-street, along eastward into Mitre-street, then into Mitre-square, round the square again into Mitre-street, then into King-street to St. James's-place, round the place, then into Duke-street, where I started from. That beat takes twelve or fourteen minutes. I had been patrolling the beat continually from ten o'clock at night until one o'clock on Sunday morning.

So Mitre Square is patrolled every 12 or 14 minutes, which means the killer's timing has to be good. In the accepted story, it is explained by saying that prostitutes were aware of the timing of police patrols. The accepted story assumes Kate was a prostitute, assumes she picked up a client on this night and assumes she made her killer aware of how little time was available.

These are not the only assumptions that have to be made to make the accepted story viable.

Coroner: Had anything excited your attention during those hours?

PC Edward Watkins: No.

Coroner: Or any person?

PC Edward Watkins: No. I passed through Mitre-square at 1.30 on the Sunday morning. I had my lantern alight and on – fixed to my belt. According to my usual practice, I looked at the different passages and corners.

Coroner: At half-past one did anything excite your attention?

PC Edward Watkins: No.

Coroner: Did you see anyone about?

PC Edward Watkins: No.

Coroner: Could any people have been about that portion of the square without your seeing them?

PC Edward Watkins: No. I next came into Mitre-square at 1.44, when I discovered the body lying on the right as I entered the square.

PC Edward Watkins describes a meticulous patrol that never takes him more than a two-minute brisk walk from where the murder took place. He checks Mitre Square at 1:30, and a mere 14 minutes later, he is back to discover the body of Kate Eddowes.

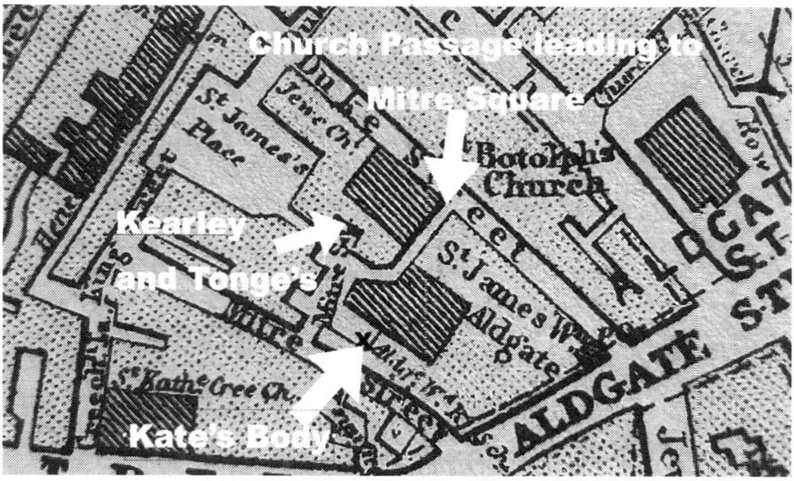

In 1888 Mitre was tiny and it wasn't a square. The darkest and most sheltered spot was where Kate's body was discovered.

Mitre Square was considerably smaller than it is today. From *Bacon's New Large-Scale Ordnance Atlas of London & Suburbs* (1888), the distance from Duke Street down Church Passage to Mitre Street is only 50 yards. The distance from the southeast corner, where Kate's body was found, to Kearley and Tonge's premises on the northwest corner was about 30 yards.

PC Edward Watkins: The woman was on her back, with her feet towards the square. Her clothes were thrown up. I saw her throat was cut and the stomach ripped open. She was lying in a pool of blood. I did not touch the body. I ran across to Kearley and Tonge's warehouse. The door was ajar, and I pushed it open, and called on the watchman Morris, who was inside. He came out.

Coroner: When you first saw the body did you hear any footsteps as if anybody were running away?

PC Edward Watkins: No. The door of the warehouse to which I went was ajar, because the watchman was working about.

Again, we have somebody close to the scene of the murder. The watchman was working behind a door that was partly open, about 30 yards from where the murder took place, and he said he heard nothing.

George James Morris, the night watchman at Messrs. Kearley and Tonge's tea warehouse, provided this testimony.

George James Morris: On Saturday, Sept. 29, I went on duty at seven o'clock in the evening. I occupied most of my time in cleaning the offices and looking about the warehouse.

Coroner: What happened about a quarter to two in the morning?

George James Morris: Constable Watkins, who was on the Mitre-square beat, knocked at my door, which was slightly ajar at the time. I was then sweeping the steps down towards the door. The door was pushed when I was about two yards off. I turned round and opened the door wide. The constable said, 'For God's sake, mate, come to my assistance.'

Coroner: Did you see any suspicious persons about?

George James Morris: No.

Coroner: Before being called by Constable Watkins, had you heard any noise in the square?

George James Morris: No.

Coroner: If there had been any cry of distress, would you have heard it from where you were?

George James Morris: Yes.

To questions from the jury and the City of London solicitor:

George James Morris: I was in the warehouse facing the corner of the square. Before being called I had no occasion to go into the square. I did not go there between one and two o'clock; of that

> I am certain. There was nothing unusual in my door being open and my being at work at so late an hour. I had not seen Watkins before during the night. I do not think my door had been ajar more than two or three minutes when he knocked.

He opened the door two or three minutes before Watkins knocked at 1:45 a.m.

Historian Donald Rumbelow says that 'Joseph Lawende saw a man talking to Eddowes.' Philip Sugden similarly asserts, 'The man Lawende saw with Kate Eddowes was reportedly rather rough and shabby.' These are presented as unequivocal statements by experts that Kate Eddowes was indeed with a man. Lawende claimed, 'It would be twenty-five minutes to two o'clock when we passed the man and woman.' (1:35 a.m.)

If this were true, then Kate was killed 50 yards from where Lawende saw them. Assuming they didn't sprint, the killer, without alarming his victim, would have had to guide her 50 yards down the narrow Church Passage to the secluded spot in Mitre Square.

Then, astonishingly, without her struggling or making any sound, he got her onto the ground before severing the left carotid artery. Then he cut her throat right across, lifted her skirts, sliced open her abdomen, pulled out her intestines, cut a piece about two feet long and placed it between her left arm and body, removed her uterus, removed her left kidney, sliced off her nose, part of her right cheek, part of her right ear, and cut two V-shapes pointing up to her eyes, before finally cutting a piece of her apron to take with him.

All completed between 1:35 and 1:44. Just nine minutes.

Dr Frederick Gordon Brown, the City of London police surgeon, stated these wounds 'might be done in five minutes. It might take him longer, but that is the least time it could be done in.'

Five minutes is the least time to complete the mutilation, so that leaves a maximum of four minutes for the killer and Kate to walk 50 yards from where Lawende said they were standing to where he had to get her onto the ground and slice the left carotid artery. And in those four minutes, he had to get out of Mitre Square before PC Watkins entered from Mitre Street.

George James Morris stated, 'I do not think my door had been ajar more than two or three minutes when he knocked' (at 1:45). This means Morris opened his door around 1:42 or 1:43. Yet, he heard nothing and saw nothing as *The Daily News* reported on Saturday, 10 November 1888:

> That such a man should again and again succeed in entrapping a woman into some lonely place and there slaughter her and yet never be seen, never be noticed, never be suspected by anyone one because of blood marks on his hands or his clothes, would certainly seem to border on the miraculous.

Truly miraculous.

The first doctor on the scene, Dr G. W. Sequeira, arrived at 1:55 a.m., stating, 'The death must have been instantaneous after the severance of the windpipe and the blood-vessels.' He estimated life had been extinct for 'Very few minutes – probably not more than a quarter of an hour.' This places the death squarely within that impossibly tight window.

Inspector Collard further confirmed, 'The head, neck, and, I imagine, the shoulders were lying in a pool of blood when she was first found, but there was no blood in front.' In answer to the question, 'There was no sign of a struggle having taken place?' Collard replied, 'None whatever.'

Dr Frederick Gordon Brown corroborated this: 'There was no blood on the front of the clothes. There was not a speck of blood on the front of the jacket.'

This confirms she was lying down when she was killed.

So, according to the accepted narrative, the killer engages Kate, brings her to the darkest part of Mitre Square, performs extensive and highly graphic mutilations, all without a struggle or a sound, and then leaves unseen and unheard just minutes before PC Watkins discovers the body.

Annie Millwood, Emma Elizabeth Smith, Martha Tabram, Polly Nichols, Annie Chapman, Liz Stride and Kate Eddowes were all murdered, and their killer(s) walked away unseen and unheard. As *The Daily News* stated, this would 'border on the miraculous'. But it ceases to be miraculous if we consider the possibility that the murders were committed by opportunists driven by 'perverted imitativeness', fuelled by a sensational media campaign.

22

How Might Kate Eddowes Have Been Murdered?

The standard explanation borders on the miraculous, and it must be clear that we cannot with absolute certainty state who killed Kate Eddowes; however, can we come up with an explanation that doesn't border on the miraculous?

Using Occam's razor, here is a more plausible explanation: Kate leaves Bishopsgate Police Station at 1:00 a.m., just four hours after arriving so drunk she couldn't walk unaided. After a few minutes in the cold night air (6°C / 43°F), her immediate thought isn't prostitution, but shelter.

She instinctively heads for Duke Street and Church Passage, an area she knows well, as it's only a 10-minute walk from Cooney's doss house in Flower and Dean Street. It's also close to where Annie Millwood, Emma Elizabeth Smith, Martha Tabram and Annie Chapman had been attacked. Crucially, this area is in the City of London, with its separate police force, and there had been no similar murders in its territory – yet.

The opportunist

She reaches the entrance to Church Passage perhaps 10 minutes before a man and woman (like Lawende's sighting) might arrive to discuss business. She walks down the narrow passage and into the square, just as a man in a nearby doorway is about to light his pipe. She might have seen him if she looked over her right shoulder, but she's focused on the darkest, most sheltered space ahead and to her left. She reaches the southeast corner, huddles into a tiny, dark heap of clothing, and within minutes, exhausted and intoxicated, she falls asleep.

The man in the doorway is 30 yards from Kate. This man steps inside and waits for the familiar sound of PC Watkins' boots at 1:30 a.m. PC Watkins, a 17-year veteran with eight more years before retirement, walks into the square with his bull's-eye lantern. He checks the square four times an hour, six days a week, rain or shine. This is his 14th check that night. All is silent. He misses the bundle of dark clothing huddled in the corner.

For the 14th time, he leaves the square. The sound of his boots fades as he paces into Mitre Street, leaving the square to darkness and the man who has now exchanged his pipe for a knife. A man who knows with certainty that no policeman will enter Mitre Square until PC Watkins returns.

He knows he has less than 15 minutes to act. His aim? To surpass the horror of previous killings, ensuring it would be reported that he had 'improved upon his example'. Risky, yes, but he completes his task, adding those two V-shaped decorations to Kate's face. Then, scurrying back to his door, he steps inside, leaving the door ajar. He disposes of the knife, the left kidney and the uterus. He waits for the sound of PC Watkins' boots echoing from Mitre Street before they turn into Mitre Square.

Dr Frederick Gordon Brown was asked, 'Would you expect to find much blood on the person inflicting these wounds?' He replied, 'No, I should not.' This killer need not worry about being suspected because he is splattered with blood.

The miraculous element

I have presented two possible scenarios to explain how a man murdered Kate Eddowes without anybody seeing or hearing him. Which one you prefer will likely depend on the narrative you find most compelling. The story of a killer who targets prostitutes has endured. This may be partly because we prefer to believe things happen for a reason. The killer in that story has a reason to kill: to rid the world of prostitutes.

What reason would this hypothetical watchman have? Perhaps he, too, believes the world would be better without prostitutes, and when he sees this woman hiding in a dark corner, he concludes she must be earning money by selling herself. Now, he can help the 'unknown warrior' in his gruesome quest.

There is another motive, one less about a moral crusade and more about infamy. Consider the phenomenon of crop circles. In the 1970s, strange circular shapes began appearing in fields, and for some, they were evidence of flying saucers. Crop circles in Wiltshire made headlines, capitalising on the prevalent UFO stories.

The 1977 film *Close Encounters of the Third Kind* effectively demonstrated the compelling nature of such narratives. Southern England became a hotspot, with crop circles evolving into complex designs, and by the 1980s, they were making headlines worldwide, with crop circles as far away as Iowa.

Then, in 1991, Doug Bower and Dave Chorley confessed. In Wiltshire, they had created hundreds of circles using ropes and wooden planks. Their motive? As they relaxed in a local pub in 1978, they said they were 'wondering what we could do for a bit of a laugh'. Reports of UFO landings and *Close Encounters* had fuelled public fascination. They decided to create a 'UFO landing site', and when it hit the papers, they were able to have 'a bit of a laugh'.

Doug and Dave continued, inspiring other young men looking for a bit of a laugh. Newspapers reported a flurry of copycat creations, with each artist vying to outdo their predecessors.

Of course, making a crop circle on a farmer's land is not in the same ballpark as cold-bloodedly murdering and mutilating a rough sleeper, at least for most of us. However, some person or persons attacked five homeless people in 2025 on the streets of Shrewsbury, and three rough sleepers were murdered in 2023 in Los Angeles.

After the Double Event of Sunday, 30 September 1888, the police were under fire. *The Star* began its piece, published the following day, proudly boasting that less than nine months since its launch, it had the 'Largest Circulation of Any Evening Paper in the Kingdom'.

> WHAT WE THINK.
> THE terror of Whitechapel has walked again, and this time has marked down two victims, one hacked and disfigured beyond discovery, the other with her throat cut and torn. Again, he has got away clear; and again the police, with wonderful frankness, confess that they have not a clue.
>
> They are waiting for a seventh and an eighth murder, just as they waited for a fifth, to help them to it. Meanwhile, Whitechapel is half mad with fear. The people are afraid even to talk with a stranger.

The Star devoted more than 13,000 words to the murders of Liz Stride and Kate Eddowes, including this section:

The night watchman's story

> The Star man next got hold of Morris, the watchman at Kearley and Tonge's. He was standing at the door, and said, first, that he had just been through the warehouse and had gone to the front door to look out into the square two moments before Watkins called to him last night.
>
> 'Do you always take a look out into the square?'
>
> 'Every night in the week, barring Saturday night, I stand at this door and smoke my pipe from one till two o'clock. It is a habit with me, and the police on the beat know it well, but on Saturday nights, I have some work to do inside that interferes with it.'

'I stand at this door and smoke my pipe from one till two o'clock.' What a shame he didn't do it on Saturday; he would have caught the killer. What was this work that was so urgent that it must be done between one and two o'clock on a Sunday morning? He was sweeping the stairs; was that enough to stop him from enjoying his nightly ritual?

The *Express and Echo*, Tuesday, 2 October 1888, reported:

> Yet within its small precincts, approachable from Mitre street, Duke-street, and St. James's-place, a woman was butchered in cold blood, not fifty yards from the quarters of a night watchman, who heard no sound of a struggle or even of footsteps, although he had alleged that, 'as a rule, he can hear the tread of the policeman passing on his beat every quarter of an hour.'

This is interesting: 'he can hear the tread of the policeman'.

The measured two-and-a-half-miles-an-hour tread of the officer on his beat. Put yourself in his position:

> I do not think my door had been ajar more than two or three minutes when he knocked… The door was pushed when I was about two yards off.

Imagine standing behind a door that opens onto a small, silent square. You are standing behind the door, which is ajar:

> **PC Edward Watkins**: I next came into Mitre-square at 1.44, when I discovered the body lying on the right as I entered the square.

His footsteps let you know that PC Watkins has entered the square. Then:

> **PC Edward Watkins**: The woman was on her back, with her feet towards the square. Her clothes were thrown up. I saw her throat was cut, and her stomach ripped open. She was lying in a pool of blood. I did not touch the body.

You hear the footsteps stop. Why has the policeman stopped? What has he found? I'd be curious. I'd be tempted to throw the door open.

> **PC Edward Watkins**: I ran across to Kearley and Long's warehouse.

Now, running footsteps. You couldn't stop me. A police officer running when I am 'about two yards off' from a door that is ajar? Come on. Open the door, saying, 'What's going on, Edward?'

Was somebody enjoying the moment?

The thought strikes me that there might be a weakness in my story. Mr Morris might be afraid to carry out the murder because – forget motive, he has opportunity. He is right there. And he knows the police patrol's timing intimately. He'll inevitably be a suspect.

But, of course, he won't be a suspect, and he knows it. The murderer the police are looking for 'has but one aim and seeks but one class in the community'. The man is a prostitute killer who killed Polly Nichols and Annie Chapman. Killed them on nights when George James Morris was taking care of business in Kearley and Tonge's warehouse in Mitre Square. He certainly didn't have the opportunity to kill those victims.

The *Morning Advertiser*, Monday, 1 October 1888, added:

> It was only on that night that he remarked to some policeman that he wished the 'butcher' would come round Mitre square, and he would give him a doing; yet the 'butcher' had come, and he was perfectly ignorant of it.

I'm not sure that he was perfectly ignorant of it, but then again, I would say that. I like my story. And that's all it will remain – a story. Had the police not become fixated on the idea that they were hunting a prostitute killer, they could have considered other alternatives.

The fact that in every case, people were close by and heard nothing must lead to the conclusion that the simplest explanation for the police was that the women were sleeping when the attack took place. Of all possible explanations, it is the one that gave the killer the simplest task.

The police were well aware that Polly, Annie, Liz and Kate were homeless, and, on the nights they were murdered, they were penniless. They were also aware that thousands of penniless people in Victorian London had no alternative but to sleep on the streets.

It is extraordinary that this was not considered a possibility.

23

Mary Jane Kelly

Mary Jane Kelly was different from the other victims in every way except one – like them, she was killed while lying down, in silence, without a struggle. The simplest explanation is that she was sleeping when attacked.

Mary Jane Kelly was the fifth victim, and she stood apart from the others. She was only 25 when she was killed – the only victim under 40. She was the only victim killed in her own home, the only one who could afford her own accommodation. She was the only victim who openly described herself as a prostitute. She's also the only victim about whose early life we know nothing for certain, and the only one for whom no photograph taken in her lifetime exists.

A woman of mystery

We know only what Mary told people after moving to Spitalfields in March 1887, and she seems to have told different stories to different people. In one version, she was born in Ireland and moved to Wales where her father worked in Carmarthen's steelworks; at 16 she married a coal miner who died in a mining accident, then she moved to Cardiff where her cousin led her into prostitution.

She told her partner Joseph Barnett she arrived in London in around 1883–84 and worked in a gay house, a high-class West End brothel. She also claimed she'd gone to Paris but stayed only a few weeks because she 'did not like the part'.

This may have been the result of human trafficking. William Thomas Stead estimated that around 250 women were sent to France or Belgium annually, mostly tricked into doing so.

People trafficking doesn't attract gentle souls blessed with empathetic natures. Ruthlessness would be a desirable trait in men organising this game, and crossing them would be dangerous. This may explain why we know so little about her early life. Did this young woman invent a new identity for herself? She certainly didn't return to the life she'd been living in London's racy West End. She must have had a reason for choosing to make her new home in the streets around the infamous Ratcliffe Highway rather than exclusive St James's Square.

Mary took a room at 79 Pennington Street, close to East London's docks, and made it her business address – the same business she'd known in the West End but with a very different clientele. Social reformer Edward Thomas observed, 'Ratcliffe and Wapping have ways of their own and in no particular could this be better illustrated than in the conduct of the sailors and the women.'

One woman who knew Mary described her as 'one of the most decent and nicest girls when sober, but very quarrelsome and abusive when intoxicated'.

In around late 1886, she attracted a 27-year-old plasterer, Joseph Fleming. They lived together briefly in Bethnal Green, but by early 1887, Mary had returned to prostitution, moving to Spitalfields to work around Commercial Street and Aldgate.

'One of the smartest, nicest-looking women'

According to Detective Chief Inspector Walter Drew:

> She would be parading along Commercial Street, between Flower and Dean Street and Aldgate, or along Whitechapel Road. Always fairly neatly dressed and invariably wearing a clean white apron, but no hat.

A missionary confirmed this description of Mary as being 'one of the smartest, nicest-looking women in the neighbourhood'.

The fatal partnership

In March 1887, Mary met 29-year-old fish porter Joseph Barnett on Commercial Street. Joseph was besotted, and within days, he'd found them a room in George Street. It was the first of four addresses they'd occupy, ending at 13 Miller's Court, just a room, 10 feet by 12 feet, for which they paid four shillings and sixpence a week.

In the summer of 1888, Joseph lost his job, and they fell into debt and began arguing. During one argument, a window was broken. It was never repaired; they just stuffed it with old clothes to keep out the wind and rain. On Tuesday, 30 October 1888, Joseph moved to Buller's Boarding House.

On Friday morning, 9 November 1888, Miller's Court landlord John McCarthy, sent his assistant, Thomas Bowyer, to collect the rent. Getting no answer, he looked through the broken window. What he saw stayed with him for the rest of his life.

He ran back to tell John McCarthy, and then they informed the police. Despite arriving by 11:00 a.m., they didn't enter the room until 1:30 p.m. as they awaited the arrival of Commissioner Sir Charles Warren, unaware that he had resigned the day before.

The post-mortem examination began at 2:00 p.m. and was the only post-mortem examination to be carried out at the scene of the crime because it was the only murder committed in a room behind a locked door. That meant for the first time, the killer was not in a public street or square, so he could take his time, and so it was the most extensive mutilation in any of the five murders as Dr Thomas Bond's report shows:

> The body was lying naked in the middle of the bed, the shoulders flat, but the axis of the body inclined to the left side of the bed. The head was turned on the left cheek. The left arm was close to the body with the forearm flexed at a right angle & lying across the abdomen. the right arm was slightly abducted from the body & rested on the mattress, the elbow bent & the forearm supine with the fingers clenched. The legs were wide apart, the left thigh at right angles to the trunk & the right forming an obtuse angle with the pubes.
>
> The whole of the surface of the abdomen & thighs was removed & the abdominal Cavity emptied of its viscera. The breasts were cut off, the arms mutilated by several jagged wounds & the face hacked beyond recognition of the features. The tissues of the neck were severed all round down to the bone.

> The viscera were found in various parts viz: the uterus & Kidneys with one breast under the head, the other breast by the Rt foot, the Liver between the feet, the intestines by the right side & the spleen by the left side of the body. The flaps removed from the abdomen and thighs were on a table.

The inquest

The inquest was held at the Shoreditch Town Hall on Monday, 12 November 1888. *The Daily Telegraph* reported it on Tuesday, 13 November 1888. Superintendent Arnold, Inspector Abberline of the Criminal Investigation Department, and Inspector Nairn were present.

The first witness was Joseph Barnett, who described his relationship with Mary and said:

> I last saw her alive between half-past seven and a quarter to eight on Thursday night last, when I called upon her. I stayed there for a quarter of an hour.

He told the inquest he had been 'on friendly terms' and wanted to give her money, but he had no work.

Thomas Bowyer and John McCarthy described how they discovered the body. A resident of Miller's Court, Mary Ann Cox, said she had seen Mary on the night before she was murdered at a quarter to midnight, going into Miller's Court. She was with a man:

Mary Ann Cox: A short, stout man, shabbily dressed. He had on a longish coat, very shabby, and carried a pot of ale in his hand.

Coroner: What was the colour of the coat?

Mary Ann Cox: A dark coat.

Coroner: What hat had he?

Mary Ann Cox: A round hard billycock.

Coroner: Long or short hair?

Mary Ann Cox: I did not notice. He had a blotchy face, and full carroty moustache.

Coroner: The chin was shaven?

Mary Ann Cox: Yes. A lamp faced the door.

Coroner: Did you see them go into her room?

Mary Ann Cox: Yes; I said, "Good night, Mary," and she turned round and banged the door.

Coroner: Had he anything in his hands but the can?

Mary Ann Cox: No.

Coroner: Did she say anything?

Mary Ann Cox: She said, "Good night, I am going to have a song." As I went in she sang "A violet I plucked from my mother's grave when a boy." I remained a quarter of an hour in my room and went out. Deceased was still singing at one o'clock when I returned. I remained in the room for a minute to warm my hands as it was raining, and went out again. She was singing still, and I returned to my room at three o'clock. The light was then out and there was no noise.

Coroner: Did you go to sleep?

Mary Ann Cox: No; I was upset. I did not undress at all. I did not sleep at all. I must have heard what went on in the court. I heard no noise or cry of "Murder," but men went out to work in the market.

The next witness lived in the room above Mary:

Elizabeth Prater, a married woman, said: My husband, William Prater, was a boot machinist, and he has deserted me. I live at 20 Room, in Miller's-court, above the shed. Deceased occupied a room below. I left the room on the Thursday at five p.m., and returned to it at about one a.m. on Friday morning. I stood at the corner until about twenty minutes past one. No one spoke to me. McCarthy's shop was open, and I called in, and then went to my room. I should have seen a glimmer of light in going up the stairs if there had been a light in deceased's room, but I noticed none. The partition was so thin I could have heard Kelly walk about in the room. I went to bed at half-past one and barricaded the door with two tables. I fell asleep directly and slept soundly. A kitten disturbed me about half-past three o'clock or a quarter to four. As I was turning round I heard a suppressed cry of "Oh – murder!" in a faint voice. It seemed to proceed from the court.

Coroner: Do you often hear cries of "Murder?"

Elizabeth Prater: It is nothing unusual in the street. I did not take particular notice.

She said she heard nothing else.

A woman who lived at 14 Dorset Street, Caroline Maxwell, said she had talked to Mary at 8:30 a.m. and then seen her with a man outside the Britannia beer house at a quarter to nine. The coroner commented that 'You must be very careful about your evidence, because it is different to other people's.' He also questioned the fact that she knew Mary's name and Mary knew her name, despite her claim that they had only spoken to each other twice.

The next witness was Sarah Lewis:

> **Sarah Lewis**: I live at 24, Great Pearl-street, and am a laundress. I know Mrs. Keyler, in Miller's-court, and went to her house at 2, Miller's-court, at 2.30 a.m. on Friday. It is the first house. I noticed the time by the Spitalfields' Church clock. When I went into the court, opposite the lodging-house I saw a man with a wideawake. There was no one talking to him. He was a stout-looking man, and not very tall. The hat was black. I did not take any notice of his clothes. The man was looking up the court; he seemed to be waiting or looking for someone. Further on there was a man and woman – the latter being in drink. There was nobody in the court. I dozed in a chair at Mrs. Keyler's, and woke at about half-past three. I heard the clock strike.
>
> **Coroner**: What woke you up?
>
> **Sarah Lewis:** I could not sleep. I sat awake until nearly four, when I heard a female's voice shouting "Murder" loudly. It seemed like the voice of a young woman. It sounded at our door. There was only one scream.

She went on to describe a man she had seen on Wednesday night who wanted her or her friend to 'follow him into an entry'. She described him as 'short, pale-faced, with a black moustache, rather small. His age was about forty.' He was wearing a high round hat, a brownish overcoat, dark trousers, and he was carrying 'a shiny leather bag'. She said that she and her friend ran away. She said she saw the same man talking with a woman in Commercial Street about 2:30 a.m.

Sarah Lewis said a little before 4 a.m., while in 2 Miller's Court, she heard a 'female's voice shouting "Murder" loudly. It seemed like the voice of a young woman. It sounded at our door.' At about the same time, Elizabeth Prater, in the room above Mary's room, heard only 'a suppressed cry of "Oh – murder!" in a faint voice. It seemed to proceed from the court.'

The next witness, Julia Vanturney, who lived at 1 Miller's Court, said,

'I could not rest at all during the night.' When the coroner asked if she heard anything during the night she said, 'I did not. I heard no screams of "Murder," nor any one singing.'

The last of these women was Maria Harvey, who said she had spent Thursday with Mary and was there when Joe Barnett visited but left before him. Asked if Mary ever spoke of being afraid of any man, she said, 'She did not.'

In his evidence, George Bagster Phillips, divisional surgeon of police, said:

> The large quantity of blood under the bedstead, the saturated condition of the palliasse, pillow, and sheet at the top corner of the bedstead nearest to the partition leads me to the conclusion that the severance of the right carotid artery, which was the immediate cause of death, was inflicted while the deceased was lying at the right side of the bedstead and her head and neck in the top right-hand corner.

Dr Bond also explained that death occurred when Mary was lying down.

Mary's room provided no security

In his evidence, Detective Inspector Abberline said:

> An impression has gone abroad that the murderer took away the key of the room. Barnett informs me that it has been missing some time, and since it has been lost they have put their hand through the broken window, and moved back the catch. It is quite easy.

Mary Jane Kelly may have been the only one of the five victims to be murdered in her own home; however, Inspector Abberline's statement shows she was no less vulnerable.

Coroner Roderick Macdonald opened and closed the inquest in one day:

> **The Coroner** (to the jury): The question is whether you will adjourn for further evidence. My own opinion is that it is very unnecessary for two courts to deal with these cases, and go through the same evidence time after time, which only causes expense and trouble. If the coroner's jury can come to a decision as to the cause of death, then that is all that they have to do. They have nothing to do with prosecuting a man and saying what amount of penalty

he is to get. It is quite sufficient if they find out what the cause of death was. It is for the police authorities to deal with the case and satisfy themselves as to any person who may be suspected later on. I do not want to take it out of your hands. It is for you to say whether at an adjournment you will hear minutiae of the evidence, or whether you will think it is a matter to be dealt with in the police-courts later on, and that, this woman having met with her death by the carotid artery having been cut, you will be satisfied to return a verdict to that effect. From what I learn the police are content to take the future conduct of the case. It is for you to say whether you will close the inquiry to-day; if not, we shall adjourn for a week or fortnight, to hear the evidence that you may desire.

The Foreman, having consulted with his colleagues, considered that the jury had had quite sufficient evidence before them upon which to give a verdict.

The Coroner: What is the verdict?

The Foreman: Wilful murder against some person or persons unknown.

Mary Jane Kelly's inquest began and ended on the same day, Monday, 12 November 1888. This contrasted sharply with the extensive inquests into the first three victims' deaths, which were presided over by coroner Wynne Baxter.

The reason was jurisdictional manipulation. Mary's body was taken north to Shoreditch mortuary instead of the closer Old Montague Street mortuary, placing her case under Dr Roderick Macdonald rather than Wynne Baxter.

An inquest's purpose is to investigate the circumstances of a death, mainly when it's not due to natural causes or when the cause is unknown. It's not a trial or blame-finding process. The aim is to establish the deceased's identity, the circumstances of their death, and the time and place of their death.

The inquests into Polly Nichols, Annie Chapman and Liz Stride's deaths, presided over by Wynne Baxter, went way beyond that and spread over weeks. Dr George Bagster Phillips, for one, felt that far more information about the nature of the murder and mutilation was put in the public domain than was necessary.

Moving Mary Jane Kelly north into Dr Macdonald's territory

massively reduced what would have been revealed under Wynne Baxter. Dr Macdonald deliberately limited the proceedings:

> My own opinion is that it is very unnecessary for two courts to deal with these cases and go through the same evidence time after time, which only causes expense and trouble.

The press, which had feasted on Wynne Baxter's detailed inquests, got almost nothing from Macdonald's single-day proceeding.

On the day of the murder, the *Manchester Evening News* showed what happened when journalists lacked hard evidence:

> One statement which had its origin with the police is to the effect that the body was literally dissected by having been cut into no fewer than 42 pieces. This is, however, unofficial, as also are wild statements to the effect that her arms and legs had been cut off.

The article also showed the miraculous nature of these crimes:

> Many loose women were shadowed every night, and the fiend, who has now found seven victims, could not conduct his ghastly operations except at the almost certain hazard of discovery.

It also showed how some would react when 'this kind of mania is in the air'.

> Since [the] Mitre Square tragedy the police have on several occasions found chalk writing on the walls in the neighbourhood, stating that "Jack the Ripper" would be at work again shortly. In many of these cases doubtless the writer was an innocent man, of that very silly class of practical jokers who find opportunities for the display of their idiocy.

The day after Mary Jane Kelly's murder, one writer listed all the attacks that had taken place in a tiny and crowded part of London. *The Daily News* published his article:

> The attention of the police authorities has been directed to that limited area for weeks and weeks back. The whole neighbourhood has been thrown into alarm and consternation. Every man and woman in the entire region must have been aroused to watchfulness and to activity. Yet the murders have been going on just the same – and we do not hear of any clue to the perpetrator of the latest any more than to the perpetrator of the earliest.

He asked how this could be.

> That such a man should again and again succeed in entrapping a woman into some lonely place and there slaughter her and yet never be seen, never be noticed, never be suspected by anyone because of blood marks on his hands or his clothes, would certainly seem to border on the miraculous.

And he answered with the simplest explanation.

> Of course there is the other possibility to which we have already drawn attention, that some at least of the later crimes may have been the mere outcome of man's perverted imitativeness. The newspapers have been full of cases of men who threatened their wives, or their sweethearts, or women who were neither their wives or sweethearts that they would treat them in the Whitechapel way.

On Monday, 12 November, the *London Evening Standard* showed what entertainment value these murders could provide.

> Yesterday people flocked from all parts of the Metropolis to the place, and the street hawkers plied a brisk trade with drinks, nuts and oranges, while strong-lunged men offered for sale the history of all the murders in a red paper back.

Then on Tuesday, 13 November, the press presented another story.

The convenient witnesses

In the evening, right after the inquest closed, George Hutchinson appeared at Commercial Street Police Station with an impossibly detailed description of a man he claimed to have seen with Mary at two o'clock on the morning she was murdered:

> Age about thirty four or thirty five; height five feet six inches; complexion pale; dark eyes and eyelashes; slight moustache curled up at each end and hair dark; very surly looking; dress – long dark coat; collar and cuffs trimmed with astrakhan and a dark jacket underneath; light waistcoat; dark trousers; dark felt hat turned down in the middle; button boots and gaiters with white buttons: wore a very thick gold chain with linen collar; black tie with horseshoe pin; respectable appearance; walked very sharp; Jewish appearance.

Hutchinson claimed he followed them to Miller's Court and saw the man give Mary a red handkerchief. How could he determine the handkerchief's colour at 2:00 a.m. on a wet November night? Conveniently, a 'red handkerchief' was a well-publicised detail from Joseph Lawende's questionable testimony about Kate Eddowes.

Like other celebrity witnesses in this case, Hutchinson displayed phenomenal recall. The simplest explanation is that Hutchinson, like Mrs Elizabeth Long before him, wanted his 15 minutes of fame and the morbid thrill of viewing the victim's body. Both succeeded in gaining this macabre privilege.

For an alternative explanation, read *From Hell: The Jack the Ripper Mystery* by Bob Hinton or *Jewbaiter Jack the Ripper* and *False Flag Jack the Ripper*, both by Stephen Senise. Bob Hinton and Stephen Senise believe George Hutchinson had murdered Mary Jane Kelly and the other victims, and was attempting to muddy the waters and give himself an alibi rather than satisfy his curiosity.

Adding more complexity as to why George Hutchinson chose to come forward certainly makes for a good story. Although, as Agatha Christie's sleuth Miss Marple said in *Sleeping Murder* (1976): 'I always think it's best to examine the simplest and most commonplace explanations first.'

The obvious suspect

While Hutchinson's mysterious foreigner captured the public imagination, the most likely suspect was Joseph Barnett.

Mary moved to Spitalfields early in 1887 and met Joseph Barnett soon after. He was sufficiently attracted that he found a room he could rent, and they both moved in. Fish porters were skilled workers, so Joseph earned good money, but in the summer of 1888, he lost his job. Financial pressure led to violent rows and the breakup of their relationship. Bruce Paley states in *Jack the Ripper: The Simple Truth* that Barnett turned to desperate measures to prevent Mary from leaving.

> Driven by his unrequited love and sexual obsession with Kelly – a twisted and overpowering emotion responsible for countless homicides to this day – Joseph Barnett concocted a desperate plan in which he would frighten Mary Jane Kelly off the streets by murdering and mutilating a series of prostitutes, leaving their disembowelled bodies lying out in the open as a warning for all to see.

Unrequited love and sexual obsession could well have driven a young man to murder his lost love. Whether it could explain murdering and mutilating a series of prostitutes to frighten Mary away from soliciting is, for me at least, a lot less convincing. There's also the fact that there's no solid evidence that Polly, Annie, Liz or Kate were prostitutes.

What is a fact is that Barnett had easy access to the murder site. As he explained to the police, after losing the door key, they would reach through the broken window and open the door from inside. This meant anyone could enter 13 Miller's Court while Mary slept.

The statistics are stark: according to the Femicide Census, 62% of women killed by men in the UK are murdered by current or former partners. One woman dies every three days from domestic violence.

The sleeping victim

Like all victims in the Whitechapel murders, Mary Jane Kelly was killed while lying down, in silence, without a struggle.

The pattern is unmistakable:

- Polly Nichols: homeless, penniless, sleeping rough
- Annie Chapman: homeless, penniless, sleeping rough
- Liz Stride: homeless, penniless, sleeping rough
- Kate Eddowes: released from police custody, intoxicated, seeking shelter
- Mary Jane Kelly: sleeping in a room accessible through a broken window

Rough sleepers today are 17 times more likely to be attacked than the general population. The first four victims were homeless on the night of their murders. Mary slept behind a broken window that provided easy access to anyone who knew the arrangement.

Whether the killer was Joseph Barnett, another ex-partner or an opportunistic predator who learned about the window access, the vulnerability was the same: a woman sleeping alone in an easily accessible space.

The extraordinary oversight

The most remarkable aspect of Mary Jane Kelly's case isn't the extensive mutilations or the mysterious circumstances; it's the complete failure by coroners, police, journalists or modern investigators to consider that she was sleeping when attacked.

This oversight reveals more about Victorian prejudices and modern myth-making than about the actual crimes.

24

The Three Who Went Before

Annie Millwood, Emma Elizabeth Smith and Martha Tabram were three homeless women who died following brutal attacks during 1888 in what became known as 'the Whitechapel murders'. All three were attacked within a five-minute walk of each other: Annie Millwood on Saturday, 25 February; Emma Elizabeth Smith on Tuesday, 3 April; and Martha Tabram on Tuesday, 7 August.

The five murders that followed these three made a total of eight victims in a single year in an area of less than one square mile. All but one were aged between 38 and 46, and all but one were homeless.

The brutal attacks on these three women were not lightly dismissed. The masses huddled in 'The Abyss' would have exchanged information while the press stoked public fear. By the time Polly Nichols was found murdered in Buck's Row on Friday, 31 August 1888, mass hysteria had reached fever pitch.

Annie Millwood

The comprehensive website dedicated to the Jack the Ripper case, Casebook: Jack the Ripper (casebook.org), gives what little is known of Annie Millwood:

> Possible victim mentioned in Sugden's *The Complete Jack the Ripper* and Hinton's *From Hell*. The widow of a soldier named Richard Millwood, Annie was thirty-eight years of age in the winter of 1888. She lived in Spitalfields Chambers, 8 White's Row, Spitalfields, and may have been supporting herself through prostitution, though that is pure speculation.

That Annie was supporting herself through prostitution is speculation. What is not speculation is that, like Sarah Delhar, she was a widow, and like all widows at that time, when her protector died, she was homeless.

Spitalfields Chambers in White's Row was a doss house, the Victorian version of a hostel for the homeless today. It was not a home. It was a temporary bed on those nights when a homeless person had the necessary fourpence doss money.

I don't think ending up living like this would have been something that many widows clinging to a little respectability would have wanted the world to know.

The *Eastern Post* of 7 April 1888 reported:

> It appears the deceased was admitted to the Whitechapel Infirmary suffering from numerous stabs in the legs and lower part of the body. She stated that she had been attacked by a man who she did not know, and who stabbed her with a clasp knife which he took from his pocket. No one appears to have seen the attack, and as far as at present ascertained there is only the woman's statement to bear out the allegations of an attack, though that she had been stabbed cannot be denied.

The woman was stabbed multiple times in one of the most densely populated areas of the East End, which was heavily patrolled by police officers, and nobody knew anything about it. A woman who receives 'numerous stabs in the legs and lower part of the body' does not remain silent. What can we make of this?

Since she obviously was not stabbed while she slept in the doss house, this was one of those nights when, to her undoubted shame, she was huddled in a doorway or dark corner. Just another vulnerable rough sleeper in Victorian London.

The attack is easy. While one hand presses hard across her mouth, a knife repeatedly plunges into her body. Shock and suffocation render her unconscious and silent as her attacker departs, perhaps to his loving wife, perhaps to his doss house and a single bed.

The Emma Elizabeth Smith case

The cases of Emma Elizabeth Smith and Martha Tabram are documented more fully. *The Ultimate Jack the Ripper Sourcebook* by Stewart Evans and Keith Skinner provides coverage.

Evans, whose fascination began in childhood after seeing the 'Dear Boss' letter at Madame Tussauds, chose a police career partly influenced by these murders. His co-author, Keith Skinner, became a respected crime historian, consulting on documentaries including *From Hell*.

Their sourcebook presents Emma Elizabeth Smith's murder as the first of 11 in police files spanning until the death of Frances Coles on Friday, 13 February 1891. Although the original police file on Emma is missing, BBC presentation notes from 1973 and press reports are still available.

On Tuesday, 3 April 1888, Emma appeared at 18 George Street between four and five in the morning, badly injured. The deputy and a lodger helped her to the London Hospital, where she died the next day. The inquest opened on Saturday, the 7th; the police only learned of the attack the day before.

Dr G. H. Hillier testified that Emma's right ear was torn, with peritoneum rupture and other internal damage caused by a blunt instrument. Though she had consumed alcohol, she wasn't intoxicated. According to Emma, three men attacked her around 1:30 a.m. near Whitechapel Church.

Curiously, no one questioned what Emma did during the three hours before reaching her lodging house, only 300 yards from the attack site. Despite the attack taking place in a densely populated area, nobody heard anything. No beat policemen reported disturbances.

The simplest explanation is that the attack took place in circumstances similar to the attack on Annie Millwood, whose death occurred just three days before the attack on Emma.

The Martha Tabram murder

On Tuesday, 7 August 1888, Martha Tabram was found on the first-floor landing of George Yard Buildings at 4:50 a.m. She had been stabbed 39 times.

The Times reported that the inquest opened on Thursday, 9 August, and quoted Dr Killeen:

> I did not think all wounds were inflicted with the same instrument. The wounds generally might have been inflicted by a knife, but such an instrument could not have inflicted one wound, which went through the chest bone.

Alfred Crow, a cab driver, passed the body at 3:30 a.m., heading home. He paid no attention because he was accustomed to seeing people lying about there. He did not then know whether the person was alive or dead.

An hour and a quarter later, at 4:45 a.m., John Reeves 'found the deceased lying on her back in a pool of blood'.

The body initially remained unidentified, despite three women claiming to recognise it under different names. A Metropolitan Police report dated Friday, 10 August 1888, noted that descriptions and photographs had been circulated unsuccessfully.

On Thursday, 16 August, Henry Tabram identified the body as his wife's. Mrs Luckhurst of 4 Star Place also identified her as Mrs Turner, saying she and Mr Turner had lodged with her until a month prior.

A police report dated 24 September revealed Henry Tabram had lived with Martha until she left 13 years earlier. She then lived with Henry Turner for nine years until three weeks before her murder:

> The deceased resided at 19 George Street (a Common Lodging House) passing there in the name of "Emma" and was looked upon as a common prostitute, and a friend of Mary Ann Connelly, alias "Pearly Poll," also a prostitute.

Mary Ann Connelly claimed she and the victim had been drinking with two soldiers – a private and a corporal – from 10 p.m. until 11:45 p.m. on Monday, the 6th. She promised to identify both men, but when corporals and privates on leave that night were paraded the next morning, she failed to appear. Found and brought to the Tower the following morning, she failed to identify anyone.

A police constable on duty in George Yard claimed he spoke with a private of the Guards at 2 a.m. on 7 August. This PC picked out two men, but both were cleared:

> They were questioned and beyond all doubt the first was not the man, and the second gave an account of himself and his time, which on inquiry was found to be correct.

Inspector Edmund Reid's report reviewing both Mary Ann Connelly's and the police officer's evidence concluded:

> Inquiries were made to find some other person who saw the deceased and Pearly Poll with the privates on the night of the 6th but without success, and Pearly Poll and the P.C. having both picked out the wrong men they could not be trusted again as their evidence would be worthless.

Reading and rereading the police reports and newspaper accounts, Inspector Reid had a valid point; their evidence was worthless. Today, eyewitness evidence faces much greater scrutiny than in 1888, yet it still largely shapes the story, perhaps because it's so colourful.

The conventional narrative

The accepted story suggests Martha Tabram sold sex and picked up a client, possibly a Guards private, possibly someone else found later. They went to the first-floor landing of George Yard Buildings, where the client went berserk, stabbing her 39 times before calmly sheathing his knife to draw a heavy-duty dagger, and smashing it through her chest bone.

This vivid tale, combined with the colourful 'Pearly Poll', makes for compelling storytelling.

An alternative theory

But could there be another story based on known facts?

Henry Turner and Martha Tabram separated. At the inquest, Henry Turner said:

> They had lived together on and off for nine years. She used to get her living, like himself, as a street hawker. He last saw her alive on the Saturday before her death, when they met accidentally in Leadenhall-street. She said she had got no money, so witness gave her some to buy stock with.

Martha struggled to survive alone in 1880s Whitechapel. Each day, she hoped to earn fourpence for a bed in a doss house. On nights without money, she found shelter by sleeping rough; George Yard Buildings was a popular and well-known option.

At 3:30 a.m., Alfred Crow passed Martha Tabram heading home. He didn't take any notice because 'he was accustomed to seeing people lying about there'.

I think even with a casual glance, Alfred would have spotted the difference between the average rough sleeper and the sprawled-out body of a woman stabbed 39 times, with her chest bone smashed through.

Perhaps, after Alfred passed, the crew that had used Emma Elizabeth Smith as entertainment months earlier – or another crew inspired by the sensational publicity – decided to check if the first-floor landing was occupied.

Seeing a middle-aged woman sleeping might have proved too tempting. One gang member secured Martha's head, clamping her mouth shut – after all, they were only a few yards from sleeping people; silence was essential. Then, like Hannibal Chollop*, one of the gang possessed a great knife, perfect for smashing through chest bones, inspiring a more lightly armed companion to demonstrate the superiority of speed over brute force. Thirty-nine stab wounds later, they walked away, gleefully anticipating inevitable headlines.

This murder could easily have occurred silently without the victim struggling. The soldier-and-prostitute story requires a less straightforward explanation. But, however I dress up my story, it's simply about another rough sleeper being abused – something that could never compete with tales of prostitutes, uniformed guardsmen and a character called 'Pearly Poll'.

It's obvious which story is more interesting. It's perhaps less obvious as to which is true. Our only evidence, as Inspector Edmund Reid said, is worthless. Neither tale might be true, so you're entitled to your own opinion about how Martha Tabram met her end.

* Charles Dickens created Hannibal Chollop in *Martin Chuzzlewit*:

> Much esteemed for his devotion to rational Liberty; for the better propagation whereof he usually carried a brace of revolving pistols in his coat pocket, with seven barrels apiece. He also carried, amongst other trinkets, a swordstick, which he called his 'Tickler' and a great knife, which (for he was a man of a pleasant turn of humour) he called 'Ripper' in its allusion to its usefulness as a means of ventilating the stomach of any adversary in a close contest.

Around the time *Martin Chuzzlewit* was first in circulation (1843–4), newspapers created the headline-grabber 'Spring-heeled Jack.' At September's end, 1888, a letter arrived at the Central News Agency, possibly inspired by Hannibal Chollop's 'Ripper' and 'Spring-Heeled Jack'; it was signed 'Yours truly Jack the Ripper'.

One of history's greatest headline-grabbers was born.

Part 3

The Dark Side

25

The Women and the Street Gangs

Late 19th-century Britain saw massive increases in gang activity in major cities. Birmingham had the Peaky Blinders. Liverpool had the Cornermen and High Rip. These gangs revelled in violence.

Michael Macilwee, author of *The Gangs of Liverpool: From the Cornermen to the High Rip*, noted:

> The High Rip were often portrayed as having some level of organisation, which they used to plan criminal activities. However, one of the most terrifying features of the gang was their willingness to engage in random acts of violence. There was often no attempt at theft. It seems that nobody could innocently walk past them without falling prey to some sort of abuse or violence.

Liverpool's extreme poverty and unemployment made its slum streets breeding grounds for crime and violence. The Cornermen appeared in the early 1880s; by mid-decade, the High Rip had established control over the streets.

Their first major crime was the Blackstone Street Murder in January 1884. Five gang members aged 18–20 attacked two Spanish sailors, beating them with belts before the sailors attempted escape. The gang caught Rodriguez Nunez as they shouted, 'Knives, boys, knives!' He died bleeding from neck wounds.

London had its gangs, too. The Blind Beggar Gang, around The Blind Beggar Pub on Whitechapel Road; the Hoxton High Rips; the Limehouse Forty Thieves; the Green Gate Gang; and a Jewish gang called the Coons. Just 15 minutes north up Brick Lane from where Annie Millwood, Emma Elizabeth Smith and Martha Tabram were attacked stood Old Nichol Street and the Old Nichol gang.

Murder in Regent's Park

In the summer of 1888, newspapers covered updates on Joseph Rumbold's murder. He was strolling with his girlfriend and another couple through Regent's Park on Thursday, 24 May 1888, when a gang of 15–17-year-olds attacked them. According to *The Globe*:

> Before the attack, one of the eight roughs said to Rumbold, 'Are you Macy?' Then, without waiting for an answer, he was grappled and twice stabbed. No sooner was the crime perpetrated than all assailants ran away, as if their object was accomplished; they made no attempt to molest any of Rumbold's companions. This resembles closely the doings of murderous gangs in some Lancashire cities who set forth after dark for the express purpose of stabbing miscellaneously.

Young thugs wandered London's streets, eager to engage in random violence against convenient, easy targets.

One police theory about the Whitechapel murders suggested that these gangs collected protection money from local prostitutes, with brutal attacks sending clear signals about timely payments.

But these homeless women were hardly worth robbing, though they could have offered cheap entertainment for gang members.

26

The Women and Their Jekyll and Hyde World

The Strange Case of Dr Jekyll and Mr Hyde was published in 1886, capturing the dual nature of Victorian society. Robert Louis Stevenson's tale emerged from nightmares but reflected the monstrous conditions that breed monsters. In one scene, two men walked through London at 3 a.m. on a black winter morning:

> I saw two figures: one a little man who was stumping along eastward at a good walk, and the other a girl of maybe eight or ten who was running as hard as she was able down a cross street. Well, sir, the two ran into one another naturally enough at the corner; and then came the horrible part of the thing; for the man trampled calmly over the child's body and left her screaming on the ground.

Interestingly, neither man questioned why an eight or 10-year-old girl was on the street at 3 a.m. on a winter morning. Stevenson felt no need to explain to middle-class readers that in Victorian London's squalor, children could be abroad at any hour.

Born in Edinburgh in 1850, Stevenson suffered health problems, possibly including tuberculosis. As a child, he would lie awake coughing, sometimes staying awake deliberately to avoid the terrifying nightmares that filled his sleeping hours.

Poor health dogged him throughout his life, although it didn't stop him from travelling extensively. In 1884, he chose Bournemouth for its clean air and a mild climate. His father, lighthouse engineer Thomas Stevenson, bought him a house where Robert lived with his

American wife, Fanny, and her 16-year-old son, Lloyd Osbourne.

Robert's deteriorating health rarely allowed him to leave the house. Still, this period produced a literary outpouring: *A Child's Garden of Verses*, *Prince Otto*, *Kidnapped*, and *The Strange Case of Dr Jekyll and Mr Hyde*.

Childhood nightmares persisted, but as a writer, he welcomed them as a source of inspiration. During one nightmare, he screamed with such horror that Fanny woke him. He had dreamed Jekyll's transformation into Hyde.

Three days of feverish writing followed page after page. When he read the finished manuscript aloud, Lloyd found it spine-chilling, but Fanny called it 'magnificent sensationalism' instead of an 'allegorical masterpiece'. Stevenson was furious, driving Lloyd from the room with his rage.

When Stevenson calmed down, he accepted the criticism. After throwing the 'magnificent sensationalism' into the fire, he rewrote it. Published in 1886, it became a bestseller, and 'Jekyll and Hyde' became a widely recognised phrase, all arising from Stevenson's nightmares.

Did those nightmares include Eugene Chantrelle? Born in France, the multilingual Chantrelle taught Latin, Greek, German and French at a private school in Edinburgh. He formed a relationship with a 15-year-old pupil, Elizabeth Dyer. They married when he was 34 and she was 16. Elizabeth had four children and endured 10 years of torment and abuse. Eugene's habits created money problems. In October 1877, he took out a life insurance policy on his wife, ensuring accidental death coverage was included.

Two months later, on New Year's Day 1878, Elizabeth was found unconscious. Chantrelle blamed poisoning from a faulty gas pipe, but Professor Maclagan at the Royal Infirmary said she'd been poisoned by morphine. The jury reached a guilty verdict in just one hour and 10 minutes.

It was discovered that Chantrelle had enjoyed serving cheese snacks to dinner guests, snacks he had poisoned with morphine. At least four other victims existed, poisoned not for financial gain but for pleasure.

Stevenson would have read the case with amazement. The erudite Chantrelle had been an urbane, entertaining companion at several Edinburgh soirées that Stevenson had attended. Eugene Chantrelle was a classic Jekyll and Hyde psychopath.

The Strange Case of Dr Jekyll and Mr Hyde was published in 1886. Two years later, German doctor Julius Koch wrote about his latest research in *A Short Text Book of Psychiatry*. He described the 'Psychopathic disposition' as a recognisable mental infirmity often leading to 'anomalies in excitability and primordial instinctive impulses'.

His use of the word 'psychopath' in his 1888 book caught on in psychiatric circles. Interesting timing: 1888 became the year of the psychopath we call 'Jack the Ripper'.

Fanny persuaded Robert to go beyond creating a piece of 'magnificent sensationalism' about a psychopath's life. She pointed him towards an allegorical masterpiece about society's existing state, a state that might have seeped into his nightmares.

The Strange Case of Dr Jekyll and Mr Hyde was a bestseller not only in Britain but also hugely successful in America, where Richard Mansfield bought the theatrical rights. He must have been exceptional – when performing the dual role in Boston, the theatre required standby doctors and nurses for those overcome by Mansfield's transformation from good doctor to monster Hyde.

Henry Irving brought the cast over from Boston to perform at his West End theatre, the Lyceum. Jekyll and Hyde was playing in the West End at exactly the same time that Jack the Ripper was playing in the East End.

Mansfield's convincing monster transformation made him a suspect. Police interviewed but quickly dismissed him.

The theatre administrator of the Lyceum watched the play many times and read newspaper accounts of the Whitechapel murders. He was a writer, so he was constantly on the lookout for inspiration, and his inspired tale about a monster spreading terror appeared in bookstores in 1897. The story was *Dracula*, and the theatre administrator was Bram Stoker.

Dracula used his teeth while 'Jack' used a knife, but both went for the throat and both went for women.

27

A Jekyll and Hyde City

William Thomas Stead, *Pall Mall Gazette* editor and campaigning journalist, reviewed a newly printed pamphlet in 1883:

> *The Bitter Cry of Outcast London* is the striking title of a small pamphlet. If this were the first time this wail of hopeless misery had sounded in our ears, the matter would be less serious. Because we've heard it so often, the case is desperate. Everyone knows what the evil is. Men, women, and children are herded together in filthy sties; there's a family in every room, morality is impossible, and in these stinking tenements are bred the stunted, squalid savages of civilisation. Some rookeries have been demolished, but those remaining are more crowded than ever. New dwellings are filled with the better class and outcasts are driven to huddle more closely together in the few loathsome places still left them. These fever dens are said to be London's best-paying properties, and owners who, if justice were done, would be on the treadmill, are drawing 50 to 60 per cent on slum tenement investments. In one district are 43 houses of ill fame, 428 fallen women and girls, many not 12 years old.

Congregational minister Andrew Mearns, who wrote *The Bitter Cry of Outcast London*, began with a warning to his readers:

> No exaggeration has been made in describing conditions – indeed we've had to tone down descriptions. To enter the squalid conditions endured by the poor, you must ascend rotten staircases threatening to give way beneath every step. You must grope along dark, filthy passages swarming with vermin. Every room in these rotten, reeking tenements houses a family, often two. In one cellar is a poor widow,

> her three children, and a child dead thirteen days. Her husband, a cabman, had shortly before committed suicide.

In such monstrous conditions, who could be surprised that monsters would rise from them?

Abject poverty was widespread throughout the 19th century, but the situation dramatically worsened with the arrival of one of the worst financial catastrophes in history. 'The Panic of 1873' led to 'The Long Depression', a 20-year period that brought about new levels of suffering for society's lowest tier.

When those around Queen Victoria worried that 'The Long Depression' might lead to revolution, she told them, 'Give my people plenty of beer, good beer, and cheap beer, and you will have no revolution among them.'

Perhaps she was wrong. Maybe all she needed was pageantry and patriotism. And good weather.

Long days of blue skies filled Queen Victoria's Golden Jubilee year, but warm weather meant the fruit harvest dried out. With no fruit to pick, unemployment rose higher still.

The homeless who came to London for celebrations and work joined those who were already homeless. Trafalgar Square became their gathering place. Social reformers arrived to give speeches, including Eleanor Marx (Karl Marx's youngest daughter), William Morris, George Bernard Shaw and Annie Besant. All spoke in Trafalgar Square to crowds. Thousands chanted and waved banners. Some thought the time had come – maybe beer and patriotism wouldn't quench the thirst for change.

On Tuesday, 8 November 1887, in Victoria's Golden Jubilee year, Metropolitan Police Commissioner Sir Charles Warren banned all meetings in Trafalgar Square. On Sunday, 13 November 1887, over 40,000 people defied the ban, protesting unemployment, coercion in Ireland and demanding the release of Irish Nationalist MP William O'Brien.

They faced the Queen's Life Guard, Grenadier Guards, and 2,000 truncheon-armed police. Two hundred were injured and two killed in what became known as 'Bloody Sunday'.

The following year was 1888, when Cecil Rhodes established De Beers as his stepping stone to becoming Prime Minister of the Cape Colony; when 10,000 matchgirls went on strike, joined by Annie Besant, to improve appalling working conditions; and Polly Nichols and seven other women would see the last year of their lives.

The murders focused attention on the appalling conditions to which many of the queen's subjects were condemned. However, the extent to which the poor benefited from that attention is questionable.

George Bernard Shaw wrote with biting sarcasm in *The Star* on Monday, 24 September 1888:

> SIR,–Will you allow me to comment on the Whitechapel murderer's success in calling attention momentarily to the social question? Less than a year ago the West-end press, headed by the *St. James's Gazette*, the *Times*, and the *Saturday Review*, were literally clamouring for the people's blood – hounding Sir Charles Warren to thrash and muzzle the scum daring to complain of starvation – heaping insult and reckless calumny on those interceding for victims – applauding the open class bias of magistrates and judges zealously doing their worst in following criminal proceedings – behaving, in short, as the proprietary class always does when workers throw it into terror by venturing to show their teeth ... The *Saturday Review* was still frankly for hanging the appellants, and the *Times* denounced them as 'pests of society.' This was still the class Press tone as late as the Bryant and May girls' strike. Now all is changed. Private enterprise has succeeded where Socialism failed. While we conventional Social Democrats were wasting time on education, agitation, and organisation, some independent genius has taken matters in hand, and by simply murdering and disembowelling four women, converted the proprietary press to an inept sort of communism.

Following murder-generated publicity, some slums were cleared, but conditions for many worsened, as Jack London described 14 years later in *The People of the Abyss*:

> We next visited municipal dwellings erected by the London County Council on the slums' site where lived Arthur Morrison's 'Child of the Jago.' While the buildings housed more people than before, it was much healthier. But the dwellings were inhabited by better-class workmen and artisans. The slum people had simply drifted on to crowd other slums or form new ones.

Part 4

Suspects

28

The Royal Conspiracy

I have done my best to explain how I interpret what I've discovered about these attacks on homeless women in 1888. Other interpretations have inspired bestselling books that continue to shape the Jack the Ripper narrative.

The most famous theory about the Jack the Ripper murders appeared in the film *From Hell.* The theory claimed that the murders were part of a conspiracy designed to protect those at Victorian society's very pinnacle.

This theory encompasses all the essential elements for compelling storytelling, which explains its prevalence in films and books. In 1973, the BBC produced a six-part programme examining the Jack the Ripper case. Two television detectives investigated while dramatised 19th-century scenes provided context.

The television detectives were Chief Superintendent Barlow (Stratford Johns) and Chief Superintendent Watt (Frank Windsor) from the hugely popular series, *Z Cars*, *Softly, Softly* and *Barlow at Large*. This proved an engaging way to present the 1888 murders to 1970s television audiences, and it still entertains today; the series DVD remains available.

Joseph Sickert's tale

Research during the BBC programme's production led to a man calling himself Joseph Sickert, who told a remarkable story. Joseph claimed to be the illegitimate son of Victorian painter Walter Sickert. Walter was allegedly a friend of 'Eddy' – Prince Albert Victor, Queen Victoria's grandson and second in line to the throne.

According to Joseph's account, Eddy and Walter enjoyed slumming in London's East End. During these adventures, Eddy fell in love with young working-class Annie Elizabeth Crook. In 1885, Alice Margaret Crook, their baby daughter, was born. Walter Sickert helped the couple by finding them a babysitter – Mary Jane Kelly, who would become the fifth and final victim.

The couple's romance was doomed when Queen Victoria discovered the affair. She was furious. Annie Elizabeth wasn't merely a commoner; she was Roman Catholic. It was feared that a Catholic marrying into the royal family could spark a revolution. Fortunately, Prime Minister Lord Salisbury was available. The love nest was raided, and Eddy and Annie were removed in separate carriages.

Queen Victoria's physician, Sir William Gull, then intervened and performed a lobotomy on Annie, conveniently causing memory loss, epileptic fits and eventually insanity. Baby Alice was more fortunate – Mary Jane Kelly rescued her and placed her under the protection of nuns.

The blackmail plot

Mary fully understood Alice's father's identity and shared this information with three friends: Polly Nichols, Annie Chapman and Liz Stride. They devised a plan to profit by blackmailing the government.

Prime Minister Lord Salisbury decided these blackmailers must be eliminated, and the perfect man to handle them was 71-year-old royal physician Sir William Gull. Despite feeble health and strokes beginning in 1887, the good doctor, alongside Metropolitan Police Assistant Commissioner Sir Robert Anderson, travelled Whitechapel's grimy lanes in a gleaming black coach pulled by two black horses, controlled by Prince Albert Victor's coachman, John Netley.

Rattling through the narrow, cobbled lanes around Buck's Row might have attracted attention, but somehow they hunted down the blackmailers, and Sir William Gull went to work with his knife.

The fourth victim, Kate Eddowes, was a mistake – they believed she was Mary Jane Kelly. Kate bore responsibility because she sometimes used the name Mary Kelly. However, the murders were successfully concealed, and they even found a scapegoat, laying blame on a young barrister, Montague John Druitt, before murdering him.

There was a happy ending – the nuns nurtured little Alice. She reconnected with Walter Sickert and gave birth to a baby who grew up learning this remarkable story. That baby was Joseph Sickert, the man BBC researchers had discovered.

Jack the Ripper: The Final Solution

Joseph's story so impressed a young journalist, Stephen Knight, that he requested an interview. Joseph was initially reluctant, but Stephen gained his trust. At one meeting's conclusion, Stephen sat in silence.

> He had been speaking in his customary and disordered manner for nearly four hours. I was saturated with names and dates, and was having a hard job working out where the facts ended and the speculation began.

Sorting facts from speculation led to the publication of *Jack the Ripper: The Final Solution* in 1976. The book explains the murderers' motive – the Establishment was nervous. Unemployment was high, living conditions abysmal and socialism was gaining support. Even Queen Victoria was problematic. She was never universally popular, and her prolonged mourning for Albert further contributed to her unpopularity. The scandalous life of her son, Edward, the Prince of Wales, also threatened support for the country's 800-year-old monarchy.

Then there was the Catholic question. Public reaction would have been explosive if it were revealed that Prince Albert Victor had not only married a Roman Catholic but fathered a child conceived out of wedlock. Therefore, it would be understandable that Annie Elizabeth would be institutionalised, and Mary Jane Kelly and her low-life friends would have to be silenced. 'The circumstances were right, and the stage was set for Sickert's drama. It remained only to see if the curtain ever rose.'

The problem with the story

The book follows the BBC programme but differs in that Stephen Knight says Walter Sickert, not Anderson, assisted Sir William Gull in the dastardly plot. It's worth understanding the background of the man who first told this tale – the man calling himself Joseph Sickert and claiming to be Walter Sickert's illegitimate son.

Joseph was one of five children born to William and Alice Gorman, who had been married for seven years when Joseph was born. However, the Gorman household was complicated because, according to Joseph's tale, his mother Alice was Prince Albert Victor and Annie Crook's love child – the child whose nanny was Mary Jane Kelly.

After 40 years, Joseph claimed that Alice Crook and Walter Sickert met again. 40-year-old Alice and 65-year-old Walter had an affair, producing little Joseph in 1925.

It's a remarkable story; however, there's one enormous problem. No evidence supports any of it, apart from what Joseph Sickert told BBC researchers and what Stephen Knight recorded in interviews – interviews he then transformed into the bestseller *Jack the Ripper: The Final Solution.*

Conspiracy is the hook on which this story hangs, with Freemasons as prime movers. A conspiracy, by definition, explains why there's no hard evidence – the conspirators destroyed it.

The theory's enduring appeal

Stephen Knight's theory remains among the most popular, inspiring other works, including the graphic novel *From Hell*, which led to the 2001 film. It delivers a compelling story of power, corruption and conspiracy – so compelling that one of its heroes, Walter Sickert, captured the imagination of two writers. Both writers produced books in which they claimed they had evidence that Walter Sickert was Jack the Ripper. One of those writers produced not just one but two blockbusters about Walter Sickert.

29

Walter Sickert: Artist, Eccentric ... and Killer?

Walter Sickert was born in Munich on 31 May 1860, and died in Bath, Somerset, on 22 May 1942, at the age of 81.

One year after the film *From Hell* turned the spotlight on Jack the Ripper and the celebrated crime novelist Patricia Cornwell visited Scotland Yard's Black Museum, *Portrait of a Killer: Jack the Ripper – Case Closed* (2002) was published. It became an international bestseller because the author excelled at writing bestsellers. Patricia Cornwell has written over 30 books, selling more than 100 million copies.

Twenty-six of her books centre around medical examiner Kay Scarpetta. Patricia Cornwell gained first-hand expertise writing these stories, employing modern forensic science techniques, and could confidently declare 'Jack the Ripper – Case Closed'.

Cornwell's theory

Patricia Cornwell believed the psychological profile of Victorian painter Walter Sickert fits that of a killer. She points to his paintings, many of which she describes as violently misogynistic. She argues that Sickert was unable to have normal sexual intercourse due to botched surgery correcting a penile fistula. However, it was the marriage and subsequent estrangement of his friend, the painter James Whistler, that ignited the fuse. At this point, his anger against women exploded.

Portrait of a Killer: Jack the Ripper – Case Closed was a bestseller, but not all reviewers were kind. Author and historian Caleb Carr, writing in the *New York Times* in 2002, said:

> *Portrait of a Killer* is a sloppy book, insulting to both its target and its audience. The only way for Cornwell to repair its damage will be to stay with this case, as she says she intends to, continuing her research, studies and tests for the years required to complete them thoroughly. Perhaps then she can do what she claims to have done already – prove Walter Sickert's guilt decisively. Failing that, she should apologize for this exercise in calumny.

Patricia Cornwell is made of sturdy stuff. Such brutal reviews didn't deter her, and in 2014, she fired a warning shot with a Kindle Single, *Chasing the Ripper*: 'People want to know why I remain convinced that Jack the Ripper was the celebrated British artist Walter Richard Sickert.'

She claimed Sickert became increasingly skilled in his murderous acts, killing 20 or more victims. However, she says her research brought her no joy, as she explained to her literary agent:

> 'I'm miserable, I don't want to do this. I want to write my novels. I don't know how the hell ... All I did was look at his paintings and his life and those letters, and one thing led to another.'
>
> I explained to her that the Ripper Investigation pulls you in like a black hole and then you can't get out. It turns you into antimatter, causes nonexistence, is the most dangerous awful thing I've ever done ... From the first moment I began this work, I sensed an entity, a terrifically negative energy that when invoked causes strange aberrations of physics. There were the electrical disturbances, the crazy computer malfunctions, the sudden floods, fog banks and wildfires ... On one occasion, an enormous 'JR' appeared in the sand at the foot of my dock at a beachfront home where I was anonymous and in seclusion working on the book.

The supernatural disturbances didn't end there; her team members began experiencing these hauntings. 'I've explained repeatedly over the years that it seems the Ripper picked me and not the other way around.'

I feel fortunate that after 18 years studying the case and guiding Jack the Ripper tours, I haven't experienced anything approaching this distress. Perhaps it's a mark against me, pointing to a lack of sensitivity. I could never make Patricia's claim:

> 'From almost the start, I believed I knew the identity of the murderer. I couldn't possibly look the other way ... Every now and

> then this small voice asks me, "What if you're wrong?" I would never forgive myself for saying such a thing about somebody and then finding out I'm wrong.'
>
> 'But you don't believe you're wrong?'
>
> 'No. Because I'm not.'

DNA doubts

Patricia does harbour doubts about some aspects of the case. She's now much less certain about DNA's usefulness in solving this mystery.

> Nonetheless, I tried multiple rounds of DNA testing, finally giving up for good in 2008... As Dr. Melton explained in 2012, mitochondrial DNA analysis isn't reliable unless biological materials can be washed and bleached to remove all contaminating modern DNA that has been introduced. This is precisely the reason I have grave doubts about a recent claim that DNA proves Jack the Ripper was a Polish immigrant named Aaron Kosminski. The origin of this genetic evidence is a large piece of blue silk material described as a 'shawl' that purportedly was found with the mutilated body of Ripper victim Catherine Eddowes. The first insurmountable problem is that no such article... is referenced in the original documentation about any of the Ripper's murders.

Although preoccupied with a project she thought could ruin her life, Patricia pressed forward. The 2014 Kindle Single was merely advance publicity for the book she published in 2017, *Ripper: The Secret Life of Walter Sickert*.

The eBook version features art and animation specifically designed to enhance this story. The cover shows the Ripper in his top hat and opera cape – an opera cape that moves in the digital breeze.

We've travelled a long way since 1888, when Walter Sickert was 28. Sadly, Walter couldn't make a living, and as Cornwell writes, 'His wife supported him as women always would. He was known for his striking good looks.'

Cornwell describes Sickert as a chameleon, able to transform his appearance just as she claims Jack the Ripper could. He could alter his handwriting, as demonstrated in letters sent to the press and police, letters claiming to be from the killer. There's no evidence he kept a diary, and he didn't date his letters, paintings or drawings. Cornwell argues he left almost no trail, which she believes was no accident.

However, he did date some sketch scraps in early August 1888, and Cornwell says they prove he was in London during August 1888, contradicting evidence claiming he was in France when some murders occurred.

Sickert authority Wendy Baron says one difficulty with Sickert's chronology is that pictures of places were sometimes created after he'd left them. Therefore, dates on sketch scraps don't prove his location.

I couldn't find a review by Caleb Carr of Patricia's new book, but *USA Today* featured a review by Matt McCarthy, no kinder than Caleb's:

> Today, she writes of Walter Sickert, he would be diagnosed a psychopath, a narcissist. I'm a physician, this is false ... *Ripper* is a fundamentally dishonest book, one that uses medical jargon and mitochondrial DNA analysis to confuse the audience and obscure the fact that its conclusions are flawed.

Jean Overton Fuller

Some might note that both reviewers are men critiquing a woman writing about male misogyny. There's a woman who made brief comments on the book: Jean Overton Fuller, author and Special Operations Executive agent during World War II, who also had an interest in Walter Sickert.

12 years before Patricia Cornwell published *Portrait of a Killer*, Jean Overton Fuller published *Sickert and the Ripper Crimes* in 1990. In the 2012 Kindle edition, she includes a section on Patricia Cornwell in which she comments, 'She said Sickert had only a small penis (perhaps interesting if true, how did she know?).'

Fuller became curious about Walter Sickert and his connection to Jack the Ripper when she and her mother discussed the painter Florence Pash.

When in her late eighties, Florence Pash told Violet Overton Fuller that Sickert knew who Jack the Ripper was and painted clues into some pictures. She claimed the murders were linked to a royal family member's illegitimate child – an illegitimate child who, as an adult, had an affair with Walter Sickert, producing another illegitimate child, christened Joseph Gorman, who called himself Joseph Sickert, the same Joseph Sickert who Stephen Knight interviewed for his 1976 book, *Jack the Ripper: The Final Solution.*

Fuller's and Knight's books would undoubtedly have appeared in any search by somebody researching the Jack the Ripper case. However, they receive no mention in Patricia Cornwell's books. Cornwell claims she knew nothing about the Jack the Ripper case until she was shown around Scotland Yard's Black Museum. Eighteen months later, she published *Portrait of a Killer*.

That seems remarkably brief for a researcher who hadn't previously considered a subject before starting fact and background searches, then organising, editing and proofreading a manuscript, not to mention publication and distribution.

There are possibly 200 Jack the Ripper candidates with varying degrees of support. Like Stephen Knight and Jean Overton Fuller, Patricia Cornwell chose Walter Sickert.

Paul Begg and Philip Sugden, writers who've extensively studied the Jack the Ripper case, contradict Cornwell's statement that 'Today he would be diagnosed a psychopath'. The psychological profile suggests Jack the Ripper would have:

- had a domineering mother and weak or absent father – in fact, Sickert had loving relationships with both parents
- developed destructive emotions in younger years – no such tendencies were noted in Sickert
- been an asocial loner – Sickert had many friends
- hated women – Sickert had numerous female lovers and friends
- had an occupation allowing violent fantasies – Sickert was an artist
- lived in Whitechapel – Sickert lived in West Hampstead.

Despite what's written in these books, there's no evidence that Walter Sickert had any active involvement in the Jack the Ripper murders.

The more straightforward explanation, that Walter Sickert was a talented artist who lived in London during a notorious crime spree but had no connection to the murders, requires far fewer assumptions and aligns with the available evidence. Sometimes the most famous suspect is simply the most famous, not the guiltiest.

30

'Oh, Without a Doubt, a Hundred Per Cent, It's Him'

Russell Edwards became interested in Jack the Ripper when he watched *From Hell* in 2001, the same year the serial killer reached out and grabbed Patricia Cornwell. In 2002, she incorporated cutting-edge forensic science, including DNA testing. The DNA was a headline-grabber, and *Jack the Ripper: Case Closed* became a bestseller.

Patricia Cornwell tested DNA from letters received by the police during the investigation to see if there was a DNA match to Walter Sickert's paintings. For DNA to help, you need a suitable object to test. When Russell Edwards learned there would be an auction of a shawl that owners claimed belonged to the fourth Jack the Ripper victim, Kate Eddowes, he bought it.

In 2014, Russell Edwards published *Naming Jack the Ripper*, which became a bestseller. The book featured DNA evidence found on the shawl, claiming to link Kate's DNA and a 23-year-old Polish Jew's DNA, and it received worldwide publicity when it was published. In 2014 and 2015, it was the book most often mentioned when I guided my Jack the Ripper tour from Tower Hill. In 2025, it became a popular topic again.

If you booked a Jack the Ripper tour, you might do some basic research. You might Google 'Who was Jack the Ripper?' I did just that. Right at the top, Google's AI provided a newspaper illustration from 1888 of the discovery of Polly Nichols' body. Next to it was a block from the Australian website news.com.au, featuring an interview with Russell Edwards, who was still promoting *Naming Jack the Ripper* 11 years after its launch.

The interviewer stated that 137 years after 1888, Russell Edwards claimed to have revealed who Jack the Ripper was. This went online in 2025, which explains why, for the first time in three years of guiding my new Jack the Ripper tour from Whitechapel, Aaron Kosminski's name was again being given to me.

Russell's claims

Russell says, 'Considering his DNA is on the shawl that was at the murder scene, and he was named, I have never considered anyone else to be the Ripper.'

The article explains that:

> Self-proclaimed 'Ripperologist' and British author Russell Edwards purchased a shawl belonging to one of the victims, Catherine Eddowes, which contained blood and semen back in 2007. Years later, it was put through forensic testing, where it was found to contain DNA from two separate people. One of them matched a descendant of the female victim. Whilst the other matched the descendants of a Polish immigrant, who would have been around 23 at the time of the murders. Upon discovering this male's name, Edwards was able to reveal the true identity of the cold-blooded killer behind the alias of 'Jack the Ripper': Aaron Kosminski.

Right next to news.com.au was a 2023 video interview with Russell Edwards from an American cable news network, NewsNation. Russell was asked how certain he was that the Ripper was Aaron Kosminski:

> Oh, without a doubt, a hundred per cent, it's him. You must remember that the name of the Ripper was given to me by Scotland Yard ... The owner, who's the great, great grandnephew of acting sergeant Amos Simpson, who was actually on Fenian duty on the night in one of the houses on Mitre Square, and he was one of the first on the scene before PC Watkins officially discovered the body.

This is remarkable because in 18 years of research, I've never found anything showing that any police officer was on watch in a house on Mitre Square the night Catherine Eddowes was murdered. This information isn't even in Russell's book, *Naming Jack the Ripper*. In the book, Russell writes, 'Simpson, being on "special duties" at the time of the double murder, had gone to Mitre Square with several other officers from both the City and Metropolitan forces.'

There is no mention of him keeping watch in a house on the square. And I was staggered to hear him say that Sergeant Simpson was 'on the scene before PC Watkins officially discovered the body'.

Russell goes on to explain what Sergeant Simpson did next.

> Seeing the shawl, he asked one of the senior officers if it was fine to take it, as he thought his wife Jane might find the silk useful for dressmaking. David believes that it was his rank, Acting Sergeant, that allowed him to have the shawl.

The NewsNation interviewer asked where the shawl is now, and Russell said, 'Well, it's in a bank vault in an undisclosed location.'

Aaron Kosminski

Aaron Kosminski was the second candidate Melville Macnaghten put forward in his 1894 memorandum listing suspects he thought possible. Sir Melville Leslie Macnaghten wasn't part of the London Metropolitan Police until the year after the murder investigation. He became assistant commissioner in 1889, and he only wrote the memorandum six years after the murders.

Kosminski was born on 11 September 1865. In the 1880s, he emigrated to England and worked as a Whitechapel barber. In 1891, he threatened his sister with a knife and was confined to the Colney Hatch Lunatic Asylum, and later moved to Leavesden Asylum.

One problem with assessing Kosminski is that he was a Jew, and tens of thousands of Jews had arrived in London's East End. At all levels of society, there was virulent anti-Semitism, and the police weren't immune to prejudice. They also struggled spelling these immigrants' names, and this suspect wasn't the only Kosminski in town – a problem exacerbated by police not recording his first name.

Assistant Commissioner Anderson's claims

Sir Robert Anderson, assistant commissioner of the Metropolitan Police, in memoirs written in 1910, said:

> Undiscovered murders are rare in London, and the 'Jack-the-Ripper' crimes are not in that category... the only person who had ever had a good view of the murderer unhesitatingly identified the suspect the instant he was confronted with him, but he refused to give evidence against him ... In saying that he was a Polish Jew I am merely stating a definitely ascertained fact.

So Sir Robert was saying he knew who the killer was because an eyewitness identified him, but refused to testify because he was a fellow Jew. Sir Robert didn't mention the witness's name, but we can narrow it down to Israel Schwartz or Joseph Lawende because they were eyewitnesses and Jews.

Some researchers believe Joseph Lawende, having walked past a couple in a narrow alley at 1:35 a.m. on Sunday, 30 September 1888, was taken to identify that individual in July 1890, 20 months after his fleeting glimpse of a man whom Lawende said, just days after the sighting, he wouldn't be able to recognise.

The Ultimate Jack the Ripper Source Book includes a passage by Paul Bonner, who worked at the BBC and became Head of Science and Features. He wrote in the 1970s about a file that soon went missing:

> Many men, at least 100 in the file, were taken to Police stations just for carrying black bags, having foreign accents, accosting women, or talking about the 'Ripper' in pubs, but then released on being able to prove their identity… There was no mention, in this file or anywhere else, either in the Scotland Yard files or the Home Office ones, to Macnaghten's candidates Druitt, Kosminski or Ostrog.

In his 1987 book *The Crimes, Detection and Death of Jack the Ripper*, Martin Fido wrote in support of Sir Robert Anderson, 'He and Monro knew, and unless positive evidence to the contrary can be produced, they must be assumed to have been justified in their certainty.'

Well, Martin Fido may assume that, but just because two men claim the Jack the Ripper crimes weren't undiscovered murders doesn't mean they were right. To make a judgement, we need the evidence on which Sir Robert Anderson and James Monro based their assertion. Neither Martin Fido nor any other researcher can produce that evidence.

31

Russell's Shawl Story

Russell Edwards writes:

> I've spent 14 years working on it, and we have definitely solved the mystery of who Jack the Ripper was. Only non-believers that want to perpetuate the myth will doubt. This is it now – we have unmasked him.

According to the vendors' family history, this shawl was removed from Jack the Ripper victim Catherine Eddowes by Acting Sergeant Amos Simpson. Russell says, 'Some commentators denounced it as a fake… Yet something made me want to find out more.'

The first challenge came when Russell became aware that there was no mention of a silk shawl amongst the detailed list of Catherine Eddowes's possessions, more than 30 separate items. How was this to be explained?

Russell says that, unlike the police list, a press report in the *East London Observer* stated, 'Her dress was made of green chintz, the pattern consisting of Michaelmas daisies.' But Russell believes the reporter got it wrong; he wasn't describing a dress, but the shawl.

Russell doesn't explain how the newspaper reporter got close enough to notice the pattern of Michaelmas daisies but failed to see that he was looking at a shawl, not a dress.

Russell also appears to have ignored the part of the description that states, 'Her dress was made of green chintz.' Examining photographs of this piece of silk, it is not green. A small section is blue, but as the auction description says, it is predominantly brown.

> Lot 235: A late 19th-century Brown Silk Screen Printed Shawl decorated with Michaelmas daisies, length 8ft (with some sections cut and torn).

Anyone investigating this case understandably wants to be the one who finally solves it, so it is difficult to resist the strong desire to make assumptions, even when we know that they can distort our interpretation of what we discover.

Apart from a family story handed down through the generations, there is no evidence that this piece of silk belonged to Catherine Eddowes. Russell obtained his story from David Melville-Hayes, the great-great-grandnephew of Sergeant Amos Simpson. Russell says that it is 'important to put the specific version of events across, as the story of the origins of the shawl has been muddled with the passing of time'.

I'm not sure how you can dig a 'specific version of events' out of a story that 'has been muddled with the passing of time', but Russell attempts it.

The Simpson story

Sergeant Simpson had been on special duties and had gone to Mitre Square and ended up accompanying the body of Catherine Eddowes to the City of London mortuary. Russell says, 'Seeing the shawl, he asked one of the senior officers if it was fine to take it.'

Would a senior officer hand this item to Sergeant Simpson? Russell says in those days, 'No importance was attached to the belongings of a victim.'

Rigorous scepticism could make us question that statement. The detailed list of Catherine's possessions seems to indicate that some importance was attached to the belongings of a victim, and we know that police surgeons complained that important information was lost because mortuary assistants would strip the clothes off the bodies of victims before the police surgeon had time to carry out a complete post-mortem examination.

Police Constable Alfred Long was sufficiently motivated to pick up a blood and faeces-soiled cloth that he discovered 600 metres from where Catherine Eddowes had been murdered. When he took it in to be examined, his senior colleagues did not take the disgusting object and chuck it into the bin. They attached sufficient importance to it that an examination was carried out.

The whole story of Sergeant Amos Simpson and the 'senior officer' becomes more challenging to our rigorous scepticism when it is remembered that Sergeant Simpson was a member of the Metropolitan Police Force, whereas the senior officer was a member of the City of

London Police Force. Writer and former City of London police officer Donald Rumbelow says there was intense rivalry between these two forces.

Also, this was the fourth brutal murder of a woman on the streets of London in less than five weeks, and it was the first one to be committed in the 'One Square Mile' that is the City of London. It's hard to believe that a 'senior officer' in the City of London Police would be so casual about anything connected to this murder.

Since there was no objective evidence to link the shawl to Kate Eddowes apart from a family story passed down through the generations, Russell faced a dilemma, which was made worse when research revealed Kate's abject poverty.

Just before Kate was brutally murdered, she and John Kelly had come back from hop-picking in Kent. It was a bad harvest, and they returned flat broke. Things were so bad that Kate left John Kelly standing barefoot outside a pawnshop whilst she pawned his boots to get some money for food and drink. If Kate had this two-and-a-half-metre-long piece of silk amongst her possessions, it would have crossed the pawnshop's counter first. Russell says, 'What if this shawl did not belong to Catherine at all? What if it had been left at the scene of the crime by the Ripper himself?'

Now, before looking into the evidence for this assumption, let's remember that there is no reliable evidence that this shawl was at the murder site.

The Michaelmas theory

However, using rigorous scepticism, let's examine Russell's reason for saying Aaron Kosminski left the shawl at the crime scene. 'I also realised that, for the Michaelmas daisies to have real significance, they had to be connected to the Ripper.'

Russell wants to find a reason that Jack the Ripper would be carrying this piece of silk, and that reason might involve the Michaelmas daisies:

> Perhaps he had left the shawl at the scene of the crime as an obscure clue to the police as to when he would strike again. Perhaps he had intended to take it away with him but was using it in his disturbed mental state because of its Michaelmas symbolism.

Perhaps, but can we first have proof that he took it there in the first place?

> Whatever he meant by leaving it there, it suddenly seemed blindingly obvious that it was nothing to do with Catherine and was entirely to do with him.

> He had taken the shawl with him on the night of 29 September, with the intention of killing, and he signalled that he would kill again, on the Michaelmas date that was (if he was Aaron Kosminski, as I strongly believed) part of his own background and the culture of his homeland, not this new Michaelmas he had had to learn in England.

So, did these Michaelmas daisies have real significance to Aaron Kosminski because of the festival of Michaelmas?

> How could I have seen this, when nobody else had? It was the two dates of Michaelmas that hit me. They were the nights of the last three murders, first the double event on the traditional Michaelmas celebrated in this country, second the final murder of Mary Jane Kelly on the night of the Orthodox Church Michaelmas. The double event deaths happened after midnight, so they were technically on 30 September, but what if Jack the Ripper set out on his mission on the evening of Michaelmas Day?

Russell has built this whole story on the fact that the *East London Observer* and other newspapers said, 'Her dress was made of green chintz, the pattern consisting of Michaelmas daisies', which Russell says was a mistake – the journalists thought they were looking at a green dress, but what they were looking at was a brown shawl.

Russell takes us on a voyage of discovery to show that this piece of silk might have been made in Poland, where Aaron Kosminski came from and where the Eastern Orthodox Church celebrate Michaelmas on a different date to the Western Church. Whilst the Western Church celebrates on 29 September, in Poland it would be celebrated on 8 November. Unfortunately, Aaron missed those dates because he was running a little late. He murdered Elizabeth Stride and Catherine Eddowes on 30 September and Mary Jane Kelly on 9 November.

Although Russell considers it 'all blindingly obvious,' I missed the section where he proved that Aaron Kosminski had taken the shawl to Berner Street and then to Mitre Square. Isn't Michaelmas a Christian festival, and wasn't Aaron Kosminski a Jew? Did the Kosminski family ever mention the loss of this piece of silk?

The problems mount

Nobody can doubt that Russell Edwards has done much research, buoyed by his commendable energy and enthusiasm. However, his enthusiasm cannot hide the fact that there is only a story handed down through the descendants of Sergeant Amos Simpson to link the silk shawl to Kate Eddowes.

It is imaginative to say that the journalists were describing a shawl and not a dress when they wrote about the Michaelmas daisy design, but it is not proof that they had mistaken a two-and-a-half-metre-long piece of brown silk for a green dress.

It is equally imaginative to suggest that this silk became associated with the impoverished Kate Eddowes because Aaron Kosminski brought it to the murder scene. It is not enough to say, 'Well, you can't prove the journalists didn't get it wrong, can you? And you can't prove Aaron Kosminski didn't bring the shawl to the party, can you?'

The scientific method for acquiring knowledge doesn't work that way. The scientific method for acquiring knowledge requires careful observation and rigorous scepticism because our desire to make assumptions can distort how we interpret what we discover. Russell has a perfectly understandable desire to make assumptions. He spent an undisclosed sum of money and invested a lot of time and energy because, as he said, 'I believed it was genuine, and I wanted it. I wanted it very badly.'

The eyewitness evidence

Apart from the shawl, Russell believes the evidence of Israel Schwartz points to Aaron Kosminski as the killer. He recounts what Alan McCormack, the curator of Scotland Yard's Black Museum, told him about identifying the suspect that the police arranged in 1890. Russell writes:

> The scenario Alan put to me is the one suggested by Anderson and apparently confirmed by Swanson. This is my summary of it. Aaron Kosminski was placed in a room at the Seaside Home. Israel Schwartz was led into the room by a police officer and confronted with Kosminski. He was then immediately led out of the room and asked if this was the man he had seen attacking Elizabeth Stride on the night of her murder. Alan McCormack was adamant that there was what he described as an unhesitating ID.

Now, we must remember the questions about the reliability of Schwartz's evidence covered in Chapter 19: The Murder of Elizabeth

Stride. But even if we accept that Schwartz did see this man attacking the woman, as Russell Edwards says, Schwartz was 'tens of feet away' at one o'clock in the morning on a very dimly lit street. Then, consider that 20 months had passed since that sighting.

Russell goes on to say:

> The police asked Schwartz if he would be willing to testify to the fact, and he refused on the grounds that he could not bear to have it on his conscience that he had sent a fellow Jew to the gallows.

This claim was made in 1910 in Sir Robert Anderson's memoirs, and it infuriated at least one Jew. Writing under the pen name of 'Mentor' in *The Jewish Chronicle* (4 March 1910):

> According to Sir Robert Anderson, the police 'formed a theory' – usually the first essential to some blundering injustice. In this case, the police came to the conclusion that 'Jack the Ripper' was a 'low class' Jew, and they so decided, Sir Robert says, because they believe 'it is a remarkable fact that people of that class in the East End will not give up one of their number to Gentile justice'. Was anything more nonsensical in the way of a theory ever conceived even in the brain of a policeman? Here was a whole neighbourhood, largely composed of Jews, in constant terror lest their womenfolk, whom Jewish men hold in particular regard – even 'low-class' Jews do that – should be slain by some murderer who was stalking the district undiscovered. So terrified were many of the people – non-Jews as well as Jews – that they hastily moved away. And yet Sir Robert would have us believe that there were Jews who knew the person who was committing the abominable crimes and yet carefully shielded him from the police. A more wicked assertion to put into print, without the shadow of evidence, I have seldom seen.

Surely, even the most ardent supporter of Russell Edwards would have to concede that 'Mentor' makes a good point. But Russell goes on to say:

> Even though Aaron Kosminski had been clearly identified, [Really? Clearly identified for Russell maybe] the manner in which this identification was made was problematical, because to present it as evidence in court it would have to have been a full line-up of men from whom Kosminski was chosen. As a result, the police had the moral proof, but the legal proof was not good enough, a matter bemoaned by Robert Anderson.

Robert Anderson may have bemoaned this failure to convict after Israel Schwartz 'clearly identified' Aaron Kosminski. However, it's possible that another miscarriage of justice was averted:

> Eyewitness misidentification has been found to be the leading cause of known wrongful convictions, contributing to approximately 70% of known wrongful convictions that have been overturned by DNA testing. Eyewitness identification error – when a witness identifies an innocent suspect.
>
> policinginsight.com on 3rd December 2022 by Dr Joanna Pozzulo, Carleton University, Ottawa, Canada.

Russell says:

> Alan McCormack stressed to me that there was no other evidence... I believe the fact there was a confrontation and not line-up is the reason why Jack the Ripper has remained such a hot topic down the years: if Kosminski had been prosecuted and convicted, the Ripper case would be of interest only to experts studying serial killers.

So, for Russell, all that was needed to make this eyewitness evidence compelling was a police line-up. Russell believes that Israel Schwartz:

> As a Jew himself, he knew the prejudice against his race that was rampant at the time: if the Ripper was Jewish, it would feed into this growing anti-Semitism. And as far as his own community was concerned, he would possibly have been regarded as a traitor to have stirred up more bad feelings towards them all.

As 'Mentor' wrote in *The Jewish Chronicle*: 'A more wicked assertion to put into print, without the shadow of evidence, I have seldom seen.'

Russell is not alone in seriously considering this story.

It is retold in a number of books that Israel Schwartz refused to give the police the evidence they needed 'on the grounds that he could not bear to have it on his conscience that he had sent a fellow Jew to the gallows'.

Why then did Israel Schwartz report this fellow Jew to the police some 18 hours after he saw him at the crime scene, 15 minutes before Liz Stride's body was discovered?

The new claims

Before looking at the DNA element in Russell's story, I want to pick up on that moment in the NewsNation interview when Russell says Acting Sergeant Amos Simpson was keeping watch in a house on Mitre Square and that he discovered the body of Kate Eddowes before PC Edward Watkins did. A few weeks after finding the interviews with Russell, I found out why he was again promoting his writing. I'm not as alert as I think because Russell published a new book in September 2024.

I ordered *Naming Jack the Ripper: The Definitive Reveal* and began reading it in April 2025. It is the same book as *Naming Jack the Ripper*, published 10 years earlier, but with two additional chapters. In one of those chapters, Russell describes how he had grounded himself in a quest for justice that led to an energetic attempt to persuade the attorney general to reopen the case. The attorney was not persuaded.

In the last chapter, he describes how Sergeant Amos Simpson was involved.

Russell begins by reproducing a piece published in the *People's Journal* in 1919. This was 31 years after the murders of 1888. In it, a Sergeant White is reported as saying he was checking on two police officers on watch in an alley off Whitechapel Road when he passed a man who made him think 'that there was something more than usually sinister about him'. Then, 'one of the police officers came out of the house he had been in' and called out that there was the body of a woman 'at the end of the cul-de-sac'.

Russell says the location Sergeant White refers to is St James's Passage. This is Church Passage. It was renamed St James's Passage on 1 July 1939. It was at the point where it met Duke Street that Joseph Lawende claimed he saw Kate Eddowes with a man nine minutes before she was found murdered and mutilated in Mitre Square. This passage is a 15-minute walk from Whitechapel Road and is not, and was not, a cul-de-sac.

Russell says about the police officer who came out of the house, 'I have been advised this officer was Acting Sergeant Amos Simpson.' Russell doesn't specify who advised him of this or what evidence they used to support this claim. But he goes on to say:

> As it is known that Amos Simpson was the first to discover the body of Catherine Eddowes, he immediately alerted Sergeant White and PC Webber, who rushed immediately to the scene. However, on hearing the approaching footsteps of City Police Constable Watkins, who is acknowledged as discovering the mutilated remains

of the body, they hid in the shadows, assuming it may have been the murderer returning to the scene of the crime.

Since Russell tells us that Acting Sergeant Simpson and PC Webber were on watch in a house on Mitre Square, how was this killer able to escort his victim to the end of this 'cul-de-sac', get her onto the ground, cut the left carotid artery, slice off part of her nose, part of her right cheek, her right ear, lift her skirts, rip open her abdomen, pull out her intestines, throw them over her shoulder, detach a piece of intestine two feet long, place it between her left arm and her body, remove her uterus, remove her left kidney, secrete both about his person, cut out a piece of apron and then walk out of the cul-de-sac without Acting Sergeant Simpson or PC Webber knowing anything about it until Acting Sergeant Simpson tripped over a mutilated corpse?

The DNA testing

Now, Russell was a savvy enough businessman to realise that he couldn't completely ignore science. He found a top scientist, Dr Jari Louhelainen, who became sufficiently excited by Russell and his project that he agreed to, as Russell writes, 'Do these tests in his own time for me, free, as long as he could write a paper on his findings when it was all over.'

This is where the DNA testing began. DNA testing is the one thing that everybody mentions when they talk about the book, the one thing featured in all those headlines that generated that massive international press launch of *Naming Jack the Ripper*.

DNA testing is science at its purest. If any scientific investigation requires total adherence to the scientific method, it is DNA testing. The scientific method for acquiring knowledge requires careful observation and rigorous scepticism because our desire to make assumptions can distort how we interpret what we discover.

Dr Jari Louhelainen was doing work for Russell, which he said was very expensive. He was doing it for free so 'he could write a paper on his findings when it was all over'. Like Russell's book, *Naming Jack the Ripper*, Jari's academic paper could generate an interest that other academic papers could only dream about. Could there be a desire to make assumptions?

The other problem is that Russell's infectious enthusiasm had alerted the good doctor to what he was looking for. The danger is that Jari would keep testing until he finally discovered what they were both looking for.

The problem could have been avoided if Russell had just handed over the silk and the DNA samples while saying, 'Please examine this.' No mention of Aaron Kosminski, Kate Eddowes or – most importantly – no mention of that guaranteed headline-grabber 'Jack the Ripper'. But then why would Jari agree to do the work for free?

Russell writes with great spirit about the search for DNA. They discovered something about the dye in the silk that reminded me of a problem I have whenever I look at the photographs of this piece of silk.

> The fact that the blue dye came off so easily told us one piece of information: the shawl could never have been used as an outer garment, because rain would have made the blue dye leak.

This proved to Russell that it could not have belonged to Catherine Eddowes:

> Just before her death she and her partner John had walked back to London from the hop fields in Kent, and because she had nowhere to live she had all her clothes on when she was murdered: there is no possibility that the shawl would never have been wet if it was hers.

And so, this was the moment when, for Russell, 'It suddenly seemed blindingly obvious that it was nothing to do with Catherine and was entirely to do with him.'

It was Aaron Kosminski who was scurrying around clutching this precious piece of silk when, as Google AI reports, 'The weather in the early hours of 30 September 1888, in London was exceptionally cold and wet, potentially with snow showers.' And we have first-hand evidence from that night from Joseph Lawende – 'It was raining, and we sat in the club till half-past one o'clock, when we left.'

Was Aaron Kosminski clutching this bundle of Michaelmas daisies when he murdered Elizabeth Stride 40 minutes before visiting Mitre Square? The weather was wet at Berner Street, as Donald Rumbelow explains in *The Complete Jack the Ripper*:

> PC 452H Smith saw Stride between 12.30 and 12.35 a.m. ... The slight discrepancies in description are understandable when it is remembered that it was a dark night and raining.

Possibly, he was toting this silk through the rainy night in a bin bag. What strikes me is who would manufacture a shawl that a woman would have to quickly remove in the event of a sudden shower of rain?

This is the description provided at the auction:

> Lot 235: A late 19th-century Brown Silk screen-printed shawl decorated with Michaelmas daisies, length 8ft (with some sections cut and torn).

Later, Russell tells us it is 25.5 inches wide.

The evidence of the blue dye running in the rain reminded me that this piece of silk, around 8 feet long and 2 feet wide, is an odd shape for a shawl. However, it is not an odd shape for a runner that might decorate the top of a dresser or a table on a special occasion.

The only reason it is described as a shawl today is that the family who entered it into the auction claimed that their ancestor, Acting Sergeant Amos Simpson, had removed Catherine Eddowes 'shawl' from her body.

Scientific scepticism

As for any other evidence that the DNA might have provided, some experts expressed scepticism that a shawl examined in the early 21st century could yield any reliable DNA deposited in 1888. A significant amount of DNA would have accumulated as the shawl was passed around over the course of more than 100 years.

More significantly, as the *Smithsonian Magazine* reported (18 March 2019):

> As Hansi Weissensteiner, a mitochondrial DNA expert, points out, mitochondrial DNA can't be used to positively ID a suspect, it can only rule one out since thousands of other people could have had the same mitochondrial DNA.

The business angle

Whilst Russell's credentials as a scientist can be questioned, his business credentials are excellent. According to the *East Anglian Daily Times*, the 'undisclosed sum' paid by Russell at the Bury St Edmunds auction in 2007 was £5,200. Seven years of research culminated in the launch of *Naming Jack the Ripper*, which garnered international publicity far exceeding the wildest dreams of most nonfiction authors.

Then, one year after the book launch, the *Daily Mail* of Thursday, 9 July 2015, reported:

> Bloodied shawl worn by one of Jack the Ripper's victims said to prove identity of serial killer goes to auction for £2.9 MILLION.

'I believed it was genuine, and I wanted it. I wanted it very badly.'

And with that kind of potential return on investment, I believe many of us would find that our 'rigorous scepticism' would wilt under our dynamic entrepreneurial 'desire to make assumptions' that this shawl 'was genuine'.

There is no available evidence that Russell managed to sell the shawl. So despite his significant investment in time and money, Russell didn't get £2.9 million, and 11 years later, he is working on his return on investment.

The news industry loves a good story, and Russell certainly has one for them. And as Mark Twain (or possibly someone else) said, 'Never let the truth get in the way of a good story.'

Of course, if you want the truth, you should never let a good story get in the way of the truth.

32

The Ease of Creating Suspects

M.J. Trow, writing in *The Mammoth Book of Jack the Ripper* (1999), singles out the son and heir to the Charrington family brewing business:

> Frederick Nicholas Charrington, aka Jack the Ripper. In his late teens, he witnessed a sight which led to a deep and lasting religious conversion. Outside one of the innumerable East End pubs to which his father's company supplied beer, he saw a wife being beaten to a pulp by her drunken husband.

Charrington said of this moment:

> I looked up and saw my own name in high gilt letters... and it suddenly flooded into my mind that that was only one case of dreadful misery and fiendish brutality in one of the several hundred public houses that our firm possessed.

Trow sketches out this man's life from a little boy raised in a schizoid family. Frederick's mother was doling out non-alcoholic cordial to the poor at the same time that his father was getting them roaring drunk.

Charrington became an evangelist campaigning outside pubs and brothels, and the madams and keepers of the brothels feared Frederick Charrington as they feared no policeman, no inspector, no other living being.

Trow builds as solid a case against Frederick Charrington as any other writer manages on his favourite suspect, then this:

> There – you fell for it. Or at least, I hope you did. I want to apologise publicly to Frederick Nicholas Charrington because he was

> a good man doing a difficult job in a difficult time, and because he was no more Jack the Ripper than I am. But isn't it easy – frighteningly easy – to put a man in the frame? To take the random jottings of a life – any life; it might be yours or mine – and build them into a sinister framework of guilt and complicity?

This perfectly encapsulates the problem with Jack the Ripper theories. When you start with the assumption that one of these historical figures was the killer, it becomes remarkably easy to construct a case by cherry-picking details from their lives and interpreting them in a sinister light.

Part 5

The World of Jack the Ripper

33

Letters from Hell

Newspaper coverage of Polly Nichols and Annie Chapman's murders – occurring just eight days apart – resulted in a feeding frenzy amongst the East End population. Queues formed at shops as first editions sold out.

A further boost to newspaper sales came from a letter written in red ink and addressed to the Central News Agency.

The 'Dear Boss' letter

Dear Boss,

I keep on hearing the police have caught me but they wont fix me just yet. I have laughed when they look so clever and talk about being on the right track. That joke about Leather Apron gave me real fits. I am down on whores and I shant quit ripping them till I do get buckled. Grand work the last job was. I gave the lady no time to squeal. How can they catch me now. I love my work and want to start again. You will soon hear of me with my funny little games. I saved some of the proper red stuff in a ginger beer bottle over the last job to write with but it went thick like glue and I cant use it. Red ink is fit enough I hope ha. ha. The next job I do I shall clip the ladys ears off and send to the police officers just for jolly wouldn't you. Keep this letter back till I do a bit more work, then give it out straight. My knife's so nice and sharp I want to get to work right away if I get a chance. Good Luck.

Yours truly Jack the Ripper

Dont mind me giving the trade name

PS Wasnt good enough to post this before I got all the red ink off my hands curse it. No luck yet. They say I'm a doctor now. ha ha

Whoever wrote the letter handed the world a gift of a headline: 'Jack the Ripper'. The writer called it a trade name; we would call it a brand name, and it's difficult to imagine the marketing departments of Apple Computers or Coca-Cola creating a better brand name. It's descriptive, memorable and has rhythm.

Many today agree that it was the work of a practical joker or a journalist. In 1931, journalist Fred Best, who began his career on *The Star*, reportedly confessed that he and a colleague, Tom Bullen, had written the 'Dear Boss' letter, the 'Saucy Jacky' postcard and other hoax messages, and together, they chose the name Jack the Ripper.

From Hell letter

Among the hundreds of letters sent that claimed to be from the Whitechapel killer is the 'From hell' letter. It was sent along with half a kidney to the chairman of the Whitechapel Vigilance Committee, George Lusk. The vigilance committee had been set up in response to the Whitechapel murders. The letter was postmarked 15 October 1888 and received by Lusk on the 16th.

> From hell
> Mr Lusk,
> Sor
> I send you half the Kidne I took from one women prasarved it for you tother piece I fried and ate it was very nise. I may send you the bloody knif that took it out if you only wate a whil longer
> signed
> Catch me when you can Mishter Lusk

The combination of a kidney and the letter's title, 'From hell', has assured it a prominent position among the many letters. *From Hell* was the title chosen for the graphic novel written by Alan Moore and illustrated by Eddie Campbell, published in serial form from 1989 to 1998 and in book form in 1999. The title was good enough to lead to a feature film, *From Hell* (2001), loosely based on the graphic novel, which itself drew inspiration from Stephen Knight's *Jack the Ripper: The Final Solution* (1976).

The letter writer was perhaps inspired by a collection of letters written by a Danish priest, Valdemar Adolph Thisted, in 1862, which was translated into English. The 1884 edition of *Letters From Hell* included a preface by the Congregational minister and writer George MacDonald.

The book explores themes of regret and the consequences of life's choices – appropriate reading perhaps for any murderer who happens to be of a thoughtful disposition.

Opinions are divided as to the authenticity of the letter George Lusk received, so you can make up your own mind.

34

The Writing on the Wall

Soon after the discovery of Kate's body in Mitre Square, a blood and faeces-soaked cloth and a chalk message were discovered in an entrance to the Wentworth Model Dwellings in Goulston Street. The message, which appeared in three different versions according to how witnesses copied it, referenced 'Juwes' and became central to Masonic conspiracy theories.

However, there's no solid evidence supporting the theory that Kate's killer was the person who dropped the cloth or wrote the message. If the killer used the cloth to wipe blood off his knife and hands, why did it take him from Mitre Square to Goulston Street to carry out that simple task? Indeed, why waste time cutting it out of the apron? Why not spend the seconds simply wiping the blade and hands on the apron and leave it intact?

Trevor Marriott in *Jack the Ripper: The 21st Century Investigation* suggests it may have been left by Kate Eddowes herself at some point in the afternoon or evening. With feminine hygiene products being what they were in 1888, it's a possibility.

35

The Macnaghten Memoranda

The police interviewed hundreds of people as suspects at the time, but without any success. It wasn't until some of the senior police officers looked back at the case that some of the names still discussed today began to be mentioned.

One of the documents that can spark a student's interest in these murders is the Macnaghten memoranda. This document was written by Melville Macnaghten, who joined the Metropolitan Police as assistant chief constable in June 1889, the year following the murders.

The memoranda begin by attacking a sensational story that had appeared in *The Sun* newspaper about a young man called Thomas Cutbush, who was charged with stabbing the rear of Florence Grace Johnson and Isabella Fraser Anderson in Kennington. The paper suggested that Thomas Cutbush was the likely suspect behind the Jack the Ripper murders.

Macnaghten wrote his memoranda partly to throw scorn on this idea, after which he said:

> Now the Whitechapel murderer had 5 victims – & 5 victims only, – his murders were
>
> 31st August, 1888. Mary Ann Nichols – at Buck's Row – who was found with her throat cut – & with (slight) stomach mutilation.
>
> 8th Sept. 1888 Annie Chapman – Hanbury St.; – throat cut – stomach & private parts badly mutilated & some of the entrails placed round the neck.
>
> 30th Sept. 1888. Elizabeth Stride – Berner's Street – throat cut, but nothing in shape of mutilation attempted, & on same date
>
> Catherine Eddowes – Mitre Square, throat cut & very bad mutilation, both of face and stomach.

9th November. Mary Jane Kelly – Miller's Court, throat cut, and the whole of the body mutilated in the most ghastly manner –

The last murder is the only one that took place in a room, and the murderer must have been at least 2 hours engaged. A photo was taken of the woman, as she was found lying on the bed, without seeing which it is impossible to imagine the awful mutilation.

With regard to the double murder which took place on 30th September, there is no doubt but that the man was disturbed by some Jews who drove up to a Club, (close to which the body of Elizabeth Stride was found) and that he then, 'mordum satiatus', went in search of a further victim who he found at Mitre Square.

It will be noted that the fury of the mutilations increased in each case, and, seemingly, the appetite only became sharpened by indulgence. It seems, then, highly improbable that the murderer would have suddenly stopped in November 1888, and been content to recommence operations by merely prodding a girl's behind some 2 years and 4 months afterwards. A much more rational theory is that the murderer's brain gave way altogether after his awful glut in Miller's Court, and that he immediately committed suicide, or, as a possible alternative, was found to be so hopelessly mad by his relations, that he was by them confined in some asylum.

No one ever saw the Whitechapel murderer; many homicidal maniacs were suspected, but no shadow of proof could be thrown on any one. I may mention the cases of 3 men, any one of whom would have been more likely than Cutbush to have committed this series of murders:

(1) A Mr M. J. Druitt, said to be a doctor & of good family – who disappeared at the time of the Miller's Court murder, & whose body (which was said to have been upwards of a month in the water) was found in the Thames on 31st December – or about 7 weeks after that murder. He was sexually insane and from private information I have little doubt but that his own family believed him to have been the murderer.

(2) Kosminski – a Polish Jew – & resident in Whitechapel. This man became insane owing to many years indulgence in solitary vices. He had a great hatred of women, specially of the prostitute class, & had strong homicidal tendencies: he was removed to a lunatic asylum about March 1889. There were many circumstances connected with this man which made him a strong 'suspect'.

(3) Michael Ostrog, a Russian doctor and a convict, who was subsequently detained in a lunatic asylum as a homicidal maniac. This man's antecedents were of the worst possible type, and his whereabouts at the time of the murders could never be ascertained.

Montague John Druitt

This is what *The Southern Guardian* wrote on Saturday, 1 January 1889, when it reported the death of Montague John Druitt:

> An inquiry was on Wednesday held by Dr Diplock, at Chiswick, respecting the death of Montague John Druitt, 31 years of age, who was found drowned in the Thames.
>
> The deceased was identified by his brother, Mr William Harvey Druitt, a solicitor residing at Bournemouth, who stated that the deceased was a barrister-at-law, but had lately been an assistant at a school at Blackheath.
>
> The deceased had left a letter, addressed to Mr Valentine, of the school, which alluded to suicide. Evidence having been given as to discovering deceased in the Thames – upon his body were found a cheque for £60 and £16 in gold – the jury returned a verdict of 'Suicide whilst of unsound mind.'
>
> The deceased gentleman was well known and much respected in his neighbourhood. He was a barrister of bright talent, he had a promising future before him, and his untimely end is deeply deplored.
>
> The funeral took place in Wimborne Cemetery on Thursday afternoon, and the body was followed to the grave by the deceased's relatives and a few friends.

Druitt was the second son of seven children. He was born on 15 August 1857 at Westfield, Wimborne, Dorset. His father was a doctor. Montague John Druitt went to Winchester College and from there to New College, Oxford.

After graduating in 1880, he took up a teaching post at a boarding school for boys in Blackheath. He played cricket and was described as one of the best players in the history of the Blackheath Club.

In 1882, he began a second career in law and, in 1885, rented chambers at 9 King's Bench Walk. Soon after this move, his father died of a heart attack, and his mother, Ann, began to show signs of mental instability. Later, she attempted suicide with an overdose of laudanum. Druitt's sister also attempted suicide, and their mother finally did commit suicide.

At the end of November 1888, Montague was dismissed from the boarding school. Then, when his brother William went to investigate why he'd been missing for a week, he found a suicide note in which Montague had written: 'Since Friday, I felt I was going to be like mother, and the best thing for me was to die.'

His body was discovered floating in the Thames at Chiswick on 31 December 1888. It was believed to have been in the water for about a month.

The inquest, which was held in Chiswick, concluded that Montague John Druitt had committed suicide whilst of unsound mind. He was buried in Wimborne Cemetery on 3 January 1889. His estate was valued at £2,600, equivalent to more than £300,000 today.

Problems with the Druitt theory

Macnaghten was wrong about Druitt's age and occupation, and also about when he committed suicide. It was not right after the murder of Mary Jane Kelly on 9 November, but three weeks after that event at the beginning of December.

In 1903, when a Sunday newspaper claimed that Jack the Ripper was a young medical student who had drowned in the Thames, *The Pall Mall Gazette* interviewed retired Chief Inspector Frederick Abberline, who said:

> Yes, I know all about that story, but what does it amount to? Simply this: soon after the last murder in Whitechapel the body of a young man was found in the Thames, but there is nothing beyond the fact that he was found at that time to incriminate him.

Michael Ostrog

Michael Ostrog was the third name that Melville Macnaghten put forward as a suspect in his memorandum of 1894.

Ostrog was born in Russia sometime around 1833, so at the time of the murders in 1888, he was in his mid-fifties.

The FBI's Violent Crimes Manual and other researchers say that the majority of serial killers are white males aged between 25 and 35, which would certainly exclude Ostrog. Of course, that alone doesn't prove his innocence.

When he was around 30 years of age, he emigrated to England and attracted police attention in 1863 when he committed a robbery at the University of Oxford. On that occasion, he was using the name Max Grief. He received a 10-month prison sentence.

Then, in 1864, just after he was released from prison, he was arrested for a series of frauds committed in Cambridge, and he served a three-month prison sentence.

He didn't learn his lesson, as in December 1864, he committed another fraud, which landed him in jail for 10 months.

Then, in August 1866, he was sentenced to seven years for stealing gold watches in Maidstone. When he was released in 1873, he immediately committed more thefts.

He was taken to Burton upon Trent Police Station, where he pulled a gun on the police officers. This earned him a 10-year prison sentence.

Released in 1883, he stayed out of prison until 1887, when he was arrested for stealing a trophy from a cricket match and was sentenced to six months in prison.

At this point, you might believe that either Ostrog was not cut out for the life of a criminal, or he had discovered that for those living in poverty, the harsh conditions of Victorian prisons were an improvement on the harsh conditions of Victorian society at large.

He was freed in March 1888, the year of the Jack the Ripper murders.

So yes, he would have been just in time to switch from petty theft and fraud to becoming a cold-blooded killer of homeless women. However, in 1888, he ended up in France, where he was sentenced to prison for robbery.

He returned to England, and in 1891, he was admitted to an asylum in Surrey. However, he spent the next three years alternating between more unsuccessful criminal activity and the inevitable time behind bars.

There are no records for him after 1904, so it is believed this is when he died after an eventful three score and 10 years.

Despite Melville Macnaghten's inclusion of Michael Ostrog in his memorandum, he would seem an improbable candidate for the role of Jack the Ripper.

Druitt requires us to assume that a successful barrister and teacher suddenly became a brutal serial killer, despite no evidence of violence in his background, and even contemporary police officers found no evidence linking him to the crimes.

Kosminski requires us to accept Anderson's claim about eyewitness identification despite the fundamental problems with such evidence, particularly after a 20-month delay.

Ostrog requires us to believe that a habitual petty criminal in his mid-fifties suddenly escalated to become a sophisticated serial killer, despite being in France during some of the murders.

The simpler explanation is that Macnaghten, writing six years after the events and under pressure to respond to newspaper speculation, named three convenient suspects based on limited information and personal prejudices of the era. All three theories require multiple unsupported assumptions.

Part 6

The Players

36

Queen Victoria

Alexandrina Victoria (1819–1901) was just 18 when her uncle died and she became queen on 20 June 1837. In 1876, she became Empress of India after a vote in the British Parliament. The people of India were not consulted. She reigned for more than 63 years.

Depending on your world view, it was either a glorious period of industrial, political, scientific and military advances, and the expansion of a mighty empire, or it was a period when an already broken society became even more dysfunctional. Some could claim that it was both.

Victoria had a far from ideal childhood, but like most, she struggled to make the best of the cards she had been dealt. However, her relationship with her children was influenced by her own upbringing. There were moments of affection and tenderness in the early years of motherhood, but for the most part, she was detached, particularly from her eldest son, Bertie (Edward VII). She was a strong-willed and often critical mother, sometimes complaining that she found motherhood a burden.

Her husband was much more hands-on. Albert valued education and strove to mould his family into an example of excellence. He would not shrink from hitting his children's fingers during piano lessons if they played the wrong notes, and whipping them if he had to instil obedience in them. Violence in the home was not the sole preserve of the poor.

The monarchy Victoria inherited had lost much of its power, and its primary function was to help prevent outright revolution through displays of ceremony and spectacle. As Walter Bagehot wrote in his 1867 book *The English Constitution*: 'The Queen is only at the head of the dignified part of the Constitution. The Prime Minister is at the head of the efficient part.' The consensus was that women were fine for set dressing, but when it came to the serious stuff, you needed a man.

Victoria did quite well. Having a woman as a figurehead was fortuitous, especially perhaps with a woman like Victoria, who operated on instinct rather than logic.

In a letter written to her uncle Leopold, king of the Belgians, in 1852, she wrote:

> Albert grows daily fonder of politics and business and is wonderfully fit for both… and I grow daily to dislike them both more and more. We women are not made for governing and, if we are good women, we must dislike these masculine occupations.

Victoria's attitude was perhaps the natural response to being the queen, and so the head of state, at a time when the state was run entirely by men. She was an essential symbol at the centre of a pageantry that held a population in awe and obedience. In those circumstances, having a head of state who was a woman and a woman who believed that women were not made for governing was fortunate.

Other women saw things differently. Mark Bostridge, in his biography of Florence Nightingale, shows a very different female character from that of Victoria. The two women met when Florence visited Victoria at Balmoral in the company of the queen's doctor, Dr Clark.

Florence felt that her contemporary society 'fritters away all that is spiritual in women'. She need not have restricted it to women. The brutal world that the Victorians inhabited meant very few of either sex were able to retain more than a shred of the spiritual.

Florence Nightingale and Queen Victoria were very different, and the differences between us all fascinated Florence from an early age. This nursing heroine of the brutal Crimean War spoke to a friend about 'the extraordinary variety there is between sisters or between brothers born under almost exactly the same circumstances', specifying, 'for want of a better, the difference between my sister and me'.

It seems Florence's sister suffered a severe breakdown as an adult, and it was Dr Clark who treated her. He believed Parthenope's 'total absorption in self, with at times, chronic delirium' indicated lunacy. Florence thought her sister's symptoms arose from being 'condemned to spend her days in a meaningless round of trivial occupations, which ate away at her vital strength'.

If Florence, Parthenope and Victoria had all been dealt the cards that Polly and the other victims had been dealt, then it is obvious who would have had the better chance of survival. Perhaps for some, that is proof that these victims did not have to end their lives sleeping on the streets of London. It was their fault. They had made their choices.

Many who have written about them have seen them as 'degraded women', 'inveigling belated drunkards', 'hawking the only thing' they had. There is no evidence to support these assumptions, and surely it takes only a minimum amount of compassion to see that the women deserved but a small amount of blame for how their lives shaped up, given the world they had to survive in.

Victoria ended up being at odds with many of her sex. She was totally against those who were campaigning for women's rights, and, in a bill outlining the punishments for homosexuality, she insisted that it omitted women as it was unnecessary because 'women don't do such things'.

However, Victoria may have been a more positive force for the advancement of her sex than she intended, as Lucy Worsley suggests in her 2018 biography *Queen Victoria: Daughter, Wife, Mother, Widow*.

> Victoria may have succeeded at least in part simply because she looked no more threatening than your own loving grandmother. But, in a passive way, she did change things for other women too. After experiencing decades of female rule, no one, wrote the journalist W. T. Stead, 'could honestly repeat the old rubbish about the natural incapacity of woman'. He thought that Victoria's silent example, simply sitting there in her landau being looked at, had ushered in an age when it was normal to see 'Woman' as well as 'Man... in the playing-field and the park, on the cycle and the street, on the platform, in business, in hospital and at the university'.

And it must be said, Victoria was no pushover. The men around her in government may have been more suited to politics and business, but they occasionally needed prodding into action, as in the events in Whitechapel in 1888.

Four days after the murders of Elizabeth Stride and Catherine Eddowes, she wrote in her diary, 'Dreadful murders of unfortunate women of a bad class, in London. There were 6, with horrible mutilations.' After the murder of Mary Jane Kelly, she wrote to the Prime Minister, Lord Salisbury: 'This new, most ghastly murder shows the absolute necessity for some very decided action... All these courts must be lit, and our detectives improved. They are not what they should be.'

Three days later, she wrote to the Home Secretary, Henry Matthews:

> The Queen fears that the detective department is not so efficient as it might be. No doubt the recent murders in Whitechapel were committed in circumstances which made detection very difficult; still, the Queen thinks that, in the small area where these horrible crimes have been perpetrated, a great number of detectives might be employed, and that every possible suggestion might be carefully examined and, if practicable, followed ... Have the cattle boats and passenger boats been examined? Has any investigation been made as to the number of single men occupying rooms by themselves? The murderer's clothes must be saturated with blood and must be kept somewhere. Is there sufficient surveillance at night? These are some of the questions that occur to the Queen on reading the account of this horrible crime.

The dreadful murders drew attention to the poor, even to the very top of society. However, conditions for those at the very bottom did not improve over the remaining years of Victoria's reign.

37

Prince Albert Victor

Queen Victoria would have been shocked to learn that her own grandson was considered a likely contender for the role of Jack the Ripper.

Prince Albert Victor, Duke of Clarence and Avondale (1864–1892), was the eldest son of the future King Edward VII and Princess Alexandra of Denmark, making him second in line to the British throne after his father. He was known to his family as 'Eddy'. Educated by tutors and later at the Royal Naval College, accounts suggest he was not particularly academically gifted.

He served as a cadet in the Royal Navy and then in the 10th Royal Hussars, though he saw no active military service. He enjoyed London's social scene, including its many brothels. There were persistent rumours about his sexuality, and he was allegedly linked to the Cleveland Street scandal involving a homosexual brothel, though no conclusive evidence supports this connection.

In his book *Edward and the Edwardians*, published in 1962, Philippe Jullian put Albert Victor forward as a possible suspect.

In 1970, Dr Thomas Stowell picked up on the allegation when he wrote an article that appeared in the magazine *Criminologist*. Although he didn't use the prince's name, simply calling him 'S', he gave enough detail that it was clear that 'S' was Prince Albert Victor.

According to Stowell, 'S' was arrested shortly after the murder of the fourth victim, Kate Eddowes. He was then certified as insane and sent to a private mental home under the care of Sir William Gull. Unfortunately, he escaped and murdered Mary Jane Kelly.

Stowell said that Prince Albert Victor contracted syphilis in the West

Indies, and it was this disease that caused him to commit the murders. Stowell said that the royal prince's experiences of deer hunting, where he would have participated in butchering deer, explained his skill at dissecting his victims.

In 1978, another writer claimed that Eddy was the Whitechapel fiend. In his book, *Prince Jack*, Frank Spiering stated that he had found a copy of Dr William Gull's notes at the New York Academy of Medicine. The notes described how the doctor hypnotised Eddy and watched in horror as he acted out the murders.

According to Spiering, Gull believed it was the pain caused by his syphilis that created fits of rage and drove Eddy to commit the murders. Spiering also suggested that Eddy's father, the Prince of Wales, together with Lord Salisbury, eventually killed Eddy with an overdose of morphine.

When Spiering first published *Prince Jack*, he challenged Queen Elizabeth II to open the royal archives to reveal the truth about Prince Albert Victor. A statement by the Palace said that several researchers had examined the royal archives, and Spiering could do the same, but the Palace did not believe that it was 'sufficiently serious to warrant a special statement by the Queen'. At that point, Spiering said he didn't want to see the files. Which certainly makes you wonder why he turned down the kind offer.

Writer and researcher Donald Rumbelow contacted the New York Academy of Medicine about the notes of Dr William Gull that Frank Spiering claimed to have discovered there. The New York Academy of Medicine said: 'None of the entries in our catalogue for works by or about Sir William Gull contain the material referred to by Mr Spiering.'

Well, despite the efforts of Philippe Jullian, Dr Thomas Stowell and Frank Spiering, experts are unimpressed, and it is pointed out that the prince cannot be shown to have been anywhere near any of the murder sites on the dates in question.

In the early hours of 31 August, when the first victim, Polly Nichols, was murdered in Buck's Row, Eddy was in Yorkshire. He was staying with Viscount Downe at Danby Lodge, Grosmont, Yorkshire, from 29 August until 7 September.

In the early morning of 8 September, when Annie Chapman's body was found in the little yard behind 29 Hanbury Street, Eddy was staying at the Cavalry Barracks in York, where he had arrived on 7 September and remained until 10 September.

Then, in the early hours of 30 September, the night of the 'double event' when both Liz Stride and Kate Eddowes were murdered, Queen Victoria wrote that the prince had lunch with her in Abergeldie Castle in the north of Scotland. So on 30 September, he was 500 miles north of where the two murders had taken place.

On 9 November, when Mary Jane Kelly was brutally murdered, he was enjoying the delights of Sandringham, where he stayed from 2 November to 12 November.

For some, however, the connection to the royal family makes this theory particularly appealing. The royal connection has also led to this high-profile suspect being mentioned in theories about others who have been proposed as suspects.

38

Lord Salisbury – Prime Minister

Robert Arthur Talbot Gascoyne-Cecil, 3rd Marquess of Salisbury, (1830–1903, known as Lord Salisbury), was the British prime minister in 1888.

He left the matter of the Whitechapel murders to the Home Secretary, Henry Matthews, and the Metropolitan Police. His main concern regarding the case appears to have been its potential to inflame social tensions in the East End of London, particularly given the anti-Semitic theories that circulated after some of the murders. He was more concerned about maintaining public order than with the investigative details themselves.

The relative silence from Downing Street was criticised at the time, with some newspapers and MPs calling for more government leadership on the issue.

The lack of dramatic pronouncements from Salisbury probably reflects both the constitutional separation between government and police operations and his own preference for working behind the scenes rather than making public declarations about ongoing criminal investigations.

It might be suggested that 'the constitutional separation between government and police operations' was appropriate when the situation concerned women at the bottom of Victorian society. When the situation involved those at the very top, then an approach that was more hands-on might be needed.

Prime Minister Lord Salisbury appeared more proactive when he was faced with the Cleveland Street scandal, which exposed activities surrounding a male brothel in 1889–1890. Salisbury was accused of orchestrating a delay in issuing an arrest warrant for Lord Alfred Somerset. Somerset and others implicated were able to flee the country to France and America. Salisbury and the cabinet ultimately decided against prosecution, a decision that drew public outrage and led to accusations of a cover-up to protect the monarchy.

39

Henry Matthews – Home Secretary

Henry Matthews, 1st Viscount Llandaff (1826–1913) was a lawyer and politician. He was home secretary from 1886 to 1892.

As home secretary, he was directly responsible for overseeing the Metropolitan Police response to the Whitechapel murders and faced considerable pressure and criticism for the handling of the case.

He regularly fielded questions in Parliament about the murders, defending the Metropolitan Police's efforts whilst acknowledging the difficulties of the investigation.

He repeatedly refused to offer a government reward for information leading to the killer's capture, arguing that rewards often led to false accusations and wasted police time. He was heavily criticised by the press, who felt the refusal showed a lack of government commitment.

On the positive side, he authorised additional police patrols in Whitechapel and supported increased lighting in the area's dark streets, and also backed the use of plain-clothes detectives and coordination between the Metropolitan Police and City of London Police.

Newspapers accused the government of not taking the East End murders seriously enough because the victims were poor women. For Matthews, it was sensational press coverage that hindered the police investigation.

40

Sir Charles Warren, Commissioner of the Metropolitan Police

The man who had the most direct responsibility for dealing with the murders of 1888 was the Commissioner of the Metropolitan Police, Sir Charles Warren (1840–1927).

He was born in Bangor, North Wales, in 1840, the son of Major-General Sir Charles Warren, who became a war hero after the Battle of Inkerman in 1854. In that same year, 14-year-old Charles entered the Royal Military College at Sandhurst.

From the age of 15, he attended the Royal Military Academy at Woolwich. In 1857, at the age of 17, he was commissioned as a second lieutenant in the Royal Engineers.

He established himself as a proficient surveyor. From 1861 to 1865, he worked surveying Gibraltar and, with support, created two scale models of Gibraltar. One of them is 26 feet or 8 metres long and is in the Museum of Gibraltar.

On 1 September 1864, he married Fanny Margaretta Haydon, with whom he had two sons and two daughters.

From 1865 to 1867, he served as an instructor at the School of Military Engineering in Chatham, after which the Palestine Exploration Fund recruited him. During his excavations in Jerusalem, he discovered a series of tunnels beneath the Temple Mount and a water shaft, now known as Warren's Shaft. He spent time in Africa, both surveying and commanding troops.

His military background certainly showed that he had a disciplined mind and energy, but he had little experience that would recommend him for the demands of police work. However, at that time, senior police officers were generally selected from the military.

To be fair to Charles Warren, the job of commissioner of the country's most prominent police force would never be easy. When Warren took over, it would have been extremely challenging for even the most qualified candidates.

His predecessor, Sir Edmund Henderson, has been in the post for 17 years, and for several years, his heart was not in the job. Consequently, police morale was low.

Added to this, they were struggling to deal with a bombing campaign organised by those fighting for Irish independence – a bombing campaign which had intensified in 1884.

The difficulties for policing were exacerbated because Britain was still reeling from the effects of 'The Long Depression', which had begun with 'The Panic of 1873'. This meant unemployment was widespread, and living conditions for millions of people in London were appalling.

Then came the West End Riots. On 8 February 1886, 100,000 demonstrators marched through London. The Carlton Club, the Devonshire Club, the offices of *The Pall Mall Gazette* and several shops had their windows smashed.

The police handling of the riot was questioned, and on 22 February 1886, Sir Edmund Henderson resigned. At this point, Colonel Charles Warren replaced Henderson. Events did not improve. Since 1884, James Monro had been in charge of the Criminal Investigation Department and covert operations against Irish Republicans.

His title was assistant commissioner for crime; however, he did not regard the commissioner as his boss. Charles Warren disagreed with Monro's view, and they clashed. Then, within months of Warren becoming commissioner, Henry Matthews became home secretary, and he sided with Monro.

At the same time, the press criticised the new commissioner not just for his chosen dress uniform but also for his concerns about the quality of the boots worn by beat police officers. Given that police officers were walking around 20 miles a day, Warren's concerns about their footwear would seem justified.

Then, in June 1887, one of his officers caused a sensation in the press. Police Constable Bowden Endacott was one of the more successful

Metropolitan Police officers at arresting women on the accusation that they were soliciting. According to the clerk at the Old Bailey, Endacott often identified two or even three women a day. On 28 June 1887, he arrested 28-year-old Elizabeth Cass as detailed earlier.

Her boss, Mrs Bowman, testified that Elizabeth Cass had been in London only a few months and had never before been out late at night. Further, she was a respectable woman in a good job.

The case was raised in Parliament, and Charles Warren was forced to hold an inquiry. Then on 19 July 1887, he issued an order that 'a Police Constable should not assume that any particular woman is a common prostitute ... unless she so describes herself'.

The following year, Charles Warren wrote this sentence: 'We have no means of ascertaining what women are prostitutes and who are not.'

This certainly shows that many of the arrests of women may well have been based on the officer's assumptions rather than hard evidence. After the Elizabeth Cass case, the number of arrests of women on the grounds of prostitution fell dramatically.

No sooner had press criticism reduced over the Cass case than a new crisis fell into Warren's lap. On Sunday, 13 November 1887, approximately 2,000 police officers, armed with truncheons, and 400 troops cleared a demonstration in Trafalgar Square.

'Bloody Sunday' turned the press against him just months before the Whitechapel murders intensified the pressure still further.

The brutal attacks on Annie Millwood, Emma Elizabeth Smith, Martha Tabram, Polly Nichols, Annie Chapman, Elizabeth Stride, Catherine Eddowes and Mary Jane Kelly filled the newspapers in 1888.

Warren was blamed for failing to offer a reward for information, and he was accused of not assigning sufficient investigators and of favouring uniformed constables over detectives.

Warren wrote a response for *Murray's Magazine*, and the Home Office reprimanded him for revealing the workings of the police department and for writing an article without permission.

In the end, it was too much for Warren, and on 8 November 1888, the day before the murder of Mary Jane Kelly, he resigned.

He then resumed his military career before retiring. Sir Charles Warren died in Weston-super-Mare on 21 January 1927, at the age of 86.

41

Dr Robert Anderson, Assistant Chief Constable of the Metropolitan Police

In September 1888, Dr Robert Anderson (1841–1918) replaced James Monro as the assistant commissioner for crime at the London Metropolitan Police headquarters at Scotland Yard.

By 8 September 1888, five homeless women had died after suffering brutal attacks on the streets of Whitechapel.

The newspapers were in full cry, demanding action from the police, so it didn't help when Robert Anderson, having accepted his new position, immediately went to Switzerland for a rest cure.

Robert Anderson came from a different social class than more junior officers such as Frederick Abberline or Donald Swanson.

He was born on 29 May 1841 in Mountjoy Square in Dublin, Ireland. His father, Matthew Anderson, was crown solicitor, a distinguished elder in the Presbyterian Church of Ireland, who acted as an intelligence officer operating against Irish Republicanism.

Robert Anderson graduated from Trinity College, Dublin, in 1862 and was called to the Irish Bar in 1863. Anderson began to practise as a barrister and became an expert on the Fenians, a group who were fighting for an independent Ireland. In 1868, he was summoned to London and appointed as an adviser on political crime to the Home Office.

Anderson was not very effective in the fight against the Fenian bombing campaign that began in 1883. In May 1884, he was forced to resign from his post at the Home Office, and Edward Jenkinson replaced him.

However, when Jenkinson resigned in 1887, Anderson was the only man available with experience in anti-Fenian activities, and he was asked to assist James Monro, who was then the assistant commissioner in charge of operations dealing with political crime.

Monro did not have a good working relationship with the Commissioner of the Metropolitan Police, Sir Charles Warren, and resigned in 1888; it was then that Robert Anderson became assistant commissioner.

However, whilst home secretary Henry Matthews accepted Monro's resignation, he immediately appointed him as head of the Special Branch over which Commissioner Sir Charles Warren had no control.

This obviously did not go down well with Commissioner Warren, especially as Anderson and his senior CID officers continued to consult with Monro behind Warren's back, particularly during the Jack the Ripper case, with the complete connivance of Matthews.

In 1910, Anderson's autobiography was published. In it, he said:

> And if the Police here had powers such as the French Police possess, the murderer would have been brought to justice I will merely add that the only person who had ever had a good view of the murderer unhesitatingly identified the suspect the instant he was confronted with him; but he refused to give evidence against him ... In saying that he was a Polish Jew I am merely stating a definitely ascertained fact.

In his copy of Anderson's autobiography, Donald Swanson wrote, 'The suspect was sent to Stepney Workhouse and then to Colney Hatch and died shortly. Kosminski was the suspect.'

Robert Anderson also said: 'When the stolid English go in for a scare, they take leave of all moderation and common sense. If nonsense were solid, the nonsense that was talked and written about those murders would sink a Dreadnought.'

His compassion for the victims can be seen in his description of them; he said they 'belonged to a very small class of degraded women who frequent the East End streets after midnight, in hope of inveigling belated drunkards, or men as degraded as themselves'.

Whilst this would be regarded today as callous, it was likely a common sentiment amongst Queen Victoria's subjects. The victims suffered the double bias: their class and their gender.

On the Subjugation of Women

John Stuart Mill's *On the Subjugation of Women* (1869) showed just how deep and widespread misogyny was at all levels in the Victorian world of white male supremacy. He presented a scathing critique of Victorian attitudes towards women and argued that the level of misogyny was both systemic and deeply entrenched.

Married women had virtually no legal rights – they couldn't own property, sign contracts or even have legal custody of their own children. This legal framework reflected and reinforced society's view of women as inherently inferior.

He said that Victorian society systematically conditioned both men and women to accept female inferiority as natural when it was artificially imposed. Mill argued that women were taught from birth to be submissive and dependent, their legal position as wives was that of slaves, and husbands had almost absolute power over their wives, including the legal right to confine them and control their actions.

He challenged the widespread Victorian belief that women were intellectually inferior to men, arguing that apparent differences were the result of denied education and opportunity, not natural incapacity. He described how women were systematically excluded from most professions and economic independence, forcing them into dependence on male relatives or marriage.

Mill's work was radical for its time precisely because it exposed how thoroughly misogynistic assumptions were woven into Victorian law, culture and social structures. He argued that this oppression harmed not just women but society as a whole by wasting half of human talent and potential.

Assumptions about the victims

It seems reasonable now to treat assumptions made about the victims of the crimes with caution.

For example, Robert Anderson did not know these women, and there is no evidence that the first four victims ever spent their nights inveigling belated drunkards.

There is, though, clear evidence that all four were homeless, and on nights when they did not have their doss money, they would sleep on the streets.

Since we know the women were not killed until they were lying on the ground, and they died without a struggle and without making a sound, the logical assumption using Occam's razor is that they were murdered whilst they slept.

An assumption that might not have sat so easily on the conscience of the average 19th-century Christian gentleman as the assumption that some degraded women brought about their own death by inveigling belated drunkards.

Robert Anderson retired in 1901. He died in 1918 during the Spanish Flu epidemic.

42

Chief Inspector Donald Sutherland Swanson

In 1888, the officer at the London Metropolitan Police Headquarters to whom Inspector Frederick Abberline reported was Chief Inspector Donald Sutherland Swanson (1848–1924).

Inspector Frederick Abberline is often cited as a police officer who saw early promotion and, as a result, was given the responsibility of supervising the investigation of the Whitechapel murders on the ground. But his boss at Scotland Yard had achieved a more impressive rise through the ranks.

Swanson was five years younger than Abberline and joined the Metropolitan Police five years later than him. After 25 years in the force, in 1888, Abberline was promoted to First-Class Inspector. After 19 years in the force, in 1887, Swanson was promoted to chief inspector. Like Abberline, Swanson was not a Londoner.

Swanson was born near Thurso in Guise, Scotland, 685 miles north of London, on 12 August 1848. He excelled academically and briefly worked as a teacher before joining his two married sisters in London. He answered an advertisement in *The Daily Telegraph* and joined the London Metropolitan Police on 27 April 1868.

His decision to apply may have been partly due to the fact that Swanson already had a family connection to the Metropolitan Police through his cousin, John Macdonald, who was a Metropolitan Police officer at the time.

There was also a Donald Swanson from Thurso, who was an inspector with the Met. It seems likely they were related, as it was Inspector Donald Swanson who authenticated the signatures on the testimonials for the young Donald Swanson.

Ten years later, at the age of 30, Swanson married 24-year-old Julia Ann Nevill on 23 May 1878, at All Saints Church, West Ham, in the East End of London.

Nine years later, in November 1887, he was made chief inspector of the Criminal Investigation Department at Scotland Yard.

Like Inspector Abberline, who had also been seconded to Scotland Yard, he was involved in preventing Fenian terrorist attacks. The brutal attacks on homeless women in Whitechapel changed all of that. However, it is perhaps more accurate to say that the newspaper coverage of those attacks forced these changes within the Metropolitan Police Force.

On 7 September 1888, *The Pall Mall Gazette* included an article titled:

A PRECEDENT FOR THE WHITECHAPEL MURDER BY MR WILLIAM WESTALL

The article about the attacks in Whitechapel included a description of the brutal murders of women in Bavaria. Readers of the article were informed that 'It was evident that after killing them, the murderer had disembowelled them and torn out their hearts.' The next morning, Annie Chapman became the first victim to be disembowelled. One week after her murder, Chief Inspector Donald Sutherland Swanson was placed in charge of the investigation. He was relieved of all other duties and given his own office at Scotland Yard. He had access to 'every paper, every document, every report, every telegram'.

The following year, when giving evidence before a department committee, he described his working day between September and December 1888:

> I had to be at the office at half-past 8 in the morning; then I had to read through all the papers that had come in, which took me till 11 pm, and sometimes 1 and 2 in the morning; then I had to go to Whitechapel and see the officers – generally getting home between 2 and 3 am.

Such pressure may have shown journalists that the Metropolitan Police took their responsibilities seriously in this case, but it was surely not an effective way to manage a major criminal enquiry.

Seven years after the Whitechapel murders, *The Pall Mall Gazette* wrote:

> The theory entitled to most respect, because it was presumably based upon the best knowledge, was that of Chief Inspector Swanson, the officer who was associated with the investigation of all the murders, and Mr Swanson believed the crimes to have been the work of a man who is now dead.

A theory that doesn't really offer us very much. Chief Inspector Donald Swanson retired in 1903 and died on 25 November 1924, aged 76.

43

Detective Inspector Frederick Abberline

Like many of those young men who became London police officers, Frederick Abberline (1843–1929) was not a Londoner. On average, boys who grew up in the foul air and cramped living conditions of London didn't often turn into vigorous, well-made young men. The diet was also generally better in the countryside than in the slums of the nation's capital.

Frederick Abberline was born on 8 January 1843, 120 miles south-west of Whitechapel in Blandford, Dorset. He was the youngest son of Edward Abberline and his wife, Hannah. Edward died when Frederick was just six years old. Hannah opened a small shop and brought up her four children alone.

Frederick worked as a clockmaker, but at the age of 19, he moved to London and, on 5 January 1863, just days before his twentieth birthday, he joined the London Metropolitan Police Force. He was described as being 5ft 9½ inches tall, with dark brown hair, hazel eyes and a fresh complexion.

By 19 August 1865, he had so impressed the force that he was promoted to sergeant and moved from the Islington Division to the neighbouring Highgate. By 1867, he was a plain-clothes officer investigating Irish Republicans. On 10 March 1873, at the age of 30, he was promoted to inspector and three days later, on 13 March 1873, transferred to H Division in Whitechapel. On 8 April 1878, Abberline was appointed local inspector in charge of H Division's CID.

On 26 February 1887, he was transferred to the London Metropolitan Police headquarters at Scotland Yard. A year later, on 8 February 1888, he was promoted to first class inspector.

On 25 February 1888, a 38-year-old homeless woman, Annie Millwood, was attacked in the Spitalfields area of Whitechapel. She was stabbed multiple times. She died five weeks later, on 31 March.

Three days later, on 3 April 1888, a 45-year-old homeless woman, Emma Elizabeth Smith, was brutally attacked again in the Spitalfields area; she made it to the London Hospital but died the next day from her injuries.

On 7 August 1888, a 39-year-old homeless woman, Martha Tabram, was found dead on the landing of a stairwell of a building in the Spitalfields area. She had been stabbed 39 times.

On 31 August 1888, a 43-year-old homeless woman, Polly Nichols, was murdered, and on 3 September, Abberline was back in Whitechapel, attending the second day of her inquest.

According to fellow police officer Walter Dew, Abberline looked more like a bank manager than a detective.

The year after the Whitechapel murders, Abberline was involved in investigating the Cleveland Street scandal. That investigation into a homosexual brothel frequented by people at the top of London society left Abberline disenchanted with his superiors. It probably contributed to his decision to retire from the Met on 8 February 1892.

He retired to Bournemouth, where he died on 10 December 1929, at the age of 86.

A modern equivalent

In 2023, retired murder squad detective Steven Keogh published *Murder Team Investigation: Jack the Ripper: A 21st Century Investigation*. Keogh drew parallels between his own career and Abberline's:

> Detective Inspector Frederick Abberline was attached to Scotland Yard at the time of these murders, and he and I shared remarkably similar careers. I finished my policing career as a Scotland Yard detective inspector, investigating murders. Prior to those roles, we both policed the area of East London preyed upon by Jack the Ripper, Whitechapel.

The concept is appealing because this ex-murder squad detective is writing to show how these crimes would be investigated today. What Steven Keogh reveals is the power of the story, as it is surprising how much of the book is written as though he were scripting a remake of the 1988 miniseries, which starred Michael Caine.

Each of the victims gets her own scene, complete with dialogue and supporting characters. This is just a tiny section of the pages devoted to Emma Elizabeth Smith:

> She stopped, then touched him on the shoulder, 'How'd you do, love? Your place or mine?' He gave a nervous laugh, 'Um, we can't go to mine, my, um...' 'Don't worry, love. I'm just pulling your leg. I know a discreet place or two. Somewhere out of this rain where we can have a little privacy.' He somehow looked relieved and nervous at the same time. Clearly, he hadn't done this before, much to her relief. She loved the first-timers. They were usually gentler and easier to squeeze a bit more cash from. Which is exactly what she did. She could almost hear her inner demon giving a little cheer. Emma took the man by his clammy hand, leading him to a spot she'd been to a hundred times before. Out of the way of prying eyes and patrolling policemen. But they weren't there for long. That was another benefit of the newcomers – things were over almost as soon as they began. She'd hit the jackpot with this one.

Why would a modern-day murder squad detective decide to investigate this cold case and devote so much of his book to fictional accounts of the events? After all, he says:

> When prosecuting killers, wild theories, speculation, and conjecture cannot form part of your case. Instead, you must rely on provable facts. So, it is upon those that I will draw any conclusions.

But he then indulges in the wildest of conjecture. Steven Keogh does not consider any other explanation for these murders other than that a prostitute killer was on the loose. The evidence of Elizabeth Long and others is delivered as an accepted fact. The evidence regarding the time of death of Annie Chapman, as provided by Dr George Bagster Phillips, is dismissed. Steven ignores the fact that on a colder night, Kate Eddowes's body was still warm with no stiffening 45 minutes after she was murdered, whereas Annie's body was cold, and stiffening had commenced. She could not possibly have been murdered 40 minutes before Dr Phillips examined her body.

Here lies the fundamental problem with Keogh's approach: despite his stated commitment to 'provable facts', he presents one theory as gospel whilst dismissing contradictory evidence. For a detective who claims to eschew speculation, this selective treatment of evidence is particularly troubling.

44

Major Henry Smith, Acting Commissioner of the City of London Police

Only one of the victims who are known to 'Ripperologists' as 'the canonical five' was murdered in the City of London. She was Kate Eddowes, and she was the fourth victim. But the City of London Police had been on heightened alert since the first of the five victims, Polly Nichols, was discovered in Buck's Row.

Buck's Row, now Durward Street, is only a 20-minute walk from the City of London Police's boundary on Middlesex Street. A brutal murder less than a mile from the City of London Police territory was a murder that they couldn't ignore.

In 1888, the year of the Jack the Ripper murders, the man in charge of the City of London Police was Sir James Fraser; however, he was absent during the time the first four murders took place. The investigation was left to Sir Henry Smith (1835–1921), who had been appointed chief superintendent of the City of London Police in 1885. In James Fraser's absence, he became acting commissioner.

In *The Crimes, Detection and Death of Jack the Ripper* (1987), Fido reveals something of the man's character:

> Strangely for a policeman and a son of the manse, Major Smith knew the Haymarket brothels rather well. He devotes one chapter of his memoirs to them and regretting their passing. He recalls Kate Hamilton, echoing the descriptions others have left of this fat, ugly procuress presiding over her ornate drawing room of elegant strumpets and fashionable young men.

Martin Fido comments:

> I should make it clear apart from the unpleasant liking for public hangings, I see nothing inherently unacceptable in Smith's character. A good companion for a night's drinking and whoring (like Falstaff) is someone to be enjoyed on the appropriate occasions.

This possibly tells us about more than just the character of Major Smith. Fido's conclusion is that:

> Sir Henry Smith's rhetoric is fun. His sense of personal involvement is engaging. And his hostility to antisemitism is appealing. But I am afraid he is almost incapable of giving us a single reliable detail.

In *The Complete Jack the Ripper*, Donald Rumbelow writes:

> Acting Commissioner Major Henry Smith was described by a contemporary as a good raconteur and a good fellow. Since August, he had been desperately keen to lay hands on the killer and, to guarantee success, had put nearly a third of the force into plainclothes, with instructions, as he candidly admitted in his memoirs, 'to do everything which, in ordinary circumstances, a constable should not do. It was subversive of discipline, but I had them well supervised by the senior officers. The weather was lovely, and I have little doubt that they thoroughly enjoyed themselves, sitting on the doorsteps, smoking their pipes, hanging about public houses, and gossiping with all and sundry.'

At the time of the murders, the City of London Police had 781 constables and 92 sergeants to keep an eye on them. A third of the force, therefore, was around 250 men.

Major Henry Smith's 250 spies were presumably not wasting their time sitting on doorsteps around St Paul's or the Mansion House. To have any chance of gathering helpful information, they had to have been smoking their pipes around the crime scenes. Close to where Martha Tabram was stabbed 39 times in the George Yard Building. Or where Polly Nichols was murdered in Buck's Row, and where Annie Chapman was discovered in the yard behind 29 Hanbury Street.

Locations that have one thing in common. They were all in Whitechapel. And Whitechapel is not in the jurisdiction of the City of London Police. The Metropolitan Police controlled it.

So, contrary to what has been suggested by some, there must have been some cooperation. Major Henry Smith could not have expected his 250 men to have gone unnoticed by the Metropolitan Police, whether or not they were in plain clothes.

It is clear that police officers did cross the invisible boundary line back then; right after the discovery of the brutally murdered and mutilated body of Kate Eddowes in Mitre Square, detectives from the City of London Police scoured the area around the crime scene, including territory in the jurisdiction of the Metropolitan Police.

Despite all this effort and even cooperation, neither police force got even close to answering the question that everybody in the country at that time wanted answered: who was the killer?

Conclusion

The simplest truth

After dismantling 137 years of mythology, examining the evidence without Victorian prejudices, and applying Occam's razor to the Whitechapel murders, a different picture emerges – one that challenges everything we thought we knew about Jack the Ripper.

The story everyone knows is wrong. Not because the murders didn't happen or weren't brutal, but because the narrative built around them rests on assumptions that were never properly questioned. These assumptions, rooted in Victorian class and gender prejudices, have distorted our understanding of what actually occurred in the gaslit streets of Whitechapel in 1888.

What Occam's razor reveals

When we strip away the sensational theories and examine the core facts, the simplest explanation becomes clear.

The victims were vulnerable not because they were prostitutes, but because they were homeless.

Four of the five victims had no beds on the nights they died. They were forced to sleep rough in doorways, yards and corners – exactly where their bodies were found.

They were killed while lying down, in silence, without struggle. The medical evidence consistently shows this across all five murders. No witnesses heard screams or sounds of conflict, despite the crimes occurring in densely populated areas.

They were easy targets. A vulnerable sleeper presents no threat, makes no noise when attacked, and requires no elaborate schemes to isolate them. One hand over the mouth and nose, a knife to the carotid artery, and the deed is done in seconds.

The location pattern reflects opportunism, not hunting. The murders occurred within a tiny area where hundreds of homeless people sought shelter. The killer(s) didn't need to hunt – they simply walked the streets until they found someone vulnerable and alone.

The copycat reality

The writer for *The Daily News* of 10 November 1888 understood what modern investigators have missed. He warned of a 'ghastly imitativeness' and a 'horrible fashion' in murder, recognising that spectacular crimes inspire imitation.

The first three attacks – on Annie Millwood, Emma Elizabeth Smith and Martha Tabram – established a template. The sensational press coverage that followed created what Loren Coleman calls 'an epidemic of similar behaviours'. Men already inclined towards violence found inspiration in the headlines.

By September 1888, *The Star* newspaper boasted of having the 'Largest Circulation of Any Evening Paper in the Kingdom'. Each subsequent murder generated more lurid coverage, more detailed descriptions of wounds, and more opportunities for copycat killers to 'improve upon his example'.

Dr George Bagster Phillips, who examined multiple victims, didn't believe all the murders were committed by one person. His professional medical opinion was dismissed in favour of a more compelling narrative.

The fact that the narrative was a fiction didn't lessen its lethal impact, as the Werther suicides revealed. Detailed media descriptions inspired waves of imitation, even when the original inspiration was fictional rather than factual.

The detailed media descriptions created in the Jack the Ripper case have gone beyond the tragedy that ended the lives of five homeless women in Whitechapel.

Ask your search engine this question. Did the Jack the Ripper murders inspire copycat killers? I've just done that. The answer?

> Yes. It is often cited as a significant example of a copycat crime event, as media coverage of his crimes inspired other criminals to commit similar acts in the early 20th century. Criminologists

observed that the increased public awareness of the Ripper's methods potentially led to a rise in replicated crimes, even influencing individuals who might not have otherwise committed such offences.

The Jack the Ripper case established a template for how serial killers are portrayed and discussed in the media, which has had a lasting influence. The case introduced the concept of the 'mysterious serial killer' into popular culture, complete with taunting letters to police and media (though many of these were likely hoaxes).

The Victorian conspiracy of assumptions

The Jack the Ripper myth was born from a perfect storm of Victorian prejudices:

Class bias

Officials like Sir Robert Anderson dismissed the victims as 'degraded women' unworthy of serious investigation. This predetermined the approach to the evidence by those in authority.

George Bernard Shaw described what victims of crime, like Francis Jones, Sarah Delhar, the Whitechapel murder victims and countless others, faced:

> Less than a year ago, the West-end press... were literally clamouring for the people's blood... applauding the open class bias of magistrates and judges.

Gender bias

In a society where women were viewed as naturally inferior, it was easy to blame female victims for facilitating their own murders.

Media sensationalism

The newly launched *Star* newspaper and its competitors needed stories to sell papers. A single mastermind was more compelling than random violence by multiple perpetrators.

Police incompetence

Faced with unsolvable crimes, it was easier to label victims as prostitutes who 'brought it on themselves' than admit investigative failures.

Procedural shortcuts

Police accepted eyewitness evidence uncritically, failed to verify basic facts (like Charles Lechmere's real name), and pursued theories that confirmed their biases while ignoring contradictory evidence.

The modern perpetuation

Today's investigators have fallen into the same trap. Writers like Patricia Cornwell, Russell Edwards and others begin with the assumption that Jack the Ripper existed and then select evidence to support predetermined conclusions.

They ignore the medical evidence about the time of death that contradicts eyewitness accounts. They accept questionable DNA evidence while dismissing expert critiques. They construct elaborate theories requiring multiple unsupported assumptions while dismissing simpler explanations.

Others who have written extensively on this subject and who treat those writers claiming to have solved the case – like Cornwell and Edwards – with disdain, will not agree with the conclusions contained in this book, but they cannot deny that the simplest explanation for how these murders occurred is that the victims were sleeping when attacked. They may prefer another explanation, but they must explain why the simplest one was not at least worth considering.

The price of mythology

This mythology has cost us more than historical accuracy. It has:

- **Dehumanised the victims:** Polly, Annie, Liz, Kate and Mary Jane became props in a story about a mysterious killer rather than women whose lives mattered.
- **Increased their vulnerability:** Each of these victims slept on streets prowled by a ruthless killer, but they were told his victims were prostitutes who accosted him. These sleeping women were not going to be accosting anybody, so they were not his chosen prey.
- **Obscured the real issues:** Victorian society's treatment of vulnerable women, the conditions that created homelessness, and the violence endemic to that world have been overshadowed by fascination with one alleged perpetrator.
- **Prevented justice:** by assuming one killer, investigators may have missed multiple perpetrators.

- **Perpetuated harmful stereotypes:** the automatic labelling of victims as prostitutes reflected and reinforced attitudes towards vulnerable women that persist today.

Obvious suspects

When we abandon the single-killer theory, obvious suspects emerge:

- **Charles Lechmere** was found beside Polly's body minutes after she was killed, gave a false name at the inquest, and told conflicting stories. In any modern investigation, he would be the prime suspect.
- **John Richardson** changed his story about finding Annie Chapman's body, couldn't explain his presence at the scene, and lied about his knife. The only reason he wasn't pursued was that Mrs Long's unreliable eyewitness evidence suggested Annie was alive after Richardson left.
- In the case of Liz Stride, there is no single candidate, but the side entrance to the International Working Men's Educational Club led straight into Dutfield's Yard. Any of those present in the club that night would have had easy access to the crime scene without ever having to appear in Berner Street.
- **George Morris**, the night watchman at Mitre Square, was perfectly positioned to attack Kate Eddowes and knew police patrol timings intimately.
- **Joseph Barnett** had easy access to Mary Jane Kelly's room through the broken window and was an ex-partner – the demographic most likely to commit a domestic homicide.
- **Gang members** could have been responsible for the earlier attacks on Annie Millwood, Emma Elizabeth Smith and Martha Tabram, establishing the violent template that individual killers later copied.

Reconstructing society

> 'The proper aim is to try and reconstruct society on such a basis that poverty will be impossible.'
>
> Oscar Wilde

The true horror of the Whitechapel murders wasn't a single mastermind stalking prostitutes, but a society so broken that multiple killers found easy targets among its most vulnerable members.

Eight homeless women were brutally attacked in one square mile during 1888. This wasn't the work of one monster, but the predictable result of:

- mass homelessness in the world's wealthiest city
- endemic violence against women
- police indifference to crimes against the poor
- a press that sensationalised violence for profit
- officials who blamed victims for their own murders.

The Whitechapel murders weren't an aberration – they were Victorian society working exactly as designed. The poor, the homeless and the vulnerable were expendable. When they died, it was their fault.

The final word

Jack the Ripper never existed. He was a creation of journalists, a convenient fiction that explained the inexplicable and shifted blame from a broken society to a single bogeyman.

The real killers were products of their environment – men shaped by poverty, violence and a culture that viewed certain women as disposable. They were enabled by police who couldn't be bothered to investigate properly, journalists who cared more about sales than truth, and a society that preferred comfortable myths to uncomfortable realities.

One hundred and thirty-seven years later, we continue to choose the myth. We buy the books and debate the suspects while ignoring the real lesson: that vulnerable people remain vulnerable, that society still fails its weakest members, and that we still prefer sensational stories to simple truths. The women of Whitechapel deserved better. They deserved protection while they lived, justice when they died and truth in how they're remembered. Instead, they became footnotes in someone else's story.

It's time to tell their story properly. It's time to abandon the myth and face the reality: there was no Jack the Ripper. There were only victims of a society that created the conditions for their deaths and then blamed them for dying.

The mystery was never who killed them. The mystery was why we convinced ourselves there was ever a mystery at all.

Map

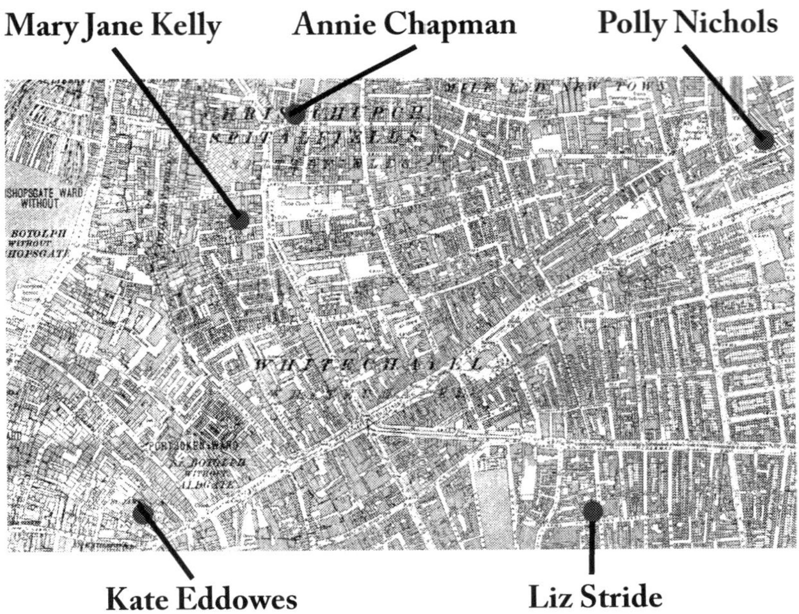

The murders took place in a densely populated area of less than one square mile.

Bibliography

Ackroyd, Peter, *Jack the Ripper and the East End* (2008)
Bagehot, Walter, *The English Constitution* (1867)
Beadle, William, *Jack the Ripper Unmasked* (2009)
Beattie, Rod, *Jack the Ripper – The Policeman* (2022)
Begg, Paul, *Jack the Ripper: The Facts* (2004)
Begg, Paul and Bennett, John, *The Complete and Essential Jack the Ripper* (2013)
Begg, Paul and Bennett, John, *Jack the Ripper – CSI: WHITECHAPEL* (2012)
Begg, Paul and Bennett, John, *Jack the Ripper: The Forgotten Victims* (2013)
Begg, Paul, Fido, Martin and Skinner, Keith, *The Complete Jack the Ripper A to Z* (London, 2015)
Blomer, Steven E., *Inside Bucks Row* (2024)
Booth, William, *In Darkest England* (1890)
Bostridge, Mark, *Florence Nightingale: The Woman And Her Legend* (2008)
Coleman, Loren, *The Copycat Effect* (2004)
Cornwell, Patricia, *Portrait of a Killer – Jack the Ripper: Case Closed* (2002)
Cornwell, Patricia, *Chasing the Ripper* (2014)
Cornwell, Patricia, *RIPPER: The Secret Life of Jack the Ripper* (2017)
Curtis, L. Perry, *Jack the Ripper & the London Press* (2001)
Edwards, Russell, *Naming Jack the Ripper* (2014)
Edwards, Russell, *Naming Jack the Ripper: The Definitive Reveal* (2024)
Evans, Stewart P. & Rumbelow, Donald, *Jack the Ripper: Scotland Yard Investigates* (2006)
Fuller, Jane Overton, *Sickert and the Ripper Crimes* (1990)

Gaskell, Elizabeth, *North And South* (1855)
Harrison, Shirley, *The Diary of Jack the Ripper* (1993)
Holmgren, Christer, *Cutting Point* (2021)
Jakubowski, Maxim, *The Mammoth Book of Jack the Ripper* (1999)
Keogh, Steven, *Jack the Ripper: Murder Investigation Team* (2023)
Knight, Stephen, *Jack the Ripper: the Final Solution* (1976)
London, Jack, *The People of the Abyss* (1903)
McNichol, Susan, *Jack the Ripper and The Women Whose Lives He Took* (2012)
Marriott, Trevor, *Jack the Ripper: The 21st Century Investigation* (2005)
Morrison, Arthur, *A Child of the Jago* (1896)
Paley, Bruce, *Jack the Ripper: The Simple Truth* (1996)
Robinson, Bruce, *They All Love Jack: Busting the Ripper* (2015)
Rubenhold, Hallie, *The Five: The Untold Lives of the Women Killed by Jack the Ripper* (2019)
Rumbelow, Donald, *The Complete Jack the Ripper* (1975)
Skinner, Keith, and Evans, Stewart P., *The Ultimate Jack the Ripper Source Book* (2000)
Stead, William Thomas, *The Maiden Tribute of Modern Babylon* (1885)
Stevenson, Robert Louis, *The Strange Case of Dr Jekyll and Mr Hyde* (1886)
Sugden, Philip, *The Complete History of Jack the Ripper* (1994)
Thorne, T. M., *The Ripper Reports* (2021)
Toughill, Thomas, *The Ripper Code* (2008)
Wescott, Tom, *Ripper Confidential* (2017)
Worsley, Lucy, *Queen Victoria: Daughter, Wife, Mother, Widow* (2018)

Index

Abberline, DI Frederick 217, 218, 220–222
  Mary Jane Kelly investigation 135
  Polly Nichols investigation 53, 58, 59
Ackroyd, Peter 16
Albert, Prince Consort 201
Albert Victor ('Eddy'), Prince, Duke of Clarence and Avondale 31, 159–161, 205–207
alcohol 19
  consumption 109, 110, 111
  drunkenness 13–14, 96, 112
alcoholism 42, 69–70
Anderson, Sir Robert 28, 160, 170–171, 177, 178, 213–214, 216
Angel, Miriam 26
animal slaughter/butchery 76–77, 206
anti-Semitism 170, 177, 178
Atherley-Jones, Llewellyn 20–21
autopsies 77, 131

Bagehot, Walter 201
Barnett, Henrietta 113
Barnett, Joseph 130, 132, 135, 139–140, 231
Barnett, Samuel 112
Baron, Wendy 166
Barry, Francis Tress 69, 70
Baxter, Wynne 91, 101–103, 136–137
Beadle, William 90
Beattie, Rod, *Jack the Ripper – The Policeman* 22
Begg, Paul 27, 40, 79, 167
Belloc, Hilaire 29
Berner Street, Whitechapel 94, 101, 103
  Dutfield's Yard 99, 100, 104
Besant, Annie 10, 155
Best, Fred 190
Bethnal Green 40
Blackwell, Dr 105–106
Blomer, Steven 24
Bloodsworth, Kirk 75
Bond, Dr Thomas 32, 77, 92, 131–132, 135
Bonner, Paul 171
Booth, Charles 41, 71
Booth, William 17
Bostridge, Mark 202
Bowman, Mary Ann 20
Bowyer, Thomas 131, 132
Brown, Dr Frederick Gordon 76, 80–81, 121, 122, 124
Brown, James 102

Buckley, Edward 12–13
Buck's Row, Whitechapel 39, 45, 46, 62
Bullen, Tom 190
Byfield, Sergeant 116

Cadosch, Albert 78–79
Campbell, Eddie, *From Hell* 162, 190
Carr, Caleb 163
Casebook Jack the Ripper (website) 23, 141
Casey, Louise 4
Cass, Elizabeth 20–21
Catholicism 160, 161
Chandler, Inspector Joseph 87
Chantrelle, Eugene 152
Chapman, Annie (formerly Smith) 17, 18, 29
  life
    alcoholism 69–70, 70–71
    childhood and youth 68
    children of 70
    homelessness 72
    husband, separation from 70
    illness 72, 78, 84
    marriage 69, 70
    and Jack Sievey 71–72
    and Edward Stanley 72
    widowhood and loss of financial support 72
    work 72
  murder 45, 60, 67
    injuries 76
    inquest 76, 82–83
    location 81–82
    suspects 89, 90–92, 231
    timeline 76, 78–80, 79, 84
    witness testimony 76, 78–83, 82–83
  prostitute, assumed to be working as 81, 89
Chapman, John 69, 70, 72
Charrington, Frederick Nicholas 184
children
  sexual exploitation of 41
  of victims 42, 43, 70, 110
City of London
  Mitre Square 99, 108, 112, 118–119, 126
  St James's (Church) Passage 179
City of London Police 174, 223–225
Clark, Dr 202
class
  bias/prejudice 12–15, 28–29, 229
  working class 8–10, 9–11, 40–41
Cleveland Street scandal 205, 208–209, 221
Coleman, Loren 34, 35
Collard, Inspector 122
Connelly, Mary Ann 144
contagion, of criminal behaviour 34–35
Conway, Catherine Annie 110
Conway, Frederick 110
Conway, George Alfred 110
Conway, Harriet 110
Conway, Thomas 109–110
Conway, Thomas Lawrence 110
copycat effect 33–35, 91, 124–125
Cornwell, Patricia 163–166, 168
  Chasing the Ripper 164–165
  Portrait of a Killer 3, 163–164, 167, 168
  Ripper 165–166
Cox, Mary Ann 132–133
Crawshaw, George 43
Crook, Alice Margaret 160, 161

Crook, Annie Elizabeth 160, 161
Cross, Charles Andrew (aka Lechmere) 60, 231
  lack of police investigation into 58–60
  at scene of Polly Nichols's death 50–52
  as suspect for Polly Nichols's murder 65, 67
  witness testimony at inquest 54–57
Crow, Alfred 143, 145

Daily News (newspaper) 32, 137, 228
Dalston 13–14
Davis, John 88
Delhar, Sarah 15, 17
Dew, DCI Walter 130, 221
Dickens, Charles 40, 43, 146
Diemschutz, Louis 94, 100
Disraeli, Benjamin, *Sybil* 8
DNA evidence 4, 74, 168, 169, 180–182
  limitations of 165, 182
  vs. eyewitness evidence 75
domestic service 42, 44, 95, 96, 97
Donovan, Timothy 72
Dorset Street, Whitechapel 71–72
doss houses 71–72, 74, 96, 110, 114, 142
  women-only 45
Dowgate School 109
Doyle, Arthur Conan 22
Drew, Thomas Stewart 43–44
Druitt, Montague John 160, 171, 194, 195–196, 197
Dutfield's Yard, Berner Street, Whitechapel 99, 100, 104

Eagle, Morris 100, 103, 104, 107
East London Observer (newspaper) 12
economic conditions 44
Eddowes, Catherine (Kate) 17, 18, 74
  life
    arrest 112
    childhood and youth 108–109
    children of 110
    drinking 109, 110, 112
    education 109
    funeral and burial 112
    poverty 111, 174
    Thomas Conway, relationship with 109–110
    work 109, 111
  murder 108
    cloth and chalk message found near 192
    as 'Double Event' (simultaneous with murder of Liz Stride) 97
    injuries 76, 77, 121
    location 99, 112
    medical evidence 121, 122
    opportunist theory of 123–124
    police discovery of 179
    and royal conspiracy theory 160
    suspects 125–127, 231
    timeline 80–81, 84, 115–116, 118, 121–122
    witness testimony 116–120
  prostitute, claimed to be working as 114–115
  shawl 4, 172–174
    blue dye, running of 181–182
    and DNA testing 168, 180–182
    doubtful authenticity of 173–174, 176
    Aaron Kosminski, possible possession of 174–175, 181–182

Michaelmas symbolism 174–175
potential financial value of 182–183
Eddowes, Emma 110
Eddowes, George 108, 109
Edwards, Russell 103, 168–170, 172–182
Naming Jack the Ripper 3, 4, 168
Naming Jack the Ripper, The Definitive Reveal 179
Edward VII, King 161, 205, 206
Ellen, Holland, 45
Endacott, PC Bowden 20–22, 22, 211
Engels, Friedrich 8, 9
Enright, DS 53
Evans, Stewart 75, 79, 142–143
evidence
ambiguity of 25
DNA 74, 168, 169, 180–182
limitations of 165, 182
vs. eyewitness evidence 75
medical 77, 121, 122, 131, 135
police 13, 14
police handling of 173, 192
quality of 23–24
selective treatment of 185, 222
for victims' work as prostitutes 23
Express and Echo (newspaper) 126

feminism 203
Fido, Martin 40, 42, 171, 223–224
Fleming, Joseph 130
Flower and Dean Street, Whitechapel 74, 96, 110
Freemasonry 90–91, 92, 162, 192
From Hell (film) 3, 4, 159, 163, 190
Fuller, Jean Overton, *Sickert and the Ripper Crimes* 166
gang crime 149–150, 231
Gaskell, Elizabeth 99
Goethe, Johann Wolfgang von, *The Sorrows of Young Werther* 35
Gorman, Joseph. *See* Sickert, Joseph (aka Gorman)
Gorman, William and Alice 161
Great Exhibition (1851) 109
Greenwich Union Workhouse 110
Griffiths, Dr Andy 61
Gull, Sir William 160, 161, 205, 206
Gustafsdotter, Elisabeth. *See* Stride, Elizabeth (Liz, formerly Gustafsdotter)

Hanbury Street, Whitechapel 67, 81–82, 84–85, 86–88
Harrison, Shirley 90
'Harry the Hawker' 72
Harvey, Maria 135
Helson, Inspector James Henry 53
Henderson, Sir Edmund 211
Higgs, Michelle 40
Hinton, Bob 139
Holland, Emily 58
Holmgren, Christer 59, 60
homelessness 59, 155, 228
and risks of violence 64–66, 128, 140–141
rough sleeping 111, 142, 146, 227
of victims 5, 15, 44, 45, 72, 227
of women 17, 27, 142
hop-picking 111
Hutchinson, George 138–139, 139

imperialism 28–29
International Working Men's Educational Club 99, 107, 231
Isaac, Susan 10

Jack the Ripper. *See also* Whitechapel murders
- geographical profile 74
- letters from 36, 146, 168, 189–190
  - 'Dear Boss' 189–190
  - 'From hell' 190
- mythology 146, 229–230
  - consequences of 230–231
  - potential financial value of 182–183
- name, origin of 190

Jack the Ripper (BBC TV series) 159
Jack the Ripper Case Reopened (BBC TV programme) 81, 105
Jack the Ripper tours 3–4, 74
Jenkinson, Edward 213
Jewish people 170, 177, 178
Jones, Frances 12–13
judges, biases of 12–15
Jullian, Philippe 205, 206

Kelly, John 110–111, 114
Kelly, Mary Jane 17, 32, 34, 74
- life
  - background 129
  - Joseph Barnett, relationship with 130, 131, 139–140
  - prostitute, work as 130
- murder 129
  - injuries 80, 131–132, 135
  - inquest 132–137
  - location 131, 135
  - medical evidence 135
  - post-mortem 77, 131
  - press coverage 137–138
  - and royal conspiracy theory 160, 161
  - suspects 139–140, 231
  - timeline 133–134
  - time of death, calculation of 80
  - witness testimony 132–134, 138–139

Keogh, Steven, *Murder Team Investigation, Jack the Ripper* 221–222
Kidney, Michael 96, 97
Killeen, Dr 143
Knight, Stephen, *Jack the Ripper, The Final Solution* 161–162, 166
Koch, Julius 152
Kosminski, Aaron 93, 214
- and DNA evidence 168–169
- and eyewitness evidence 176–178, 197
- and Kate Eddowes's shawl 174–176
- in Macnaghten memoranda 170, 194
- mental illness of 31

Lambeth Union Workhouse 43
Lamb, PC Henry 100–102
Lave, Joseph 104, 107
Lawende, Joseph 116–118, 121, 171
Lechmere, Charles. *See* Cross, Charles Andrew (aka Lechmere)
legal system, biases in 12–15
Levy, Joseph Hyam 118
Lewis, Sarah 134
Llewellyn, Dr Rhys 39, 47, 48, 49
Lloyd's Weekly (journal) 50–52, 55, 56
Lobulsk (Lipski), Israel 26
lodging houses. *See* doss houses
London Evening Standard (newspaper) 138
London, Jack 43
- *The People of the Abyss* 11, 15, 71, 96, 156

'The Long Depression' (financial depression) 44
Long, Elizabeth 79–80, 80, 81–84, 88–89
Long, PC Alfred 173
Louhelainen, Dr Jari 180, 181
Lusk, George 190
Lyceum Theatre, *The Strange Case of Dr Jekyll and Mr Hyde* 77

Macdonald, Roderick 135–137
Macilwee, Michael 149
Macnaghten, Sir Melville Leslie 170, 171
  memoranda 193–195, 197–198
Maessen, Jurriaan 12, 13
magistrates 20
  biases of 12–15
Manchester Evening News (newspaper) 137
Mansfield, Richard 77, 153
Marriott, Trevor 192
Marshall, William 101
Marx, Eleanor 155
match girls 10–11, 155
Matthews, Henry, 1st Viscount Llandaff 21, 208, 209, 211, 214
Maxwell, Caroline 133
Maybrick, James 31, 90, 93
Maybrick, Michael 90, 93
McCarthy, John 131, 132
McCarthy, Matt 166
McCormack, Alan 176, 178
Mearns, Andrew 41
  The Bitter Cry of Outcast London 154–155
Melville-Hayes, David 173
mental illness 152, 170, 195, 202, 205
Metropolitan Police 173
  Casey Report 4
  City of London Police, cooperation with 224
  complaints to 20
  Criminal Investigation Department 211, 218
  patrols 46
  protests, policing of 44
  Whitechapel murders, investigation of 31, 193, 224–225
    contradictions in 54–59
    eyewitness testimony, reliance on 74
    omissions in 59–61, 230
Miller's Court, Dorset Street, Whitechapel 74, 131
Mill, John Stuart 215
Millwood, Annie 27, 45, 141–142, 231
misogyny 4, 28–29, 163, 214–215, 229, 231
Mitre Square, City of London 99, 108, 112, 118–119, 126
Mizen, PC Jonas 46, 47, 52–53, 53, 54, 57, 59
Monro, James 211
Moore, Alan, *From Hell* 162, 190
Morning Advertiser (newspaper) 127
Morris, George James 120–121, 121, 126, 127, 231
Morris, William 155
Mortimer, Fanny 104
mothers 9
murder
  frequency of 26
  of homeless women 27
  by street gangs 149–150

Neil, PC John 39, 45, 46, 47–49, 51, 54, 56
Netley, John 160
Newton, Robert Milnes 20
Nichols, Polly (Mary Ann, formerly Walker) 16, 17, 18, 45
life
burial and memorial 45, 67
childhood and youth 40–42
children of 42, 43
in domestic service 44
drinking problem ascribed to 42
education 41
homelessness 45
in Lambeth Union Workhouse 43
loss of financial support from William Nichols 23–24, 43
marriage 42
separation from husband 42
theft from employers 45
murder 39
Charles Cross at scene of 50–52, 54–57
injuries 39, 47, 48–49, 63, 92
inquest 42, 50, 53, 54–56
location 46
method of 63, 65
press reports 50–52
silence at time of 46–47, 49
suspects 64–65, 231
timeline 45, 47–50, 51, 59, 62
witnesses 46–47, 50–52, 53, 58
prostitute, assumed to be working as 40, 53
arguments against 62
Nichols, William 23–24, 42, 43, 58
Nightingale, Florence 202
Notting Hill 71

Occam's razor 5–7, 227–228
Ostrog, Michael 171, 195, 196–197, 198

Paley, Bruce 26
Pall Mall Gazette (newspaper) 27, 92, 218
Palmer, Amelia 72
Pash, Florence 166
Paul, Robert 50–52, 53, 54, 54–57, 55, 56, 57, 58
Peabody Trust 42
People's Journal (newspaper) 179
Phillips, David P. 35
Phillips, Dr George Bagster 32, 68, 228
on Annie Chapman 76, 78, 79, 80, 84, 91–92
on Mary Jane Kelly 77, 135
on Liz Stride 106
'phossy jaw' (phosphorus necrosis) 11
police. *See also* Metropolitan Police; *See also* City of London Police
criticism of 211, 212
demonstrations and protests, management of 212
evidence 13, 14
failures/incompetence 53, 116, 229
patrols 34, 46, 62, 65, 100, 118–119, 211
additional, during Whitechapel murders 22
in Mitre Square 169–170, 179
press criticism of 27
prostitution arrests 20–21
protests/riots, management of 211
as suspects 22
victims' possessions, handling of 173

women identified as prostitutes by 20–21, 23
Police Review and Parade Gossip (journal) 21
post-mortems 77, 131
poverty 8–10, 109–110, 154–156, 211
abject 41
destitution 19, 111
morality, impact on 41
and violence 30
of women 17
Prater, Elizabeth 133, 134
press coverage 99
assumptions about victims 23
graphic detail of murders in 34, 35, 228
'Jack the Ripper' single perpetrator theory, promotion of 31, 36, 125–127
newspaper sales boost from 189
police investigation, impact on 218
sensationalised 26–28, 137–138, 229
prostitutes, victims assumed to be 4–5, 16–17, 22–23, 116, 144, 145
prostitution 16–18, 19, 114–115
arrests for 20–21, 212
official inquiry into 21
prevalence of 41
red-light districts 62
sex trafficking 18, 130
psychological profiling 163, 167
psychopathy 152–153

Ratcliffe Highway 130
Reeves, John 144
Reid, Edmund 144, 146
Renfrew Road Workhouse 44
respectability 40–41
loss of 71
Rhodes, Cecil 28
Richardson, Amelia 84, 86
Richardson, John 78, 85, 86–89, 89, 231
Ripperology 23–24
Robinson, Bruce 90, 90–91, 92
Robinson, PC Lewis 115
Rubenhold, Hallie 23, 43, 110
Rumbelow, Donald 98, 174, 206
on Dr Thomas Bond 32
on Annie Chapman 75, 79
on Kate Eddowes 121
on Polly Nichols 63
on Sir Henry Smith 224

Salisbury, Robert Gascoyne-Cecil, 3rd Marquess of 160, 206, 208
Schwartz, Israel 103–104, 171, 176–178
Senise, Stephen 139
Sequeira, Dr George 77, 122
serial killers
typical profile of 196
Whitechapel murders theory 17, 23
criticism of 30–32
imaginative attractions of 35–36
modern research, perpetuated by 230
and murder of Polly Nichols 64
police focus on 67
press coverage of 228
sexuality 163, 205
sexual violence 4, 18, 41, 42
sex work. *See* prostitution
Shaw, George Bernard 12, 29, 155, 156, 229

Sickert, Joseph (aka Gorman) 159–161, 166
Sickert, Walter 3, 31, 93, 159–161, 163–167, 168
Sievey, Jack 71
Simpson, Amos 169–170, 172, 173–174, 179
Sims, George R. 27, 36
Skinner, Keith 142–143
Smith, Annie. *See* Chapman, Annie (formerly Smith)
Smith, Emma Elizabeth 27, 45, 142–143, 231
Smith, George 68–69
Smith, Horace 13, 14
Smith, Miriam 70, 72
Smith, Ruth (formerly Chapman) 68–69
Smith, Sir Henry 223–225
Smith, PC William 100, 101
social reform 155
societal factors
  alcohol consumption 69
  class prejudice 12, 28–29, 229
  duality of 151–153
  economic conditions 44
  gender bias 215, 229
  imperialism, informed by 28
  respectability, women's loss of 12, 71–72
Somerset, Lord Alfred 208
Spelthorne Sanatorium, Feltham 70
Spiering, Frank 206
Spitalfields Chambers, 8 White's Row 141, 142
Spitalfields Market 86, 88, 89
Spratling, Divisional Inspector John 39, 47, 52
Stamford Street 42
Stanley, Edward 72
Star, The (newspaper) 26–28, 125–126
St Botolph's without Aldgate ('Prostitutes' Church') 117
Stead, William Thomas 18, 41, 130, 154
Stevenson, Fanny 152, 153
Stevenson, Robert Louis, *The Strange Case of Dr Jekyll and Mr Hyde* 77–80, 151–153
St James's Passage, City of London 179
Stoker, Bram, *Dracula* 153
Stowell, Dr Thomas 205
street gangs 149–150
Stride, Elizabeth (Liz, formerly Gustafsdotter) 16, 17, 18, 74
  life
    burial 107
    childhood 95
    in domestic service 95, 96, 97
    marriage 95
    Michael Kidney, relationship with 96
    pregnancy and stillbirth 95
    prostitute, work as 95
    separation from husband 96
    syphilis contracted by 95, 106
  murder 94, 97
    as 'Double Event' (simultaneous with murder of Kate Eddowes) 97
    injuries 76, 97, 105–106
    inquest 100–102, 105–106
    location 99
    press coverage 104–105
    suspects 231
    timeline 99, 105
    witness testimony 100–104
Stride, John 95

Sugden, Philip 16, 17
 on Annie Chapman 29, 79, 81, 82
 on Kate Eddowes 115, 121
 on Polly Nichols 55, 61, 62, 63, 64
 on Walter Sickert 167
 on Liz Stride 100
Sullivan, Peter 75
Sunday People (newspaper) 13
suspects 31, 231. *See also* Whitechapel murders, theories
 Albert Victor ('Eddy'), Prince, Duke of Clarence and Avondale 31, 159–161, 205–207
 Barnett, Joseph 139–140, 231
 for Annie Chapman's murder 89, 90–92, 231
 Cross, Charles Andrew (aka Lechmere) 65, 67, 231
 Cutbush, Thomas 193
 Druitt, Montague John 171, 194, 195–196, 197
 ease of creation of 184–185
 for Kate Eddowes's murder 125–127, 231
 Endacott, PC Bowden 22
 Gull, Sir William 160, 161
 Hutchinson, George 139
 for Mary Jane Kelly's murder 231
 Kosminski, Aaron 93, 214
  and DNA evidence 168–169
  and Kate Eddowes's shawl 174–176
  and eyewitness evidence 176–178, 197
  in Macnaghten memoranda 170, 194
  mental illness of 31
 lack of evidence for 197–198
 Mansfield, Richard 153
 Maybrick, James 31
 Maybrick, Michael 90, 93
 missing police files of 171
 Morris, George James 127, 231
 for Polly Nichols's murder 64–65, 65, 67, 231
 Ostrog, Michael 171, 195, 196–197, 198
 Richardson, John 78, 85, 86–89, 89, 231
 Sickert, Walter 3, 31, 159–161, 163–167
 for Liz Stride's murder 231
 unidentified 53
Swanson, Chief Inspector Donald 104, 214, 217–219
Swanson, Inspector Donald 217
syphilis 95, 106, 205, 206

Tabram, Henry 144
Tabram, Martha 27, 45, 52, 78, 143–145, 231
Taverner, Thomas 43
temperance movement 69, 70
Thain, PC John 46, 47, 48
Thisted, Valdemar Adolph, *Letters From Hell* 190
Thomas, Edward 130
time of death, calculation of 76, 79
Tomkins, Henry 58
Trafalgar Square 155
Trow, M. J. 184
Tucker, David 14
Turner, Henry 144, 145
Tye, Jonathan 12, 13

unemployment 161, 211

Vanturney, Julia 134
victim-blaming 12–15, 16–18, 203, 229, 232
victims
  as alien/other 29
  assumptions about 4, 215–216, 229–230
  class prejudice against 28–29
  dehumanization of 230
  financial/social background of 19–20
  geographical proximity of 74
  homelessness/insecure housing of 5, 15, 227
  killed while lying down 5, 63, 135, 140–141, 227
  lack of compassion for 214
  loss of male partners of 17, 19, 42, 70, 96
    financial impact of 23–24, 43, 72
  prostitutes, assumed to be 4–5, 16–17, 22–23, 23, 144, 145
  viewing of remains of 81, 83, 100, 105
  vulnerability of 227
Victoria, Queen 155, 160, 161, 201–203, 205
  Golden Jubilee 20, 44, 155
  Whitechapel murders, response to 203–204
violence against women
  assaults 12–15
  legal class bias against 12–15
  prevalence of 30, 34
  sexual violence 4, 18, 41, 42

Walker, Edward 40, 41, 42, 44, 58
Walker, Polly (Mary Ann). *See* Nichols, Polly (Mary Ann, formerly Walker)
Warren, Sir Charles 16, 21, 31, 131, 155, 210–212, 214
Watkins, PC Edward 108, 118–119, 179
weapons 86, 87, 104
Webber, PC 180
Weissensteiner, Hansi 182
Werther Effect 35
Wescott, Tom 24, 25, 63
Westall, William 92
Whistler, James 163
Whitechapel
  Berner Street 94, 101, 103
    Dutfield's Yard 99, 100, 104
  Buck's Row 39, 45, 46, 62
  community 112–113
  Dorset Street 71–72
  Flower and Dean Street 74, 96, 110
  Hanbury Street 67, 81–82, 84–85, 86–88
  International Working Men's Educational Club 99, 107, 231
  Jewish population 96
  Miller's Court, Dorset Street 74, 131
  Wilmott's Lodging House, Thrawl Street 45
Whitechapel Church 143
Whitechapel murders 193–195
  anatomical/medical knowledge required to commit 76–77
  assumptions about 4
  'Double Event' 97, 99
  as entertainment 138
  government response to 208–209
  locations of 5, 74, 228
  motives for 98
  mutilations 76, 90–91, 92, 121
  police investigation 31, 193, 224–225

contradictions in 54–59
eyewitness testimony , reliance on 74
omissions in 59–61, 230
public hysteria 67–68
silence, carried out in 63, 106, 121, 146
social factors in 215, 229–230, 230, 231–232
struggle, no evidence of 5, 63, 106, 121, 122, 146, 227
Victoria's response to 203–204
weapons 86, 87, 104
Whitechapel murders, theories
copycat theory 32–36, 122, 228
investigators' ignoring of 35–36
press coverage, facilitated by 35, 228
Freemasonry theory 90–91, 92, 162, 192
multiple perpetrator theory 29, 231
opportunist theory 5, 123–124
royal conspiracy theory 159–161, 205–207
serial/single killer theory 17, 23
criticism of 30–32
imaginative attractions of 35–36
modern research, perpetuated by 230
and murder of Polly Nichols 64
police focus on 67
press coverage of 228
simple vs. complex 5–7
Whitechapel Vigilance Committee 190
Wilde, Oscar 30, 231
Wilkinson, Frederick William 114, 115
Wilmott's Lodging House, Thrawl Street, Whitechapel 45
witness testimony
character witnesses 20
contradictions in 84, 88–89, 104
inconclusive 144–145
killer allegedly identified by 171
police evidence contradicted by 14, 15
police reliance on 74
reliability 80, 82–83, 117
doubts about 138–139, 176–178
lack of 74–75, 84, 103, 104–105
women
lack of rights of 214–215
lone 17, 19, 42, 70, 71, 96, 142
financial position of 23–24, 43, 72, 145
mothers 9
in nineteenth-century Britain 201–203
pregnancy 42, 95
prostitutes, categorised as 20, 20–21, 22–23, 23, 144, 145
reputation/respectability
importance of 40–41
loss of 71–72, 73
violence against
assaults 12–15
domestic/marital 11, 96
legal class bias against 12–15
prevalence of 30, 34
sexual 4, 18, 41, 42
in the workplace 10
work. *See also* prostitution
domestic service 42, 44, 95, 96, 97
hop-picking 111
of women 9–11, 10–11, 109, 111, 155
workhouses 43, 44, 110, 111

working class
  living conditions of 8–10
  reputation/respectability, importance of 40–41
  women 9–11
Worsley, Lucy 203

If you enjoyed this book, please take a moment to review it online!

Printed in Great Britain
by Amazon

2a3162d9-da44-42ee-84c3-105129282a13R01